But what of the people of Britain.

Who they, what do, and why?

KT-152-006

145985
791 4372 LUC

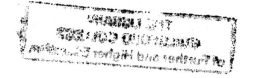
THE LIBRARY
GUILDFORD COLLEGE
of Further and Higher Education

WITHDRAWN

THE LIBRARY
GUILDFORD COLLEGE
of Further and Higher Education
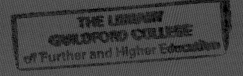

Little BRITAIN

145985
791.4372 LUC

Little BRITAIN

Written by

MATT LUCAS
AND
DAVID WALLIAMS

HarperCollins*Publishers*

Britain, Britain, Britain, land of technological achievement. We've had running water for over ten years, an underground tunnel that links us to Peru and we invented the cat.

But none of these innovations would have been possible were it not for the people of Britain and it is those people we do look at today.

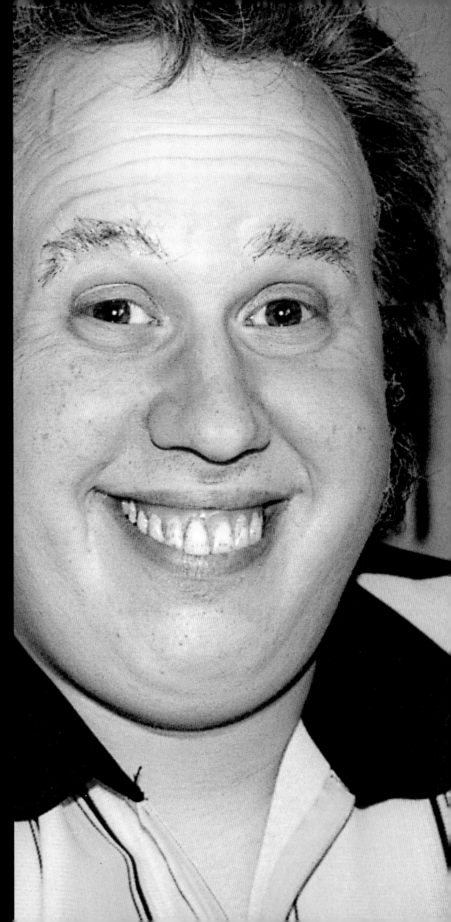

HarperEntertainment
An Imprint of HarperCollins*Publishers*
77–85 Fulham Palace Road,
Hammersmith, London W6 8JB
www.harpercollins.co.uk

Published by Harper*Entertainment* 2004
9 8 7 6

Text and Little Britain copyright
© Matt Lucas
and David Walliams 2004

The Authors assert the moral right to
be identified as the authors of this work

Design by Harry Green

ISBN 0 00 719302 5

Set in Rotis and Akzidenz

Printed and bound by Butler and Tanner

All rights reserved. No part of this publication
may be reproduced, stored in a retrieval system,
or transmitted, in any form or by any means,
electronic, mechanical, photocopying,
recording or otherwise, without the prior
permission of the publishers.

This book is sold subject to the condition that it
shall not, by way of trade or otherwise, be lent,
re-sold, hired out or otherwise circulated without
the publisher's prior consent in any form of
binding or cover other than that in which it is
published and without a similar condition
including this condition being imposed on the
subsequent purchaser.

Photographs on pages 3 (top), 20, 27, 28, 31,
38, 49, 54, 55, 99, 100, 101, 133, 136, 143,
144, 147, 148, 164, 187 (right), 193, 194,
199, 226, 227, 229, 230–31, 235, 238
© BBC Photo Library

Ruth Madoc image:
Photograph © Eddie Wing/Rex.

Worzel Gummidge image:
Photograph © Telewest Communications/Rex.

All other photographs © David Walliams
and Lisa Cavalli Green

Britain. Britain. Britain. Population: one millions. Number of towns: nine. Average height: thirty. Shoe size . . . But just who are Britain? Over the next eleventeen pages, we aim to find out — by following the lives of ordinary British folk. What do they? Who is them? And why?

acknowledgements

Matt and David would like to thank the following: Ashley Blaker, John Pidgeon, Helen Boaden, Caroline Raphael and everyone at BBC Radio 4, Paul Putner, Samantha Power, Jean Ainslie and Tom Baker for their brilliant performances in the radio series, David Arnold for his wonderful music, Stuart Murphy and Jane Root for commissioning the series for television, our executive producer Jon Plowman, Graham Linehan and Gareth Carrivick for directing the pilot, Steve Bendelack for directing the series, assistant director Mel Nortcliffe, Tracey Gillham who cast it, script supervisor Chrissy Bibby, assistant producer Andrew Wiltshire, production secretary Julia Weedon, production executive Jez Nightingale, location manager Jodi Moore, Mykola Pawluk for editing it, Mark Gatiss for script-editing, Dennis de Groot who designed it, director of photography Rob Kitzmann, Bob Newton our sound man, Martin Hawkins and Dave Bowden our cameramen, our lovely production assistant Nerys Evans, Annie Hardinge for costume design, Lisa Cavalli-Green for make-up design, Chris de Witt and all at Carlo Manzi's, Richard Mawbury and all at Wig Specialities, Bronwyn Nolan at The Business, Pat Farmer for making some fantastic costumes, all at the BBC Wig Store, all the crew and the cast, especially Tony Head, Ruth Jones, David Foxxe, Steve Furst and Ted Robbins and everyone else who worked so hard on the show. Thanks also to Melanie Coupland and all at Talkback Management, Faye Webber, Paul Stevens at ICM and, of course, Trevor Dolby and the team at HarperCollins.

Finally, we would like to say a very special thank you to our longtime producer and friend Myfanwy Moore.

SIR TOM BAKER, OBE, 1, BRITAIN

Once in a lifetime a book comes along that changes the way we think, the way we feel, the way we perceive the world. This is not that book. Hello. I am a man. Instead Matt Lucas and David Williams (I will not call him 'Walliams'. It irritates me and Williams is his real name anyway) have cobbled together this volume of 'sketches' or 'skits' or 'sketches' from the televisual series 'Little Britain', or, as it was known in France, Merde.

Oh my sweet potatoes!

Thirdly, it is a great honour for me to write this foreword. I regard 'Little Britain' as one of the finest pieces of work I've ever been associated with — even better than that Super Noodles advert I recently voiced. I greatly admire the work of Lucas and Wolliams. The way they dress up as either women or gays over and over again never fails to bring a smile to my beautiful face. I will always look back with great fondness on that morning I spent in a voiceover booth reading off what I can only describe as verbal excrement and for which I was paid forty pounds and the opportunity to observe Lucas and Welliams engaging in a sexual act (an offer I took up, incidentally, but would advise others to pass on).

To be honest, this show isn't really my thing. If I want a good laugh I'll watch 'Animal Hospital'. There's nothing I like more than seeing a hedgehog that's been run over and left for dead at the side of an A-road or a much-loved dog that has gone blind and needs to be put down. Ha ha. But I hope you enjoy this book. Apparently there is a joke on page 85, though I haven't been able to find it yet.

God bless me.

Tom Baker

Sir Tom Baker OBE

PS.   Wasn't I good in 'Doctor Who'?

EPISODE one

TOM V/O: Britain, Britain, Britain, land of technological achievement. We've had running water for over ten years, an underground tunnel that links us to Peru, and we invented the cat.

But none of these innovations would have been possible were it not for the people of Britain, and it is those people we do look at today.

Let's do it.

VICKY POLLARD — CLASSROOM 1

EXT. DAY. INNER CITY COMPREHENSIVE. SIGN – 'INNER STATE SCHOOL'. UNDERNEATH – 'HEADMASTER: GRAHAM 'SKIDMARK' STEVENS'. IN THE PLAYGROUND, SOME TEACHERS ARE FIGHTING, SURROUNDED BY A GROUP OF CHEERING KIDS.

TOM V/O: It's half past Rene at this comprehensive school in Darkley Noone . . .

INT. DAY. CLASSROOM. THE BELL RINGS AND THE CLASS IMMEDIATELY PACK THEIR BAGS AND BEGIN TO EXIT.

MR COLLIER: Projects in by first thing next week. Vicky Pollard, stay behind.

WE REVEAL VICKY IN SCHOOL UNIFORM BUT WITH MAKE-UP. SHE IS SMOKING. SHE TUTS AND PUTS OUT HER CIGARETTE ON THE FLOOR. VICKY'S FRIEND KELLY LURKS BY THE DOOR.

KELLY: Good luck, Vicky.

MR COLLIER: Yes, thank you Kelly.

THE DOOR SHUTS. EVERYONE ELSE HAS LEFT.

MR COLLIER: Right, come here please, Vicky.

VICKY SLOUCHES OVER, KICKING HER BAG IN FRONT OF HER AS SHE DOES SO. SHE SITS DOWN AT THE DESK IN FRONT OF THE TEACHER.

MR COLLIER: Vicky, it's been two weeks now and I still haven't received your essay on Lord Kitchener.

VICKY: No because what happened was was I was going round Karl's but then this whole fing happened right because Shelley Todd who's a bitch anyway has been completely going around saying that Destiny stole money out of Rochelle's purse but I ain't never even talked to Rochelle 'cause she flicked ash in Michaela's hair.

MR COLLIER: Vicky, I'm not interested in that. I'm more interested in your coursework.

NobecausewhathappenedwaswasIwas
goingroundKarl'sbutthenthiswholefing
happenedrightbecauseShelleyToddwho'sa
bitchanywayhasbeencompletelygoing
aroundsayingthatDestinystolemoneyoutof
Rochelle'spursebutIain'tnevereventalkedto
Rochelle'causesheflickedashin
Michaela'shair.

VICKY: No but what happened was was this whole fing happened what I don't even know nuffin' about because Ashley Cramer has been going around saying that Samantha's brother smells of mud but anyway shut up 'cause I ain't never even not even stole no car so shut up.

MR COLLIER: Vicky, have you even started this essay?

 ## Don't go givin' me evils!

VICKY: No but yeah but no but yeah but no but yeah but no because I'm not even going on the pill because Nadine reckons they stop you from getting pregnant.

MR COLLIER: You know if I don't get this essay by the end of the week you do know I'm going to have to fail you?

VICKY: Yeah but Louise Farren emptied a whole bottle of Fanta into Shannon's bag but anyway Luke reckons he fingered Emma Bacon in the language lab.

MR COLLIER: Vicky, do you want to pass your GCSE?

VICKY: GCS what? (PAUSE) Don't go givin' me evils!

SEBASTIAN AND MICHAEL – GREGORY

EXT. DAY. NO. 10 DOWNING STREET.

TOM V/O: Inside 10 Downing Street the Prime Minister is having a meeting with one of his aides.

RUNNING JOKE OF DISTRACTED POLICEMAN. WE HEAR AN ICE-CREAM VAN APPROACH. POLICEMAN IN TURMOIL ABOUT WHETHER HE CAN LEAVE HIS POST BUT RESOLVES NOT TO.

Of course if I was Prime Minister I'd knock through to No. 11 and have a sort of larger living area, really open up the space.

INT. PRIME MINISTER'S OFFICE. THE PRIME MINISTER IS SITTING ON THE SOFA WITH GREGORY MERCHANT, A NEW HANDSOME AIDE FROM THE TREASURY. THEY ARE SKIMMING SCHEDULES.

GREGORY: So, Prime Minister, the meeting with the Trade and Industry Secretary has now been rescheduled for six fifteen.

MICHAEL: Fine. So the Chancellor's been moved to seven?

THE DOOR OPENS. SEBASTIAN APPEARS. HE IS UPBEAT AND INFORMAL.

SEBASTIAN: Hiya!

THE PRIME MINISTER AND GREGORY LOOK UP. SEBASTIAN'S FACE DROPS.

SEBASTIAN: Oh. Hello.

GREGORY: Yes?

MICHAEL: Ah, Sebastian. This is Gregory Merchant. He's come to us from the Treasury.

GREGORY OFFERS HIS HAND.

GREGORY: Hello Sebastian. Nice to meet you.

SEBASTIAN TURNS AWAY.

SEBASTIAN: Whatever. (TO PRIME MINISTER) Um, sorry, Prime Minister. Can I have a word?

MICHAEL: Well, can't it wait?

SEBASTIAN: It's kind of important, Prime Minister.

MICHAEL: Ah, Gregory, would you . . .

GREGORY: Of course.

GREGORY EXITS

SEBASTIAN: Who was that?

MICHAEL: Gregory – new boy at the Treasury. He's rather good.

SEBASTIAN: Oh, is he?

MICHAEL: Yes, got a double first at Cambridge. Really knows his stuff.

SEBASTIAN: I don't like him.

MICHAEL: Why's that?

SEBASTIAN: I see the way he looks at you.

MICHAEL: What about it?

SEBASTIAN: He was looking at you . . . like he loves you.

(PAUSE)

MICHAEL: I don't think so.

SEBASTIAN: It's sad. He's obviously got some kind of mad crush on you, Prime Minister. Ha ha ha.

MICHAEL: I think it is very unlikely.

SEBASTIAN: He gets all kind of nervous when he's around you.

SEBASTIAN LAUGHS UNCONTROLLABLY AND TOSSES A FILE IN THE AIR. THE PAPERS SCATTER AND LAND AT MICHAEL'S FEET. SEBASTIAN KNEELS DOWN IN FRONT OF MICHAEL, PICKS UP THE PAPERS, AND LINGERS.

MICHAEL: Is that everything?

SEBASTIAN: Yes.

MICHAEL: Do you want to get up?

SEBASTIAN: No.

MICHAEL MOVES AWAY.

MICHAEL: Could you call Gregory back in?

SEBASTIAN CALLS EXCEPTIONALLY QUIETLY.

He was looking at you . . . **like he loves you.**

SEBASTIAN: 'Gregory?' I think he's gone. So anyway, um – as I was saying . . .

MICHAEL: (RAISES VOICE) Gregory, come in please.

THE DOOR OPENS. GREGORY ENTERS.

MICHAEL: Sebastian's just leaving. Could you show him out?

GREGORY OPENS THE DOOR FOR SEBASTIAN, IN A QUIETLY VICTORIOUS MANNER. SEBASTIAN EXITS. AS HE DOES SO, HE TURNS TO GREGORY.

SEBASTIAN: Bitch.

THE DOOR CLOSES. WE HEAR SOBBING AND FOOTSTEPS RUNNING AWAY.

MICHAEL: Sorry about that. Er, where were we?

GREGORY: Oh, your meeting with the Chancellor.

MICHAEL: Oh yes, right.

(PAUSE)

GREGORY: Ooh, you smell nice.

EMILY HOWARD — PUB

EXT. SEASIDE PUB. SUNNY DAY. WE SEE EMILY WALK DOWN THE STREET TOWARDS THE PUB, PRETENDING 'CINDERELLA'-LIKE TO LOSE HER SHOE ON THE WAY.

TOM V/O: People in Britain do all manner of things for kicks. Some lick stamps, others sit on chairs. This fellow, who calls himself Emily Howard, likes to dress up as a lady. Takes all sorts, I suppose.

EMILY APPROACHES PUB, HESITATES OUTSIDE, AND THEN FINALLY SUMMONS UP THE COURAGE TO ENTER.

INT. PUB. EMILY ENTERS, ACTING AS IF SHE IS DRENCHED FROM THE RAIN, SHAKING HER PARASOL, ETC., AND TRYING TO ATTRACT LOTS OF ATTENTION.

EMILY: Ooh, ah! Ooh, ah! Absolutely tipping it down out there. That's the only reason I came in here alone, without a chaperone. I am a lady, you see. Please – pay me no heed.

EMILY GOES TO THE BAR.

EMILY: I have never been in a 'perb' before. Tell me, what does one do?

LANDLORD: Well, you can order a drink if you like, mate.

EMILY: Yes, I'll have a lady's drink, s'il vous plaît.

LANDLORD: What can I get you?

VIC: *I'd* like to buy the lady a drink.

EMILY IS SHOCKED.

EMILY: What?

VIC: I said I'd like to buy you a drink, if that's OK.

EMILY: But I am a *lady*.

VIC: Yeah, I know. And I'd like to buy you a drink.

EMILY: Oh. A drinkypoopoo. Yes, I'll have a slimline tonic water, please.

LANDLORD: (SUSPICIOUS) Right you are.

EMILY: And um, two packets of crisps. Do you have the Barbecued Beef variety? Merci beaucoup.

THE LANDLORD NODS AND GIVES EMILY TWO BAGS OF CRISPS.

VIC: Cheers.

EMILY: Chin chin!

EMILY TAKES A TINY SIP.

EMILY: Ooh! Goes straight to my head.

VIC: So tell me a little bit about yourself.

EMILY: Well, my name is Emily. Emily Howard. And I am a lady. And because I am a lady, I like to do ladies' things, like attend the operettas and les ballets imaginaries. Do you like the theatre?

VIC: No, but I like you.

EMILY: You must know that I am a lady! I press flowers and stroke kittens and swim in rivers wearing dresses and hats . . . and shit.

VIC: You're a very lovely looking lady.

EMILY LAUGHS COQUETTISHLY FOR TOO LONG.

EMILY: (COY) You embarrass me. I must go and powder my nose.

EMILY EXITS TOWARDS THE TOILETS.

LANDLORD: 'Ere, you wanna be careful with that one.

VIC: She's gorgeous. Here, watch me pint, I'm off for a slash.

VIC HEADS TO THE GENTS.

INT. GENTS LAVATORY. VIC ENTERS AND GOES TO STAND AT A URINAL. WE SEE EMILY, URINATING, STANDING UP AT THE NEXT URINAL.

EMILY: Hello again.

EMILY DASHES OUT, LEAVING A QUIZZICAL VIC.

LOU AND ANDY — THE OPERA

EXT. DAY. ANDY'S HOUSE.

TOM V/O: Meanwhile, southeast of Northwestshire, lies the little town of Herby.

A POLICEMAN RUNS PAST BEING CHASED BY A ROBBER. THE PAIR WORK OUT THEY ARE CHASING EACH OTHER IN THE WRONG ORDER AND SWITCH ROLES.

INT. ANDY'S FRONT ROOM. LOU SITS NEXT TO ANDY, WITH A NEWSPAPER ON HIS LAP.

TOM V/O: Andy's birthday is just over a year away and his friend Lou has decided to do something special.

LOU: Right there's your milk. Now you know it's your birthday coming up and I said I'd take you up to London to see a show.

ANDY: Yeah, I know.

LOU SHOWS ANDY THE NEWSPAPER.

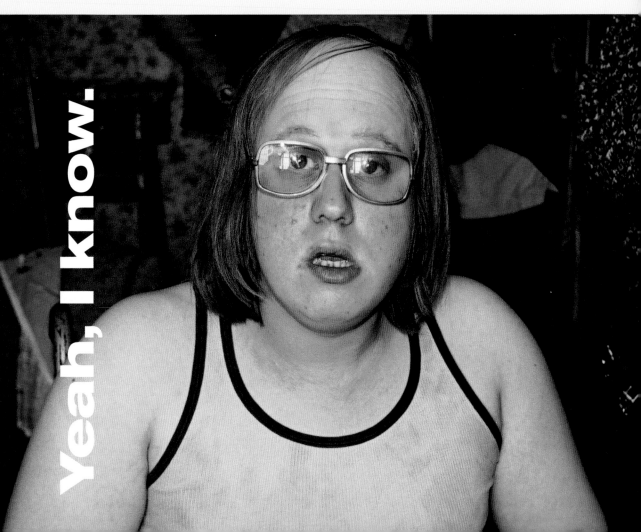

Yeah, I know.

LOU: Well, all the shows are advertised here. Now which one do you want to see, 'cause I'm gonna have to book?

ANDY POINTS INDISCRIMINATELY.

ANDY: That one.

LOU: That's the Royal Opera House. I don't think you'll enjoy that.

ANDY: That one.

LOU: Well, what about *Chitty Chitty Bang Bang*? You like the film and this one's got Michael Balls in it. You like Michael Balls.

ANDY: Yeah, I know.

LOU: So which one do you want to see?

ANDY: That one.

LOU: It's *La traviata*. It's an opera.

ANDY: Yeah, I know.

LOU: Well, it's very expensive. It's about a hundred pounds a ticket.

ANDY: That one.

LOU: Alright. We'll go to the opera.

CUT TO INT. BOX AT THE OPERA HOUSE. LOU AND ANDY – IN THEIR USUAL CLOTHES – ARE SITTING, ACCOMPANIED BY A FEW VERY WELL-DRESSED PEOPLE (I.E. DINNER JACKETS, ETC.). THERE IS BRIEF CHATTER, FOLLOWED BY A HUSH. THE LIGHTS DIM. THE MUSIC STARTS. WE HEAR JUST A FEW NOTES BEFORE . . .

ANDY: I don't like it.

KELSEY GRAMMAR SCHOOL – *GREAT EXPECTATIONS*

EXT. DAY. SCHOOL. WE SEE A SIGN – 'KELSEY GRAMMAR SCHOOL'.

THE BELL RINGS. SEVERAL BOYS RUN OUT EXCITEDLY INTO THE SCHOOL PLAYING FIELDS. THE BELL RINGS AGAIN ALMOST IMMEDIATELY AND THEY HEAD BACK TO THE CLASSROOM.

TOM V/O: This is Kelsey Grammar School in Flange. Schools are where tomorrow-adults, or 'children', are harvested.

INT. CLASSROOM IN A BOYS' PUBLIC SCHOOL. TWENTY BOYS (11/12 YEARS OLD) ARE SITTING READING FROM COPIES OF DICKENS'S *GREAT EXPECTATIONS*. BOREDOM HANGS IN THE AIR.

TOM V/O: For these boys the first lesson of the day is on Charles Dickens's *Great Expectations*.

BOY 1: ' . . . but now I was frightened again, and ran home without stopping'.

TEACHER: Palfrey, you take over. (PAUSE) Top of page 116.

BRIEF PAUSE AS THE BOY FINDS HIS PLACE.

BOY 2: 'My sister, Mrs Joe Gargery, had brought me up by hand. Knowing her to have a hard and heavy hand –'

TEACHER: Johnson, you take over.

BOY 3: ' . . . in the habit of laying it upon her husband as well as upon me –'

TEACHER: Clark.

BOY 4: 'I supposed –'

TEACHER: Back to Johnson.

BOY 3: 'supposed that Joe –'

TEACHER: Pelham, you take over.

BOY 5: ' . . . that Joe Gargery and I were both brought up by hand. –'

TEACHER: Worms!

BOY 6: ' . . . Not a good-looking –'

TEACHER: Meacher!

BOY 7: '. . . woman.'

PAUSE. THE TEACHER LOOKS UP.

TEACHER: Read on, boy!

BOY 7: 'My sis–'

TEACHER: Rolands!

BOY 8: '–ter and I had –'

TEACHER: Honkeytonk!

BOY 9: 'I had a general impression that she must have been making Joe Gar –'

TEACHER: Phillips! Nash! Papathasaniou!

(PAUSE)

TEACHER: Go on! Read!

(PAUSE)

TEACHER: Yes – all of you.

(SLIGHT PAUSE)

3 BOYS: 'Joe was a fair man, with curls of –'

TEACHER: Melling! Ashworth! Join them!

5 BOYS: '. . . of his smooth face, and with eyes –'

TEACHER: Scotch accents.

5 BOYS: (ATTEMPTED SCOTTISH ACCENTS) '. . . of such a very undecided blue that they – '

TEACHER: In the style of 'The Elephant Man'!

7 BOYS: (IN THE STYLE OF 'THE ELEPHANT MAN') '. . . seemed to have somehow got mixed with their own whites – '

TEACHER: (CLAPS HANDS) Right stop! We're not getting anywhere. *I* will read. Page 117. 'Joe was a milled . . . , mild, mild, . . . mild, mild . . . good-natter'ed'

HE PICKS UP A VIDEO TAPE OF *GREAT EXPECTATIONS* FROM HIS DESK.

TEACHER: Shall we just watch the video? Yeah, yeah, better.

JASON AND NAN – FIRST MEETING

EXT. DAY. INNER-CITY COUNCIL FLATS. SIGN – 'RICHARD VRANCH HOUSE'. WE SEE GARY AND JASON ARRIVE AT GARY'S FLAT.

TOM V/O: Unlike other countries, Britain has people of two genders – women *and* men. Gary and his friend Jason are two *men*. Write it down. *Men*.

INT. COUNCIL FLAT. A MUM, HER DAUGHTER (JULIE) AND HER GRANNY ARE WATCHING TELLY. WE HEAR A KEY OPENING A DOOR.

MUM: (OFF-SCREEN) That you, Gary?

GARY, A TEENAGE BOY, POPS HIS HEAD ROUND THE DOOR.

GARY: Yeah, Mum. I'm with me mate Jason.

MUM: (OFF-SCREEN) Oh. Bring him in.

GARY ENTERS THE ROOM WITH JASON BEHIND HIM.

GARY: All right? This is Jason. This is me sister, Julie.

JASON: All right?

JULIE: Hello.

JULIE IS MILDLY FLIRTATIOUS. JASON IS OBLIVIOUS.

GARY: This is me Mum.

JASON: Hello.

MUM: How d'you do?

Right stop! We're not getting anywhere. I will read. Page 117. 'Joe was a milled . . . , mild, mild, . . . mild, mild . . . good-natter'ed'

GARY: And this is me Nan.

JASON'S MANNER CHANGES.

JASON: Hel-*lo*!

WE SEE A SHOT OF NAN FROM JASON'S POINT OF VIEW: SOFT FOCUS, WEARING MAKE-UP, ROMANTIC MUSIC.

JASON: Gary never told me he had such a beautiful grandmother.

MUM: I'll just go and put the kettle on.

JASON SITS NEAR TO NAN. MUM EXITS. PAUSE.

JASON: Why, I haven't seen you around. Where do you normally hang out?

NAN: Day Centre.

JASON: Must check it out. (PAUSE) You smell nice. What is it?

NAN: Murray Mints.

JULIE NUDGES GARY.

JULIE: (TO GARY) Oi, tell him about the party.

GARY: (TO JASON) Oh yeah. Julie's mate's havin' a party tonight, Jay. Do ya wanna go?

JASON: (TO NAN) Er, what do you reckon, Nan? Are you up for it?

NAN: Eh? What me? Oh no. I don't think she'll want me there. It's for the younger generation.

JASON: Yeah, I think I'll give it a miss. Ta.

JASON MOVES CLOSER TO NAN.

JASON: So, er, I bet you're a woman of experience.

NAN: Well, I've lived through two world wars. (CALLING) Maureen?

MUM: (OFF-SCREEN) Yes, Mum?

NAN: Can you take me to the toilet?

MUM: I'm just making the tea, Mum. Julie, be a good girl, take your Nan to the toilet.

JULIE SIGHS AND STARTS TO RISE.

JASON: It's okay. I'll do it.

JASON HELPS NAN OUT OF HER CHAIR AND WALKS HER OUT OF THE ROOM. AS HE DOES SO, HE WINKS AT GARY.

NAN: Careful.

JASON: Oh, sorry. I thought that was your elbow.

PIANIST

TOM V/O: Meanwhile, at the Uncle Albert Hall, a recital is taking place.

INT. ROYAL ALBERT HALL. ONSTAGE, A RESPECTABLE LOOKING PIANIST STOPS IN THE MIDDLE OF A PIECE.

PIANIST: Oh no, I had a bag! Where's me bag?

HE SPOTS IT NEXT TO HIS PIANO.

PIANIST: Ah, here it is!

HE RESUMES PLAYING.

KENNY CRAIG – RESTAURANT

TOM V/O: Meanwhile, in Troby, stage hypnotist Kenny Craig is on a date.

INT. CHINESE RESTAURANT. KENNY IS SEATED OPPOSITE HIS DATE, CATHY, A WOMAN OF A SIMILAR AGE. THEY ARE STUDYING THEIR MENUS.

KENNY: I usually just have a starter and find that's enough.

CATHY LOOKS AROUND THE PLUSH RESTAURANT.

CATHY: It's nice here. (JOKILY) It's funny – I don't remember saying I'd go on a date with you. (PAUSE) (KENNY LOOKS GUILTY) I don't know what to have. It all looks so nice.

KENNY: The er, the er, set menu is very reasonable.

CATHY: Oh, they do baked lobster. I've never had lobster before. I'll have that.

KENNY IS PUT OUT. HE LOOKS UP FROM HIS MENU AND HYPNOTIZES CATHY.

KENNY: Look into my eyes. Look into my eyes. The eyes. The eyes. Not around the eyes. Don't look around the eyes. Look into my eyes. (CLICKS FINGERS) You're under. In a moment the waiter will appear and when he does you will order from the set menu. Three courses, eight ninety-five. You will not order the lobster . . .

Three – two – one . . .

. . . you're back in the room.

CATHY COMES OUT OF HER TRANCE. SHE STUDIES THE MENU AGAIN.

CATHY: Ooh, there's lots of things I like on the set menu. You don't mind ordering from the set menu, do you?

KENNY: Hey, hey, whatever you want. That's fine. Do you, er, know what you want to drink yet?

CATHY: Seeing as it's a special occasion it'd be lovely to have a bottle of bubbly.

KENNY ROLLS HIS EYES.

KENNY: Look into my eyes. Look into my eyes. The eyes. The eyes. Not around the eyes. Don't look around the eyes. Look into my eyes. (CLICKS FINGERS) You're under. You will choose a soft drink. You will not, repeat *not*, order champagne. I know it's our first date but I don't even fancy you that much and I really resent you bleeding me dry here. Three – two – one – you're back in the room.

THE WAITER APPEARS.

WAITER: Are you ready to order, madam?

CATHY: Yes, I'll order from the set menu, please. I'll have the spring roll and chicken chow mein.

WAITER: And to drink?

CATHY: Just a glass of water.

KENNY: Tap!

WAITER: And for sir?

KENNY: Er, I'm not really hungry. I'll just have the lobster and a bottle of champagne, thanks.

DENNIS WATERMAN – SHAKESPEARE

EXT. DAY. WEST END OFFICE, NEAR A THEATRE. A 'LITERAL MIME' ARTIST IS PERFORMING OUTSIDE.

TOM V/O: Above this theatre here in Sneddy is the office of theatrical agent Jeremy Rent.

INT. JEREMY RENT'S OFFICE. JEREMY IS STROKING HIS LITTLE DOG. THE RECEPTIONIST BUZZES JEREMY.

JEREMY: Yes!

RECEPTIONIST: Dennis Waterman to see you.

JEREMY: Lovely, do send him in.

DENNIS APPEARS AT THE (BIG) DOOR.

DENNIS: Hello.

'Lots of things are happening in Albert Square do do do do do do . . .'

JEREMY: Hello.

DENNIS: Ooh, that's a big dog!

JEREMY: Oh, have you never met Wolfitt? (TO DOG) Shake his hand.

A FRIGHTENED DENNIS SHAKES WOLFITT'S (GIANT) PAW.

JEREMY: Who's a good boy?

JEREMY PUTS WOLFITT INTO A LITTLE BASKET. WITH GREAT DIFFICULTY, DENNIS CLIMBS ONTO THE CHAIR.
HE IS NOW EXHAUSTED.

DENNIS: Woooh. Tired.

JEREMY: Now I'm glad you've popped in because I've just had a call from the Troot Theatre Company.

DENNIS: Oh. Not telly?

JEREMY: No. I'm afraid as long as you insist on writing and singing your own theme tunes, telly won't touch you.

DENNIS: What about that part in *EastEnders*?

JEREMY: They've already got a theme tune.

DENNIS: Mine's much better. (SINGS) 'Lots of things are happening in Albert Square do do do do do do . . .'

JEREMY: Yes, thank you Dennis. Now the Troot Theatre Company are doing a production of *Macbeth* and they want you for the lead.

JEREMY PASSES OVER A (BIG) COPY OF THE PLAY, IN BOOK FORM.

DENNIS: Ooh, heavy.

JEREMY: Just one thing – they do start rehearsals on Monday.

DENNIS: Well, that's not much time, is it? To write a new feem toon.

JEREMY: No, Dennis, it's a straight play. No music. So yes or no?

DENNIS : (SINGS)

'Mr Mac Beff is a naughty man.
Do do do do do
He gone and killed another man
Do do do do do
I hath a good idea
Just thou keep me near
I'll be so good for the Scottish Play.'

(PAUSE)

JEREMY: I'll tell 'em you're busy.

DENNIS: Could you, er, give me a hand down please?

JEREMY LIFTS DENNIS DOWN FROM THE CHAIR.

DENNIS: Oh don't drop me, don't drop me!

JEREMY: I've got you. Off you pop.

DENNIS HEADS FOR THE DOOR. JEREMY PATS HIM ON THE HEAD WITH WHAT IN DENNIS'S WORLD IS A GIANT HAND.

DENNIS: Don't patronize me.

MARJORIE DAWES/FATFIGHTERS – BROKEN SCALES

EXT. EARLY EVENING. MODERN SUBURBAN COMMUNITY CENTRE. WE SEE A GROUP OF NAZIS EXITING, CHEERFULLY.

TOM V/O: Community centres in Britain are used as meeting places for all kinds of groups. Until a law is passed to imprison fat people, the gluttons of Britain are free to walk the streets and attend special diet classes like this one.

INT. A SMALL COMMUNITY CENTRE. SITTING IN A CIRCLE ARE MEERA, PAUL, TANIA, AND HALF A DOZEN OTHERS. NEARBY ARE A SET OF SCALES, A NOTICEBOARD WITH PLENTY OF DIFFERENT FATFIGHTERS LEAFLETS ON IT, AND A TABLE NEARBY WITH LOTS OF FATFIGHTERS PRODUCTS – CEREALS, SELF-HELP VIDEOTAPES, CRISPS, CHOCOLATES,

ETC. MARJORIE STANDS BY A LARGE WHITE BOARD ON AN EASEL, JUST OUTSIDE THE CIRCLE. IT IS MARKED 'WEIGHT BOARD' AND HAS THE NAMES OF ALL THE MEMBERS IN ONE COLUMN AND THEIR WEIGHT OVER A NUMBER OF WEEKS IN ANOTHER.

MARJORIE: Yeah, I would say . . . twelve stone six. Oh, you've gone up half a pound. Bad luck.

MARJORIE FILLS IN THE AMOUNT NEXT TO MEERA'S NAME. PAT ENTERS AS MARJORIE IS TALKING.

PAT: Sorry I'm late, Marjorie.

MARJORIE: That's alright, Pat. Now the, er, scales are broken so I'm just having to estimate people's weights so er, so er, I'll tell you what – just lift up your arm.

PAT REMAINS STANDING. MARJORIE STUDIES HER FIGURE.

MARJORIE: Yeah, you look about seventeen stone to me.

PAT: I weighed myself this morning. I was sixteen stone five.

MARJORIE: Oh well, turn round. (PAT TURNS ROUND) No, definitely seventeen I'm afraid. Oh, it's not easy is it?

MARJORIE FILLS IN THE INFO ON THE BOARD.

MARJORIE: OK, last but not least . . . Paul.

PAUL: What are you gonna make me then, eh? Twenty stone?

MARJORIE: Don't be silly, Paul.

MARJORIE STUDIES HIM AND WRITES DOWN THE AMOUNT.

MARJORIE: Nineteen stone eleven. OK, our buzzword for today is 'cravings' – 'cravings'.

MARJORIE GOES OVER TO A SECOND BOARD AND WRITES DOWN 'CRAVINGS'.

MARJORIE: Not John Cravings. We're not talking 'John Craving's News Roundup' – no, we're talking cravings. What foods do we get cravings of? Tania, start us off.

TANIA: Chocolate.

MARJORIE: Chocolate. Yes. Well done. Chocolate, lovely, OK.

MARJORIE WRITES DOWN 'CHOCLIT'. A FEW PEOPLE PUT THEIR HANDS UP.

MARJORIE: Johansen?

MAN: No, it's Dave.

MARJORIE: Oh sorry, Dave. I always get those two names mixed up . . .

MAN: Chocolate.

Cake. Yes. Cake. We all like a bit of cake, don't we? I know I do. I love a bit, I do. I love a bit of cake. I do. I just like cake. I'm just one of those people. I come home and all I want is a slice of cake. I just love cake. I just love cake. I just love a bit of cake. CAKE. I love a bit of cake. Cake. Lovely.

MARJORIE: Yeah , we've sort of had chocolate.

MAN: Chocolate biscuits.

MARJORIE POINTS TO THE BOARD.

MARJORIE: Yeah, they're sort of covered in chocolate.

PAUL: Yeah, that's why he likes 'em.

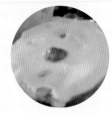

THE OTHERS CHUCKLE.

MARJORIE: (TO PAUL) Yeah, you see that's why you're so fat, because you don't take it seriously. Pat?

PAT: Cake.

MARJORIE WRITES DOWN 'CAKE'.

MARJORIE: Cake. Yes. Cake. We all like a bit of cake, don't we? I know I do. I love a bit, I do. I love a bit of cake. I do. I just like cake. I'm just one of those people. I come home and all I want's a slice of cake. I just love cake. I just love cake. I just love a bit of cake. CA-AKE. I love a bit of cake. Cake. Lovely. Mary?

MEERA: Fish and chips.

MARJORIE: Sorry, do it again . . .

MEERA: Fish and chips.

MARJORIE: She doesn't make sense . . . do it again.

MEERA: Fish and chips.

MARJORIE: Do it again.

MEERA: Oh forget it.

MARJORIE WRITES DOWN 'CURRY'.

MARJORIE: Well it must be some sort of dish that we don't get over here . . . OK, so how can we eat the food we crave and still lose weight?

MARJORIE TURNS OVER THE PAGE WITH THE LIST OF CRAVINGS ON TO REVEAL A PAGE WITH THE WORDS 'THE FATFIGHTERS HALF THE CALORIES DIET' ON IT.

MARJORIE: Introducing the all-new 'FatFighters Half the Calories Diet'. Yeah? Yeah? Take the food you like, whether it's your chocolate or your biscuits or your cake – ooh man, I love the cake! (TO MEERA) Or your . . . thing. Cut it in half and it's just half the calories. Yeah? And because it's only half the calories, you can have twice as much.

PAUL: That's just stupid.

MARJORIE: Excuse me?

PAUL: You're never gonna lose weight by doing that.

MARJORIE GOES OVER TO THE WEIGHT BOARD AND ADDS A POUND TO PAUL'S WEIGHT.

MARJORIE: Oh dear. Nineteen stone twelve.

RAY McCOONEY — SOUP

EXT. NIGHT. ISOLATED HOTEL AMIDST DRAMATIC LANDSCAPE IN SCOTLAND. HOTEL SIGN – 'YE OLDE HOTELE'. WE SEE A COUPLE IN SWIMMING COSTUMES ON SUN-LOUNGERS SUNBATHING OUTSIDE.

TOM V/O: If you're thinking of going on holiday and the Arctic is fully booked, why not try Scotland?

INT. DINING ROOM. THERE IS A VAGUE GROTTO-LIKE FEELING – E.G. MASKS, STUFFED ANIMALS, ANTIQUE MUSICAL AND MEDICAL INSTRUMENTS, ETC. A FEW PEOPLE ARE HAVING DINNER.

MORAG: This is very good.

DONALD: Yes, it's very good. I assume it was all freshly made on the premises.

THE PROPRIETOR – RAY MCCOONEY – APPEARS UNEXPECTEDLY, DRESSED IN A WAISTCOAT AND CRAVAT.

RAY: Enjoying your stay?

DONALD: Yes, very much.

MORAG: We were just saying how much we like the soup. Did you make it?

RAY: Maybe I did and maybe I didn't.

RAY PULLS OUT AN ODD LITTLE FLUTE-LIKE INSTRUMENT AND PLAYS IT.

DONALD: Well, did you?

RAY: Yeeeees.

DONALD: Well it's delicious. We would love to be able to make it ourselves.

RAY: You'd like to know my secrets, would you? (PLAYS FLUTE)

MORAG: Well, yes.

RAY: Have you ever heard of a thing called butterrrrrr?

DONALD: Yes.

RAY: Gold in colour and slippery to the touch.

DONALD: Yes, butter. Anything else?

RAY: Yes. Did ye ever hear the legend of the seeded fruit that is often mistooken for a vegetable?

DONALD: The tomato.

RAY: Red in colour and fleshy within, but beware o' the pips. (PLAYS FLUTE) They call it the tom-matto.

DONALD: Right. The tomato. Anything else?

RAY: Have ye ever heard of such a thing as a cow? A cow, mind, oh ha ha ha ha.

DONALD: (WEARILY) Let me think. Yes. I have.

RAY: Ah, but did ye know the cow secretes a liquor from its udder?

MORAG: Yes, milk.

RAY: Ye know too much. Ye know . . . (RAY DIPS HIS FINGER IN MORAG'S SOUP AND LICKS IT) Too much . . . (PLAYS FLUTE)

RAY LEAVES, PLAYING THE 'COUNTDOWN' THEME ON HIS FLUTE.

DONALD: (TO MORAG) So anyway, we start off by the castle . . .

RAY RETURNS.

RAY: I leave ye with a riddle.

DONALD AND MORAG SIGH.

RAY: I'm hard yet soft, I am coloured yet clear, I am fruity and sweet. I am jelly. What am I?

DONALD: Jelly.

RAY: Muse upon it further. I shall return.

DONALD: It's jelly though, isn't it?

RAY: Yeeeees.

I am fruity and sweet. I am jelly. What am I?

LOU AND ANDY — DIVING BOARD

EXT. DAY. SWIMMING POOL IN RUNDOWN AREA. PEOPLE ARRIVING IN SWIMMING COSTUMES.

TOM V/O: If you have a verruca, and you would like to share it with others, then why not pop down to your local swimming pool?

INT. SWIMMING POOL. LOU WHEELS ANDY FROM THE CHANGING ROOMS TO THE POOLSIDE. BOTH ARE IN SWIMMING COSTUME.

ANDY: I wanna get in.

LOU: Yes, I'll get you in in a minute. I've just got to find a lifeguard to help get you in. You wait there. OK?

ANDY: I wanna get in.

LOU: In a minute.

LOU APPROACHES THE LIFEGUARD. ANDY, UNSEEN BY LOU, GETS UP, CLIMBS THE STEPS LEADING TO THE TALLEST DIVING BOARD AND JUMPS OFF. HE SWIMS TO THE STEPS, GETS OUT AND SITS BACK DOWN IN THE WHEELCHAIR.

LOU: (TO LIFEGUARD) Excuse me, I wonder if you could give me a hand. I'm here with a friend, who you may have seen is in a wheelchair. And I need a little bit of help getting him in and out of the pool. Now I mean, getting him in the pool is not really a kerfuffle, getting him out of the pool isn't a real kerfuffle. I mean it's relatively kerfuffle free. But he does have a slight fear of water. You know, he likes the water but he's not a strong swimmer – it's really doggy paddle if anything. And really we just need help to get him in and out because I like him to go swimming because it's good exercise. You know what I mean?

LIFEGUARD: Yes, I do.

LOU: And so really I think it's just a case of me maybe taking the upper body and you maybe taking the . . .

LIFEGUARD: The legs.

LOU: Yeah, the legs, the lower body. And just lowering him in very gently. So shall we go help him in? Right, oh, how we going to do this? (TO ANDY) Have you showered?

ANDY: Yeah.

DAFFYD — HYWEL

EXT. NIGHT. VILLAGE PUB. SIGN: 'THE SCARECROW AND MRS KING'. A MINER APPEARS CARRYING A TRAY OF FOUR PINTS. A MAN BUMPS INTO HIM, BUT THE MINER MANAGES TO AVOID SPILLAGE. HE THEN TRIPS OVER SOMEONE'S BAG AND GOES FLYING. THE TRAY IS UPTURNED VIOLENTLY BUT THE DRINKS STAY STUCK TO THE TRAY AND UNSPILLED – I.E. PROP DRINKS STUCK TO TRAY. THE MINER TILTS THE TRAY IN BEMUSEMENT.

TOM V/O: It's Julia o'clock here in the Welsh mining village of Llandewi Breffi, and out gay man Daffyd Thomas is enjoying a drink.

INT. COSY OLD-FASHIONED VILLAGE PUB. DAFFYD THOMAS IS SITTING ALONE AT THE BAR, MOPING, IN ONE OF HIS TIGHT-FITTING PVC OUTFITS. MYFANWY, A FRIENDLY YOUNG BARMAID, APPROACHES WITH A SMILE.

DAFFYD: Can I have another Bacardi and Coke please, Myfanwy?

MYFANWY: Coming right up.

MYFANWY PREPARES THE DRINK.

DAFYDD: Oh, bloody hell, Myfanwy. I'm so down.

MYFANWY: Oh, why is that, Daffyd?

DAFFYD: It's so hard being the only gay in the village. Oh, I just dream of the day when I could meet other gays who understand what it's like to be a gay.

MYFANWY: Oh, I was going to tell you. I was talking to Old Ma Evans and she's got a new lodger from Cardiff and guess what – he is a gay.

DAFFYD: What, in the village?

MYFANWY: Apparently, yes. I told her to send him over here tonight so you could meet him.

HYWEL ENTERS. HE IS DRESSED IN AN OUTRAGEOUSLY CAMP WAY.

MYFANWY: This must be him now.

HYWEL APPROACHES THE BAR AND SITS NEXT TO DAFFYD. HE ADDRESSES MYFANWY.

HYWEL: Hello. Can I have Bacardi and Coke, please?

PAUSE. HYWEL TURNS TO DAFFYD.

HYWEL: Oh, you must be Daffyd.

MYFANWY: There you go. I'll leave you boys to it.

MYFANWY DISAPPEARS TO THE OTHER END OF THE BAR, WITH A KNOWING SMILE.

DAFFYD: No, don't go . . . I . . . Just passing through are you?

EPISODE

That's exactly the kind of homophobic attitude I've come to expect in this village.

GOOD DAY!

HYWEL: Oh no, I've got a job here at the florist and I'm looking for somewhere to live. I saw a very nice cottage, but that's another story!

DAFFYD: Is it?

HYWEL: Yes.

DAFFYD: And you claim to be a gay do you?

HYWEL: Yes I am. Mrs Evans said I should come and talk to you because you're the only gay in this village. Well, now you're not. Now there's two of us.

DAFFYD: No, you are not a gay. I am gay.

HYWEL: I am gay.

DAFFYD: Alright then, if you're gay who played Dorothy in the film *The Wizard of Oz*?

HYWEL AND MYFANWY: Judy Garland!

DAFFYD: How do *you* know that?

MYFANWY: It's easy, everyone knows that.

DAFFYD: Alright then, this'll get you. Who is the gay character in *Are you Being Served*?

ALL: Mr Humphries!

DAFFYD: Was it?

ALL: Yes!

DAFFYD: Well, that's very subtle then. I always thought it was Captain Peacock – he's the one with the moustache.

HYWEL: Well, I seem to have passed your gay test, so I must be gay!

DAFFYD: No, you are not a gay. I am the gay. You're probably just a little bit poofy.

HYWEL: I am gay. I've had sex with men and everything.

MYFANWY IS LISTENING AT THE OTHER END OF THE BAR. SHE CALLS OVER.

MYFANWY: That's more than you've had, Daffyd.

DAFFYD: Shut up, Myfanwy! I am the only gay in this village and that's that.

HYWEL: Well, maybe I should go.

DAFFYD: Yes, back to Cardiff. We've already got one gay in Llandewi Breffi. We don't need another one.

HYWEL: Well, goodbye then. Provincial queens!

HYWEL EXITS. MYFANWY RETURNS.

MYFANWY: Daffyd Thomas, you bloody fool! You could have had a bit of cock there! 'Oh, I'm the only gay in the village!' You're full of shit, you are!

DAFFYD: That's exactly the kind of homophobic attitude I've come to expect in this village. Good day!

DAFFYD LEAVES DRAMATICALLY.

VICKY POLLARD — CLASSROOM 2

INT. CLASSROOM. VICKY SITS OPPOSITE MR COLLIER. THERE IS A LARGE BOTTLE OF CIDER ON HER DESK.

MR COLLIER: Now about this essay . . .

VICKY: *I done it!*

MR COLLIER: Yep, I have, er, one or two problems with it. 'What was Lord Kitchener's role in World War One?' – 'No but yeah. In World War One or summink there was this bloke right called Kitchen or summink or nuffin' who done this fing but he ain't not even not done it so shut up. Anyway Kathy reckons she saw Candice getting off with Tony . . . 'Tozer?

MR COLLIER LOOKS AT VICKY QUESTIONINGLY. VICKY NODS.

VICKY: Tozer, yeah.

MR COLLIER: '. . . in Foot Locker but anyway don't listen to her because she's got one tit bigger than the other'. Vicky, this simply won't do.

VICKY: Why? Is there a problem with spellin'?

BLACK AND WHITE MINSTRELS

INT. KITCHEN. TWO MINSTRELS ARE EATING BREAKFAST. THE RADIO IS ON.

NEWS REPORTER: (ON RADIO) So, Home Secretary, what are your priorities for the next twelve months?

HOME SECRETARY: (ON RADIO) I would say the biggest challenge we face now is the increasing influx of minstrels.

There are too many minstrels in this country and I would say there is a case for saying that a good deal of them should be sent back to Minstrel-land. In my constituency over the weekend . . .

DOWNCAST, ONE OF THE MINSTRELS GETS UP AND CHANGES THE STATION. THE RADIO NOW BROADCASTS A FAMOUS MINSTREL SONG, 'SWANEE'. THE MINSTRELS SING ALONG JOYFULLY AS THEY CONTINUE TO EAT THEIR BREAKFAST.

WORLD RECORD ATTEMPT – BATH OF BEANS

INT. CONFERENCE HALL. WE SEE A BANNER WITH 'BATH OF BEANS – WORLD RECORD ATTEMPT'. WE SEE IAN 1 SEATED IN A LARGE WHITE BATH. IAN 2 POURS A CAN OF BEANS INTO THE BATH.

IAN 1: I think we're gonna need another tin.

IAN 2 HEADS FOR THE DOOR.

IAN 1: (CALLING) In fact, get two.

THE CREDITS ROLL.

TOM V/O: I hope you've enjoyed tonight's programme. If you haven't, you might like to jot down the names currently appearing on your screen and make obscene phone calls to them. There's mine now, quick, until next time, goodbike!

PHONE RINGS.

TOM V/O: Hello? No, I'm not wearing any knickers.

EPISODE

'SUGGESTED FEEM TUNE FOR 'CRIME WATCH'
BY D. WATERMAN'

'Lots of crimes are happening across
the country
Do do do do do do do do
It's presented by Nick Ross and a fat
Policeman does a bit as well
I'll be so good for —
Goodnight and remember don't have
nightmares.'

'SUGGESTED FEEM TOON FOR
SWISS TONY' BY D. WATERMAN'

Do you remember that
programme called The Fast Show?
Do do do do do do do do
It had a character that sold
cars who was called Swiss Toni.
Do do do do do do do do
Well now he's got his own show.
But you have to get BBC 3
I'll be so good for —
He's always says 'selling a car
is like making love to a
beautiful woman.'

Dennis Waterman
'Prospero'

*D*ennis is one of Britain's best-loved actors, singers, and wearers of denim. He first came to the public's attention in *The Sweeney* (1975–78), in which he starred with Morse. The feem toon was just an instrumental and although Dennis liked to sing along at home, unfortunately his vocals did not appear on the actual programme. In 1979 he took the role of minder Terry McCann, who was a minder in the hit series *Minder*, opposite Flash Harry out of *St Trinian's*. The show is best remembered for its feem toon, 'I Could Be So Good For You', which was an international hit and was the biggest selling single of all time until Michael Ball's 'Love Changes Everything' come along and ruined it.

Dennis done *Minder* for ages and then they brought in another bloke called Gary something, but it wasn't as good. Then he done *On the Up*, in which he wrote the feem toon and sung the feem toon. Gary Webster, that was him. Then he done that one on the boat with that woman from *Just Good Friends*. After that he done *My Fair Lady* with Tiffany out of *EastEnders* and that bloke who was a baddie in one of the Bond films (not one of the earlier ones, one of the rubbish later ones with that guy out of *Remington Steele*). More lately he can be seen in the BBC series *New Tricks*, in which he stars in it, writes the feem toon, and sings the feem toon, alongside the one out of *At Home with the Braithwaites*, the one out of *The Likely Lads*, and Alun Armstrong. He is currently writing his autobiography, *Come Back Rula*, and this autumn will be releasing a compilation album of his greatest hit.

Ruth Madoc

'Miranda'

'Hi-De-Hi'

'SUGGESTED FEEM TOON FOR 'BIG BROTHER'
BY D. WATERMAN

'They get some people and lock them in a house
Do do do do do do do do
And they really really hope that they have sex.
Do do do do do do do do do
But they never do,
I should know. I've watched them all.
I'll be so good for—
My favourite one was Sandy.

'SUGGESTED FEEM TOON 'THE REALLY WILD SHOW'
BY D. WATERMAN

'On BB1 at about 4.40
Do do do do do do do do
There's a show presented by Terry Nutkins
Do do do do do do do do
He's got a bald head
With long hair at the sides.
I'll be so good for—
Oh yeah and a sealion in the boot of his car.'

'SUGGESTED FEEM TOON FOR 'ROOM 101'
BY D. WATERMAN

This show is presented by Paul Merton
Do do do do do do do do do
It used to be presented by Nick Hancock
Do do do do do do do do
But now he just does 'They Think It's all Over'
Which used to have that guy Lee Hurst in it.
I'll be so good for—
Anyway it's the one where they have to
say things they don't like.

EPISODE *two*

TOM V/O: Britain, Britain, Britain. Land of tradition. Fish and fries. The changing of the garden. Trooping the coloureds. But have you ever wondered about the people of Britain? Nor have I. But this show aims to find out by following the lives of ordinary British folk. What is them? Who do they? And why?

DAFFYD — GAY TIMES

EXT. SMALL VILLAGE NEWSAGENT. DAFFYD APPROACHES. HE IS SINGING 'WEST END GIRLS'.

TOM V/O: Have you ever done it gay wise? I have – it's a hoot. It's late three, and woolly woofter Daffyd Thomas is popping into his local newsagents.

DAFFYD: Hello, Mrs Llewellyn.

MRS LLEWELLYN: Oh, hello, Daffyd.

DAFFYD PERUSES THE MAGAZINE SHELF ON THE WAY TO THE COUNTER.

MRS LLEWELLYN: And what can I do you for today?

DAFFYD: I'll have a quarter of bonbons and a copy of *Gay Times* please. It's my only outlet.

MRS LLEWELLYN: Is it not on the rack, love?

DAFFYD: I couldn't see it.

MRS LLEWELLYN: Oh, it must have gone then.

DAFFYD: I'm sorry?

MRS LLEWELLYN: Well, we only get the one in for you, so I imagine somebody must have bought it.

DAFFYD: I don't think so. I think you'll find I am the only gay in this village.

MRS LLEWELLYN: Oh, I remember. Somebody definitely came and bought it yesterday. It's got Hazel Dean on the cover and a very informative article on rimming.

DAFFYD: Who bought it?

MRS LLEWELLYN: Do you know, I can't remember.

DAFFYD: Think.

MRS LLEWELLYN: Well now, erm . . .

DAFFYD: Come on woman!

MRS LLEWELLYN: Well now, let's think. Who came in yesterday? Dai Davies, the music master – he might have bought it.

DAFFYD: He's not gay.

MRS LLEWELLYN: Ooh well, he does share a cottage with the English master.

DAFFYD: They're just friends.

MRS LLEWELLYN: No, come to think of it, he just bought *Vogue*.

DAFFYD: See – he's not gay! Who else? Quickly!

MRS LLEWELLYN: Father Hughes.

DAFFYD: A gay priest? What planet are you on, woman?

MRS LLEWELLYN: Oh, I remember.

DAFFYD: Go on.

MRS LLEWELLYN: Yes, I was quite surprised actually, because I had absolutely no idea he liked cock.

DAFFYD: Who? Who?

MRS LLEWELLYN: Well, I'd just popped next door to the tea rooms for a bun and when I came back . . .

DAFFYD: For the love of God, woman, tell me!

MRS LLEWELLYN: Noel Jones.

DAFFYD: Who?

MRS LLEWELLYN: The blacksmith.

DAFFYD: Right!

DAFFYD EXITS, STORMS OUT INTO THE ROAD AND FLAGS DOWN A FRIENDLY OLD GENTLEMAN ON A PUSH BIKE.

GENT: Hello, Daffyd.

A gay priest? What planet are you on, woman?

EPISODE

DAFFYD: I'm commandeering this vehicle.

DAFFYD PULLS THE OLD MAN OFF, JUMPS ON, AND CYCLES OFF.

DAFFYD: I'll give him a piece of my gay mind!

EXT. BLACKSMITH'S. DAFFYD LEAPS OFF THE BIKE AND DASHES INTO THE BLACKSMITH'S.

INT. BLACKSMITH'S. A MAN, WITH HIS BACK TO US, IS HAMMERING SOME METAL.

DAFFYD: Right, I want a word with you!

THE BLACKSMITH TURNS ROUND. WE SEE HE IS VERY HANDSOME, RUGGED, GLOWING WITH SWEAT, ETC. DAFFYD IS TAKEN ABACK BY THE MAN'S ATTRACTIVENESS AND IMMEDIATELY MELTS.

DAFFYD: What's this I've been hearing about . . . Ooh, Daffyd, Daffyd Thomas. You must be Noel.

BLACKSMITH: No, I'm his brother Rhys. (HE CALLS) Noel!

DAFFYD WAITS IN ANTICIPATION. NOEL EMERGES FROM THE BACKROOM, READING A COPY OF *GAY TIMES*. HE LOOKS UP. WE SEE THAT HE IS VERY UNATTRACTIVE. WE SEE DAFFYD'S FACE DROP.

DAFFYD: I left something in the oven.

DAFFYD RUNS OFF.

LOU AND ANDY — SMURF OUTFIT

INT. ANDY'S FRONT ROOM. HE IS WATCHING THE TELLY, LOU APPEARS.

> **TOM V/O:** It's late early evening and Lou is taking his friend Andy out for dinner.

> **LOU:** The, er, table's booked for seven. We'd better get you dressed then, hadn't we?

> **ANDY:** Yeah.

> **LOU:** Now what do you want to wear?

> **ANDY:** Smurf.

> **LOU:** Smurf? You want to wear your Smurf outfit?

> **ANDY:** Yeah.

I look a **pillock**.

LOU: It's quite a smart restaurant. I'm not really sure a Smurf outfit is appropriate for where we're going.

ANDY: Yeah, I know.

LOU: So what do you want to wear?

ANDY: Smurf.

INT. CHINESE RESTAURANT. LOU AND ANDY ARE SITTING AT A TABLE FOR TWO, EATING. ANDY IS DRESSED IN A HOMEMADE SMURF OUTFIT, WITH HIS FACE PAINTED BLUE.

LOU: This Chinese food is delicious.

ANDY: I look a pillock. Do you do crisps?

VICKY POLLARD — SWIMMING POOL

EXT. SWIMMING POOL.

TOM V/O: Swimming pools in Britain have very strict rules: no bombing, no petting, no ducking, and no fondue parties.

WE SEE A MAN BEING VIOLENTLY EJECTED FROM THE POOL. HIS ARMBANDS ARE THROWN AFTER HIM.

INT. SWIMMING POOL. WE SEE VICKY IN THE WATER TALKING TO TWO BOYS. A LIFEGUARD IS COMFORTING A YOUNG GIRL, WHO IS CRYING. SHE POINTS AT VICKY.

LIFEGUARD: Excuse me, can I have a word?

VICKY TUTS AND STUBS HER CIGARETTE OUT IN THE POOL.

LIFEGUARD: I've just been speaking to a little girl who says you pushed her in the pool. Did you?

VICKY: No but yeah but no because what happened was you know the Redmond sisters? Well they found a verruca sock in the girls' bogs and put it in Carrie's bag and she completely had an eppy and turned up to Kamal Sharma's party with a compass and stabbed Kamal Sharma but anyway Shelley Bentley gave Craig Herman a blowy in the shallow end for a bite of his Funny Foot.

LIFEGUARD: I asked you if you pushed that girl in the pool.

VICKY: No because I couldn't have done because I was with Michaela the whole time because she was crying because you know Dominic Malone? Well he was supposed to be meeting her down at the swings to go third base but anyway Ian Papworth who I like once got off with as a joke nicked a whole bottle of Dubonnet off Stacy Manning's Mum and hid it in the woods but then he couldn't find it but then he did find it but he didn't like it so he threw it at a family of gyppos.

LIFEGUARD: Did you push her in or not?

VICKY: No because I would never do that because once I heard this fing right that a man pushed a man, and the man died and that's true and if you don't believe me you can ask him yourself and anyway Johno tripped up Dean Hurst by the waterslides and he had to have three hundred stitches in his face and when his Mum found out she went down Johno's dad's car showroom and went up to a Vauxhall Astra and done her dirty business on it.

LIFEGUARD: Get out and go and get changed.

VICKY: I'm just going to have a wee first and then I'll get changed.

LIFEGUARD: Be quick.

VICKY WAITS A FEW SECONDS. IT BECOMES CLEAR SHE IS URINATING.

VICKY: Right, I'll go and get changed.

VICKY LOOKS AT ANOTHER GIRL IN THE POOL.

VICKY: Don't go giving me evils. (VICKY SPLASHES THE GIRL) Bitch.

LIFEGUARD BLOWS WHISTLE.

VICKY: Oh shut up!

KELSEY GRAMMAR SCHOOL – TEST

INT. CLASSROOM.

TOM V/O: At Kelsey Grammar School in Flange the boys are preparing to take a test.

THE TEACHER WALKS ROUND, HANDING OUT SHEETS OF A4 PAPER.

TEACHER: Absolute silence while the test is in progress please. I don't want to hear a pin drop.

THE TEACHER SITS AND CHECKS HIS WATCH.

TEACHER: Right, now – you may begin.

THE BOYS HURRIEDLY TURN OVER THEIR EXAM PAPERS. THE TEACHER GETS OUT A SAXOPHONE AND PLAYS A NICE JAZZ RIFF. THE BOYS ARE DISTRACTED.

DR LAWRENCE AND ANNE – OFFICE

EXT. MEDICAL INSTITUTION. SIGN – 'A STEVEN SPIELBERG HOSPITAL'.

TOM V/O: Moonwhile at this institution in Flatley, Dr Lawrence is showing an Inspector round.

INT. HOSPITAL OFFICE. DR LAWRENCE IS SEATED AT HIS DESK TALKING TO DR BEAGRIE. A FEMALE PATIENT WEARING A NIGHTDRESS COMES INTO THE ROOM.

DR LAWRENCE: Currently we have forty residential patients and, as you can see, we do like to keep things very relaxed here.

ANNE COMES ON, TAKES THE PAPERWEIGHT FROM THE TABLE.

ANNE: Eh eh eh!

ANNE WALKS OFF WITH THE PAPERWEIGHT.

DR LAWRENCE: I'm not one of those who subscribe to the school of keeping everyone under lock and key.

ANNE WALKS ON AND TAKES DR LAWRENCE'S GLASSES OFF HIS FACE.

ANNE: Eh eh eh!

ANNE WALKS OFF WITH HIS GLASSES.

DR LAWRENCE: I am going to need those glasses back, Anne. Ultimately it's all about trust.

PHONE RINGS.

DR LAWRENCE: Do excuse me.

DR LAWRENCE REACHES FOR THE PHONE. ANNE ENTERS, PICKS UP THE PHONE AND SPEAKS INTO THE RECEIVER.

ANNE: Eh eh eh?

ANNE PUTS DOWN THE RECEIVER. ANNE EXISTS TAKING THE PHONE WITH HER.

DR LAWRENCE: Fortunately, when I came here, I was able to gain, quite quickly, the respect of everybody and, er – it's all in the folder.

ANNE ENTERS AND DRAGS OFF THE TABLE.

ANNE: Eh eh eh!

DR LAWRENCE RESCUES HIS TEACUP AND SAUCER AS THE TABLE IS REMOVED BUT IS OTHERWISE UNFAZED.

SEBASTIAN AND MICHAEL – BRIEFING

EXT./INT. NO. 10 DOWNING STREET.

TOM V/O: Inside 10 Downing Street, the Prime Minister is in the middle of his morning briefing.

MICHAEL: Have the results of the opinion poll come through, Sebastian?

SEBASTIAN: Yes, I've got them right here, Prime Minister.

MICHAEL: What sort of things are people saying?

SEBASTIAN: Well, they are very happy with your work on Northern Ireland. Um, there's strong approval on your Health Service reforms. Um, they would like to see you in shorts.

MICHAEL: Shorts?

SEBASTIAN: Yes, Prime Minster, in just a pair of cycling shorts or something, Prime Minister. Oh, um, they like the fact that you're assuming a tough stance on crime and they like it when your hair's a bit wet because you look kind of soppy, Prime Minister. They would like to see you wrestle a man.

MICHAEL: I'm sorry?

SEBASTIAN: Bosnia, good. Education could do better. Wrestling men, I've covered.

MICHAEL: Can I have a look at them?

SEBASTIAN: Yeah, just right here (HE SHOWS IT TO HIM TOO QUICKLY). Um, now um, Railtrack . . . Oh, oh, you've got an eyelash. Stay still. Stay still. Make a wish.

SEBASTIAN PICKS THE EYELASH OFF.

PRIME MINISTER'S WIFE BREEZES IN.

WIFE: Darling, there's your suit for the Treasury dinner. Now we are running very late so you'll have to get changed here.

MICHAEL: Oh, thank you, darling, yes.

WIFE: Have you seen my earrings? Oh hello, Sebastian.

SEBASTIAN IS VERY UNFRIENDLY.

SEBASTIAN: Hi.

WIFE: How are you?

SEBASTIAN: Fine. Sorry we're having a meeting here.

MICHAEL: Have you tried the bathroom?

WIFE: Of course. Now don't be long.

MICHAEL: See you later, darling.

SEBASTIAN: I'm not going.

MICHAEL: I was talking to my wife.

SEBASTIAN: Oh.

WIFE: Bye, Sebastian.

SHE EXITS.

SEBASTIAN: Whatever. So anyway, um, oh God, I've completely forgotten what I was going to say. Ha ha ha!

MICHAEL: Thanks for coming in and, um, I really should get changed now.

SEBASTIAN: Oh yes, of course, of course.

MICHAEL: And you'll have a word with the Foreign Secretary about Tuesday?

SEBASTIAN: Yeah, I'll get straight onto it Prime Minister.

MICHAEL: Great.

SEBASTIAN LEAVES. THE PRIME MINISTER STARTS TO UNDRESS. SEBASTIAN RE-ENTERS AND EYES MICHAEL UP.

SEBASTIAN: Oh yes, can you approve the budget overspend by first thing on Monday because it's quite . . . big?

MICHAEL: Yes, Sebastian, now if you don't mind, um . . .

SEBASTIAN: Oh, quick Prime Minister, get down!

> Well, they are very happy with your work on Northern Ireland. Um, there's strong approval on your Health Service reforms. **Um, they would like to see you in shorts.**

SEBASTIAN JUMPS ON TOP OF THE PRIME MINISTER. THEY FALL ON TO THE SOFA. PAUSE.

MICHAEL: What's going on?

SEBASTIAN: I thought there was a sniper, Prime Minister.

MICHAEL: Where?

SEBASTIAN: By the window, but there isn't.

MICHAEL: Can we get up now?

PAUSE.

SEBASTIAN: Give it a minute.

DR LAWRENCE AND ANNE — GARDEN

EXT. MEDICAL INSTITUTION. GARDEN.

DR LAWRENCE: This is the, er, communal garden and we all look after it together.

ANNE APPEARS AND STARTS TO RIP SOME FLOWERS OUT. THIS, AND HER SCREECHING, CATCHES THE PAIR'S
ATTENTION MOMENTARILY.

ANNE: Eh eh eh!

DR LAWRENCE: Anne there has decided those flowers might look better . . . , where are you going to put them, Anne?

ANNE RUBS THEM ON HER BOTTOM. SHE LETS THEM FALL TO THE GROUND THEN STAMPS ON THEM,
SHOUTING GIBBERISH.

DR LAWRENCE: Just there. Visitors often say 'Do we have a team of professional gardeners?'

ANNE RETURNS WITH A SMALL TREE, SCREECHING.

DR LAWRENCE: Oh yes, Anne is particularly fond of this tree.

ANNE WAVES THE BRANCH AROUND. AS SHE DOES, WE HEAR A MOBILE PHONE RING. ANNE PUTS THE BRANCH
DOWN, PULLS OUT A MOBILE FROM HER POCKET, AND ANSWERS IT COMPLETELY NORMALLY.

ANNE: Hello. I'm just in the middle of something at the moment. Can I call you back? OK. Bye bye.

ANNE HANGS UP, PUTS THE PHONE BACK IN HER POCKET, AND RETURNS TO HER MAD BEHAVIOUR,
PICKING UP THE SMALL TREE, SCREECHING AND EXITING FRAME.

DR LAWRENCE: Clients do find it very therapeutic too.

WE HEAR A SCREECH. A WHEELBARROW IS THROWN AND LANDS IN FRONT OF THE PAIR.

KELSEY GRAMMAR SCHOOL

INT. KELSEY GRAMMAR SCHOOL. AN EXAM IS IN PROGRESS. A BOY DROPS A PENCIL.

TEACHER: Sssshhh! Come on!

SUDDENLY HE STARTS TO HOOVER NEAR THE BOYS' FEET. BOYS LIFT THEIR FEET AND HE HOOVERS UNDERNEATH THEM.

LOU AND ANDY — BATHROOM

TOM V/O: In Herby, Lou is making some changes to his friend Andy's bathroom.

INT. ANDY'S BATHROOM. LOU IS DOING SOME DIY. HE HOLDS TWO RAILS.

LOU: So I'm gonna put these here and here, okay?

ANDY: Yeah. Why?

LOU: So you can do toilet when I'm not here.

ANDY: Yeah, I know.

LOU: So we think, one here, yes?

ANDY: Yeah.

LOU: And one here – yeah?

ANDY: Yeah.

LOU: Because I'm gonna have to drill into the wall, you know?

ANDY: Yeah, I know.

LOU: Could you pass me the drill?

ANDY: No. I can't reach it.

LOU SOMEHOW MANAGES TO KEEP THE RAIL IN PLACE WHILE GRABBING THE DRILL.

NIGHT. ANDY IS WATCHING *MONSTER TRUCKS* AND EATING CRISPS. LOU ENTERS, SLEEVES ROLLED UP, CARRYING A DUSTPAN AND BRUSH.

LOU: Right, I've finished. Do you wanna come and have a look?

ANDY: Yeah.

THE TWO RAILS ARE NOW IN PLACE. LOU WHEELS ANDY IN.

LOU: Right, here we go! Ta-da. What do you reckon?

ANDY: Yeah, I like it. What's it for?

LOU: So you can do toilet when I'm not here.

ANDY: Yeah, I know.

LOU: Do you want to try it out?

ANDY: Yeah.

LOU: Alright, I'll leave you to it.

WE FOLLOW LOU AS HE EXITS THE BATHROOM, CLOSES THE DOOR AND STANDS OUTSIDE. WE HEAR THE TOILET FLUSH.

LOU: How are you getting on?

ANDY IS STANDING UP HAVING A WEE.

ANDY: Yeah, fine.

WE SEE LOU, SMILING PROUDLY.

DAME SALLY MARKHAM

EXT. DAY. STATELY HOME SET IN ACRES OF LAND. A GARDENER IS TRIMMING A HEDGE IN THE SHAPE OF A HAND GIVING THE FINGER.

TOM V/O: This is the home of romantic novelist Dame Sally Markham. Books were introduced into Britain in the nineteen fifties. Early books had no words or pictures, but nowadays the book world is thriving, with over seven books published every year.

THE ROOM IS VERY POSH, FULL OF ANTIQUES, ETC. DRAPED ON A CHAISE LONGUE IS AN ENORMOUSLY FAT NINETY-YEAR-OLD WOMAN, DRESSED ALL IN PINK, WITH BLUE-RINSED HAIR, ROTTEN TEETH, LOTS OF MAKE-UP, AND SOME CHOCOLATE ROUND HER MOUTH. THERE ARE LOTS OF TRUFFLE WRAPPERS ON THE FLOOR. IN THE CORNER OF THE ROOM, AT AN OLD TYPEWRITER, SITS A VERY PLAIN-LOOKING, DOWDILY DRESSED SECRETARY.

DAME SALLY: '. . . and with that, Clarence took Amelia into his arms, held her and kissed her, like a woman had never been kissed before. The End.' Truffle, I think.

DAME SALLY POPS A TRUFFLE IN HER MOUTH.

DAME SALLY: How many pages, Miss Grace?

MISS GRACE: Oh. Seventy-six.

DAME SALLY: Oh. 'Then they went to the shops for a bit. Didn't really see anything they liked, came home and had a bit of a kiss and cuddle. The End.' Do you know, I think I'll have a truffle. Oh, there was a full box here this morning. You've been scoffing again haven't you, Miss Grace?

Well, let's start another one. '*The Lady in Mauve*. Chapter One. The End'. How many pages?

MISS GRACE: I haven't touched them.

DAME SALLY: I've got my eye on you. 'Then they watched a very long television programme, which took up lots of pages. The End'. How many pages?

MISS GRACE: Still not enough, I'm afraid.

DAME SALLY: Oh well, let's come back to that one. What's it called again?

MISS GRACE: *Lady in White.*

DAME SALLY: Well, let's start another one. '*The Lady in Mauve.* Chapter One. The End'. How many pages?

ST GOD'S HOSPITAL — DAVID SOUL

TOM V/O: This is the newly built St God's Hospital in Shireshire, which was opened just last year by Dame Rhona Cameron.

EXT. HOSPITAL. A MAN WITH HIS ARM HANGING OFF APPROACHES A NURSE FOR DIRECTIONS. SHE RESPONDS VERY CALMLY.

NURSE: Go through there and downstairs.

INT. HOSPITAL WARD. ROD AND JOAN ARE SITTING BY THEIR DAUGHTER KATY'S HOSPITAL BED. SHE IS ON A LIFE-SUPPORT MACHINE. THEY LOOK BORED.

JOAN: We'll give it another minute, then we'll go.

THE DOOR OPENS AND DAVID SOUL POKES HIS HEAD ROUND THE DOOR.

DAVID: Hello. Is this Katy's room?

JOAN AND ROD LEAP UP.

JOAN: Oh, David. David Soul! Thank you so much for coming.

DAVID ENTERS, CARRYING FLOWERS.

DAVID: Not at all, I got your letter, thought if I could be of any help . . .

ROD: Oh, you just being here is going to make a huge difference.

DAVID: How are you, sweetheart? How's she doing?

JOAN: Oh, she's alright. But David Soul, tell us about you. Any more *Starsky and Hutch* in the pipeline?

DAVID: Not currently.

ROD: What about a new album? 'Cause it's been a while since 1997's 'Leave a Light On'.

DAVID: Maybe, er, maybe next year. I'm focusing on acting right now.

JOAN: Oh yeah, yeah, coz we saw you in *Holby City*.

ROD: Yeah, we couldn't believe it. We said 'Look, there's David Soul in *Holby City*'. Couldn't believe it. No. That's what we said.

JOAN: You, you still in touch with Huggy Bear?

DAVID: Christmas cards.

ROD: Better get the address right.

DAVID: Yeah, why's that?

ROD: Otherwise it might go to Yogi Bear – ha ha ha!

JOAN: Don't mind him, David.

ROD: I'm just having a laugh with you, Dave.

JOAN: It's just his way. He's just playing with you.

ROD: I'm a bit of a joker, you know.

DAVID: So tell me, what does Katy want to do when she grows up?

JOAN: Don't know, David. She's quite ill.

JOAN/ROD: (SINGING) 'Don't give up on us baby, just give us one more try'. 'Come on Silver Lady, say the words do da do'. 'When I need you, I just close my eyes and I feel you, I never knew' . . .

DAVID: Leo Sayer.

ROD: (TO JOAN) Stupid cow.

JOAN: Oh, I nearly forgot. Pass the LP.

ROD: Ooh yeah, yeah. Ask him to sign . . .

JOAN: David Soul. Would you mind signing an LP for us, please? Thank you.

You, you still in touch with Huggy Bear?

EPISODE

DAVID TAKES THE LP AND STARTS TO WRITE.

DAVID: Is that Katy with a 'y'?

JOAN: No, it's Joan with a 'J'.

ROD: And Rod. Just Rod.

NURSE: Hi, David Essex is in reception.

JOAN: We're going to have to hurry you out, David.

ROD: I hope you don't mind.

DAVID: It's been a real pleasure to meet you both.

ROD: Yeah, absolutely.

DAVID: And I do hope that Katy gets better soon.

JOAN: Yeah, I'm sure she will.

ROD: Thank you, David Soul.

JOAN: Thank you, David Soul. (POINTS) Through there.

DAVID EXITS.

JOAN: What's he put?

ROD: 'To Rod and Joan. Screw You. David Soul.'

JOAN: Must be an American thing.

MARJORIE DAWES/FATFIGHTERS — SLIMMER OF THE YEAR

EXT. EARLY EVENING. MODERN SUBURBAN COMMUNITY CENTRE. JESUS AND HIS DISCIPLES EXIT THE BUILDING.

TOM V/O: Community centres in Britain are ideal places for all kinds of groups to meet. It's half past Tula and Marjorie Dawes is taking her weekly FatFighters Class.

SITTING IN A CIRCLE ARE MEERA, PAUL, TANIA, PAT, AND HALF A DOZEN OTHERS. NEARBY ARE A SET OF SCALES, A NOTICEBOARD WITH PLENTY OF DIFFERENT FATFIGHTERS LEAFLETS ON, AND A TABLE NEARBY WITH LOTS OF FATFIGHTERS PRODUCTS — CEREALS, SELF-HELP VIDEO TAPES, CRISPS, CHOCOLATES, ETC. MARJORIE STANDS BY A SET OF SCALES JUST OUTSIDE THE CIRCLE.

MARJORIE: Now, a little bird told me that somebody, and I'm not going to name any names, has been going around saying they've been following the diet and they haven't been losing any weight, and that FatFighters is just a rip off. Well, in answer to this shit-stirrer . . . (MARJORIE GLARES AT PAUL) . . . we've got a special visit from the FatFighters

Slimmer of the Year. His name is Cliff Roberts. Now before I bring him out, just have
a look at this. This is what he used to look like (MARJORIE PRODUCES A LIFE-SIZE CUT-OUT OF HOW
CLIFF ROBERTS USED TO LOOK). Here we go, have a look at that.

MARJORIE: And these, would you believe, are his trousers. Ha ha ha!

MARJORIE HOLDS UP A VERY LARGE PAIR OF TROUSERS.

MARJORIE: So please welcome the FatFighters 'Slimmer of the Year', Cliff Roberts.

And these, would you believe, are his trousers. Ha ha ha!

A TROUSERLESS MAN ENTERS FROM THE KITCHEN DOOR. HE IS SLIGHTLY SLIMMER THAN IN HIS CUT-OUT BUT STILL VERY OVERWEIGHT. THE GROUP APPLAUD.

CLIFF: Can I have my . . .

MARJORIE: Yes.

MARJORIE HANDS HIM THE TROUSERS. HE PUTS THEM ON.

MARJORIE: Now you are Slimmer of the Year because you lost the most weight out of anybody. How much did you lose?

CLIFF: About three stones and nine pounds.

MARJORIE: Three stones and nine pounds. (MARJORIE LEADS THE APPLAUSE) See! And how much do you weigh now?

CLIFF: Er, nineteen stones and one pound.

MARJORIE: Nineteen stones and one pound. Yeah. (MARJORIE APPLAUDS. NO ONE ELSE JOINS IN) OK. Let's just get this into perspective. Come and stand by your cut-out for a minute.

CLIFF DOES SO – THERE IS VERY LITTLE DIFFERENCE.

MARJORIE: There we go. Yeah. See? You would hardly recognize him, would you? Sit back down. Now what we all want to know is, how you came to lose all this weight?

CLIFF: Well, basically, I just ate sensibly and exercised.

MARJORIE: Yeah, and you found the special FatFighters range helped?

CLIFF: No, they're a waste of –

MARJORIE (INTERRUPTS): Good, so what would you say to someone who's a bit of a Judas and who is thinking of leaving FatFighters?

CLIFF: Well, I think being around other people who are also . . .

MARJORIE: Yeah, don't say it to me, say it to him.

MARJORIE INDICATES PAUL. CLIFF ADDRESSES HIM.

CLIFF: Having other people around you who are also trying to lose weight gives you that extra boost really, so if you want to lose weight then keep coming.

MARJORIE: Yeah, you fat shit.

CLIFF: Well, I wouldn't call him that because that will lower his self-esteem.

Yeah, you fat shit.

MARJORIE: No. So um . . .

MARJORIE REACHES OUT AND FEELS THE WEIGHT OF CLIFF'S BREAST.

MARJORIE: Ooh, they're like tits, aren't they?

DR LAWRENCE AND ANNE – DINING ROOM

INT. DINING ROOM. DR LAWRENCE IS CARRYING HIS TRAY ALONGSIDE DR BEAGRIE.

DR LAWRENCE: We do eat together and I think that that's good for everybody.
We're not trying to implement any sort of hierarchical structure here.

ANNE ENTERS SCREECHING AND TAKES A BREAD ROLL FROM A PLATE.

ANNE: Eh eh eh!

DR LAWRENCE: Thank you, Anne. Yes, I think it's no, it's no small tribute that when people come and see us here they do say, um, who are the doctors and who are the patients? I know that . . .

ANNE COMES OVER, SCREECHING, AND HELPS HERSELF TO DR LAWRENCE'S SOUP.

ANNE: Eh eh eh!

DR LAWRENCE: . . . when the Chief Medical Officer came to see us – I think it was either August or, was it August? – he said only the same thing, and that that was a real, that was a real lift to everybody who works here, you know. 'Cause . . . er . . .

ANNE: Eh eh eh!

ANNE TIPS DRINKS OVER THEIR MEALS AND ALL OVER THE PLACE.

DR LAWRENCE: We're not quite ready for coffee just yet, Anne, but thank you. Or tea.
We don't want tea now – Dr Beagrie, do you?

DR BEAGRIE: No.

DR LAWRENCE: No, I do find that if you can break down some of these barriers you can, you really would be amazed at some of the results. We had somebody come and see us recently . . .

ANNE COMES IN AND POURS MILK OVER DR BEAGIE.

DR LAWRENCE: . . . it was a troubled time. They were quite distressed when they came to see us. And they'd been in and out of hospital for a number of years and I think . . . we'll talk about this later.

ANNE DRAGS DR LAWRENCE'S CHAIR AWAY WITH HIM ON IT.

something

JASON AND NAN — SUNDAY LUNCH

EXT. COUNCIL ESTATE. JASON HEADS TOWARDS A BLOCK OF FLATS.

TOM V/O: Meanwhile, Jason is joining his friend Gary for Sunday luncheon. It is the law in Britain that on Sundays everybody must eat a roast. The most popular meats are beef, lamb, pork, and bat.

INT. FLAT. LIVING ROOM.

GARY: You'd better come in.

JASON: Something smells nice.

HE TAKES HIM THROUGH TO THE DINING AREA WHERE THE TABLE IS LAID FOR LUNCH.

GARY: You know Julie.

JASON: All right?

JULIE: Hi.

GARY: And you, er, remember me Nan.

JASON: Oh yeah!

WE SEE NAN FROM JASON'S POINT OF VIEW, IN SOFT FOCUS. WE HEAR ROMANTIC ORCHESTRAL MUSIC.

GARY: Have a seat.

MUM: Grubs up. Hi, Jason.

JASON: Hiya. Sorry I'm late.

MUM: S'all right . . . Oh, I forgot the salt.

JASON: Oh, let me, Mrs Leigh.

JASON GOES OVER TO THE SIDEBOARD NEARBY AND GRABS THE SALT CELLAR. ON THE WAY BACK TO HIS SEAT HE SLIGHTLY TOUCHES NAN'S HAIR.

MUM: I can't remember the last time we had someone over for Sunday lunch.

JASON: Well, it's just nice to spend time with you . . . all. Wine anybody?

GARY: Not for me, thanks.

JASON POURS THE WINE AND FINISHES BY POURING THE MOST INTO NAN'S GLASS.

GARY: Nice potatoes, Mum.

NAN: Is that the dog?

JULIE: Is what the dog?

NAN: I can feel something under the table.

GARY: I put him out earlier.

JULIE: So you, er, got a girlfriend then, Jason?

JASON: No, I haven't. I'm single currently.

MUM: Mum, you've got gravy all down yourself!

NAN: Ooh dear.

MUM: Honestly!

JASON TAKES HIS NAPKIN AND STARTS TO WIPE IT OFF. HE DOES THIS A BIT TOO LOW, AND FOR A BIT TOO LONG. EMBARRASSING SILENCE FOLLOWS.

MUM: I've got more meat, I've got more peas, more carrots, and I can do more gravy if anyone wants.

GARY: I'm all right for the minute, thanks Mum.

JULIE: Yeah, I'm fine.

MUM: Well, there's more if anyone wants.

NAN STARTS TO COUGH.

MUM: What's the matter, Mum?

JULIE: Something must have gone down the wrong way.

IT BECOMES EVIDENT THAT NAN IS CHOKING.

MUM: Mum, you all right? Oh Gary, get your Nan a glass of water.

JASON: It's OK. It's OK.

GARY RUSHES INTO THE KITCHEN. JASON STARTS TO PAT NAN ON THE BACK. SHE CONTINUES TO CHOKE. JASON RISES, STANDS BEHIND NAN, LIFTS HER AND GIVES HER THE HEIMLICH MANOEUVRE. GARY RETURNS WITH A GLASS. AFTER A SHORT WHILE SHE RECOVERS, BUT JASON CARRIES ON REGARDLESS. IT STARTS TO LOOK LIKE HE MIGHT BE GETTING SEXUAL GRATIFICATION FROM THIS. THE FAMILY WATCH OPEN-MOUTHED. JASON MAKES GROANING NOISES.

JASON: That's got it.

JASON SITS DOWN AND COOLLY LIGHTS A CIGARETTE. THE FAMILY LOOK AT HIM IN STUNNED SILENCE.

EPISODE

KELSEY GRAMMAR SCHOOL

INT. CLASSROOM. AN EXAM IS TAKING PLACE. A PUPIL COUGHS.

TEACHER: Sssshhh!

THE TEACHER GOES TO THE WINDOW TO LIGHT THE FUSE OF A FIREWORK. OUTSIDE WE HEAR
THE FIREWORK EXPLODE.

LIZ AND CLIVE — ORDERING

EXT. CHINESE RESTAURANT. WE SEE THERE IS A PUBLIC TOILET OUTSIDE, EXPOSED FOR ALL TO SEE.

TOM V/O: Chinese food was invented by Professor Stewart Tennant in 1986 and has been very popular ever since.

INT. CHINESE RESTAURANT. A MIDDLE-AGED COUPLE — LIZ AND CLIVE — PERUSE THE MENU.

CLIVE: We're just out for a nice quiet meal. Can you please try not to mention the whole . . . you know what?

LIZ: What's that?

CLIVE: You know what I'm talking about, Liz.

LIZ: What, that I was Molly Sugden's bridesmaid?

CLIVE: Yes.

LIZ: Well, sometimes it just comes up naturally in conversation.

CLIVE: Well, let's just see if we can have an 'I was Mollie Sugden's bridesmaid'-free night tonight.

LIZ: All right then, Clive.

WAITER: Can I take your order?

LIZ: 'Are you being served', or shall I go first?

CLIVE: Liz.

LIZ: Um, I'll have the seaweed please to start. 'That's my boy!'

CLIVE: And I'll have the sesame prawn toast.

LIZ: Oh, prawns. That's what I had at Mollie's wedding. Mollie Sugden's wedding, where I was the bridesmaid.

WAITER: And for the main course?

CLIVE: We'll have a 27, a 108, and the egg fried rice, please.

LIZ: Yes, she's very nice. Very down to earth. Quite different from her character, the snooty Mrs Slocombe. And before you ask, no the wedding dress wasn't from Grace Brothers – perish the thought, ha ha. (TO OTHER DINERS, LOUDLY) *From Grace Brothers!* Ha ha ha.

CLIVE: Liz . . .

LIZ: People want to know!

CLIVE: Well, it's boring.

LIZ: Well, 'that's life'. Now do us all a 'Grace and Favour' and shut up about it.

WAITER: And to drink?

CLIVE: I'll just have a beer, please.

LIZ: And I'll have a glass of Mollie, oh I mean water. Oh sorry, did someone say Mollie Sugden?

WAITER: Excuse me, are you talking about that woman from *Are You Being Served*?

LIZ: Um ,I think she's in that one. Is that the one she's in, Clive?

WAITER: She's very funny with all those jokes about her cat. I'll get you a drink.

LIZ: If he asks me one more question about Mollie Sugden I shall scream.

SHE COUGHS LOUDLY AND SPEAKS AT THE SAME TIME.

LIZ: Mollie Sugden!

ST GOD'S HOSPITAL – LES McKEOWN

EXT./INT. HOSPITAL. THE MAN WITH THE MISSING ARM LOOKS THROUGH SOME BINS TO FIND SOME PROSTHETIC LIMBS. HE FINDS A LEG, PUTS IT INTO HIS ARM SOCKET, RESOLVES THAT IT WILL DO, AND EXITS WITH IT.

TOM V/O: Meanwhile, at St God's Hospital.

ROD AND JOAN ARE SEATED ON ONE SIDE OF THE BED, WEARING TARTAN SCARVES, ROSETTES, AND OTHER BAY CITY ROLLERS SOUVENIRS. ON THE BED LIE A FEW BAY CITY ROLLERS ALBUMS AND ANNUALS. ON THE OTHER SIDE OF THE BED IS BAY CITY ROLLERS LEAD SINGER LES MCKEOWN WITH A GUITAR. THEY LOOK AND SEE THAT KATY IS STILL UNCONSCIOUS.

LES: 'Bye bye baby, baby, goodbye. Bye bye baby baby don't make me cry.'

JOAN LOOKS AT KATY.

JOAN: Nothing.

ROD: Do do do do another one.

LES: I'll do um 'Give a little love, take a little love'.

JOAN: No, she doesn't really like that one.

LES: 'Shang a lang'?

JOAN: Oh yeah yeah. She likes that.

ALL: 'Shang a lang, shang a lang, shang a lang'.

ROD AND JOAN MERRILY WAVE THEIR SCARVES AND SING ALONG.

LINDSAY AND SAM — DRIVING LESSON

EXT. STREET. ROW OF TERRACED HOUSES. LINDSAY DE PAUL, IN FULL POLICE UNIFORM,
HEADS TOWARDS ONE OF THE HOUSES. HE RINGS THE BELL. THE DOOR IS OPENED BY SAM,
A SHOCKED SEVENTEEN-YEAR-OLD BOY.

TOM V/O: Roughly one second later in the northern town of Scoffage.

SAM: Yeah?

LINDSAY: Sam?

SAM: Yeah.

LINDSAY: Sam Bailey?

SAM: Yeah.

LINDSAY: I'm here to give you your driving lesson.

SAM: Oh, I thought you'd come to arrest me! I'll just get me jacket.

LINDSAY: There isn't time for that. I'm afraid you'll have to come now.

LINDSAY LEADS SAM DOWN THE STREET.

SAM: So you're not a policeman, then?

LINDSAY: Not any more, son. Took early retirement. Forced into it. Terrible business.

SAM: Are you still allowed to wear the uniform?

LINDSAY: Er, all me other clothes are in the wash. Here she is, the Duchess.
Get in soft, lad. Thick as a puddle!

THE PAIR ARRIVE AT LINDSAY'S CAR. IT'S A TYPICAL DRIVING INSTRUCTOR'S BROWN METRO WITH AN L-PLATE ON THE BACK AND FRONT AND 'LINDSAY'S DRIVING SCHOOL, SCOFFAGE TEL 999' ON IT . THERE ARE ALSO BLUE POLICE STRIPES AND 'POLICE' PAINTED AMATEURISHLY DOWN THE SIDE. A STANDARD LIGHT BULB HAS BEEN PAINTED BLUE AND STUCK ON THE ROOF WITH GAFFER TAPE. WIRE EXTENDS FROM THE LIGHT BULB INTO THE CAR WINDOW. LINDSAY OPENS THE DRIVER'S SIDE DOOR.

EXT. ROAD. THE CAR IS TRAVELLING FAST.

LINDSAY: Put your foot down!

SAM: What?

LINDSAY: Faster!

SAM: Isn't it a 30-mile-an-hour limit?

LINDSAY: Well, what speed are you doing?

SAM: Er . . . 72.

LINDSAY: Stop the car!

SAM SLOWS DOWN AND PARKS. LINDSAY GETS OUT OF THE CAR THEN WALKS AROUND THE BACK. HE PULLS A BOOK OF STOLEN LICENCE PLATE NUMBERS FROM HIS POCKET AND CHECKS THE NUMBER PLATE. HE KICKS ONE OF THE REAR TYRES BEFORE GOING ROUND TO THE DRIVER'S SIDE. HE TAPS ON THE WINDOW AND MOTIONS FOR SAM TO WIND IT DOWN.

LINDSAY: Is this your vehicle, sir?

SAM: No, it's yours.

LINDSAY: Drivers' licence?

SAM: I was rather hoping you could help me out on that one!

LINDSAY: Oh dear, we've got a comedian. Blow into this.

LINDSAY HANDS SAM SOMETHING. SAM STARTS BLOWING. WE REVEAL THAT IT IS IN FACT A LONG BALLOON. LINDSAY TAKES IT FROM SAM, TIES IT UP AND TURNS IT INTO A FAIRLY ABSURD BALLOON SCULPTURE.

LINDSAY: What's this?

SAM: A poodle?

LINDSAY: No, I'll tell you what it is. It's boy racer. Just turned seventeen, gets into a car, thinks he's Nicky Lauder. I've got me eye on you.

SAM: All right, all right.

LINDSAY: Now on your way, you black bastard.

LINDSAY STANDS SMUGLY AS SAM DRIVES OFF IN HIS CAR. HIS FACE DROPS.

WORLD RECORD ATTEMPT — TALLEST MAN

INT. CONFERENCE CENTRE. IAN 2 RUSHES DOWN SOME STEPS.

IAN 2: Ian, I've just spoken to Mr McWhirter and he says they're only measuring from the top of the head down.

WE SEE A BANNER READING 'TALLEST MAN – WORLD RECORD ATTEMPT'. WE REVEAL IAN 1 IS WEARING AN EXTREMELY TALL TOP HAT.

IAN 1: What shall we do?

IAN 2: Go and have a drink.

TOM V/O: So what have we learned from this evening's programme? Some ducks have bells and some don't, that murder isn't morally wrong and, most importantly, we've learned how to tell a goblin from a hobgoblin. Goodbyeeeeee!

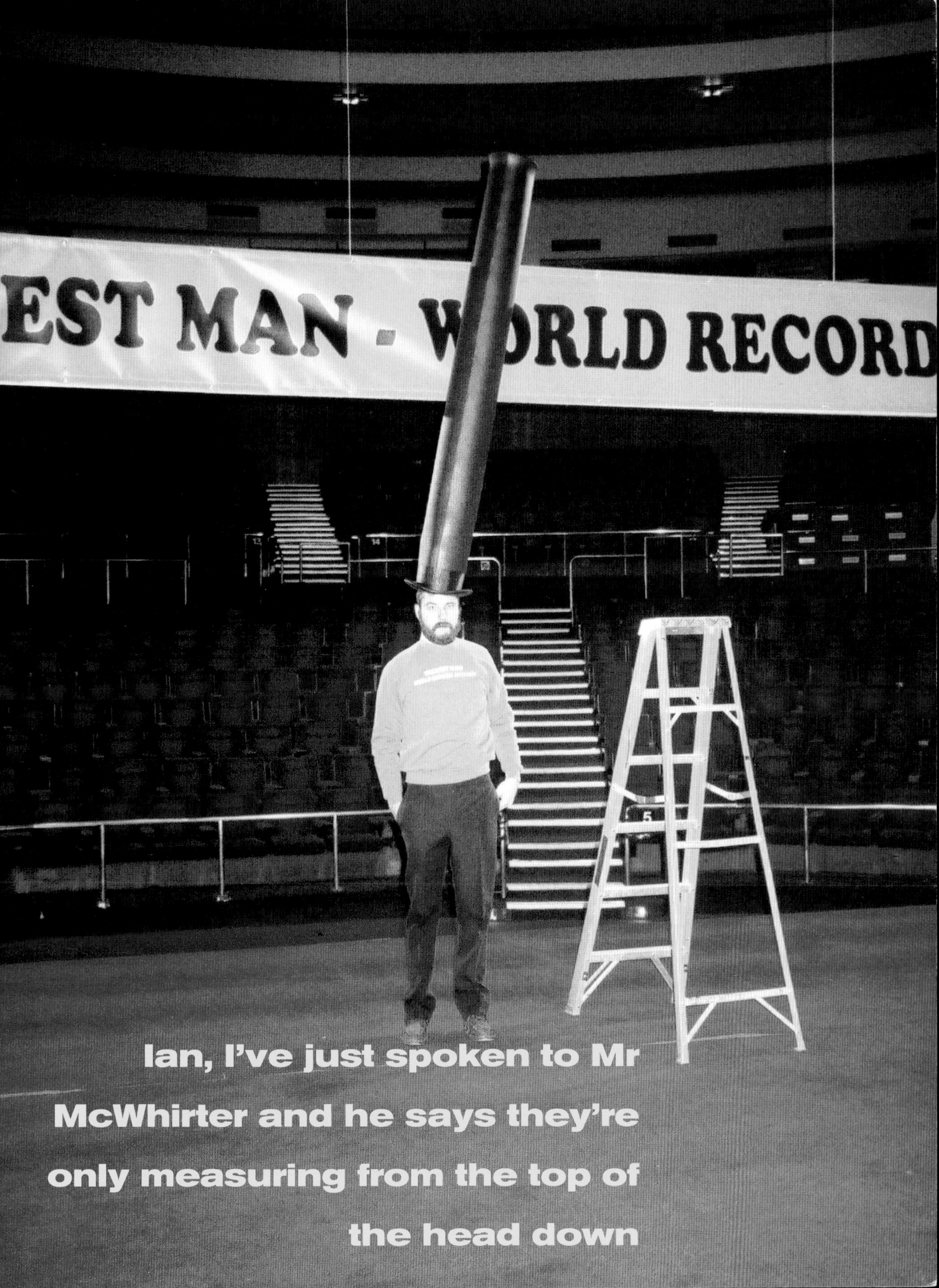

Ian, I've just spoken to Mr McWhirter and he says they're only measuring from the top of the head down

GCSE English

Name: Vicky Pollard

Class: Lower

Date: Stop getting involved

Answer ONE of the following TWO questions.

1. Discuss how Chaucer uses the theme of courtly love in *The Canterbury Tales*.

No but yeah but no because I can't believe you just said that because I have read all of that Chaucer but I haven't because what happened was I was I lost my book because we was all down the reservor and Tony Tozer said there was Piranas in there cause he saw this film once where there was all these fish in some water and they well ate people up. Anyway he got David Wu in a headlock and David Wu was going GET OFF ME. What are you. A bummer. and then Hannah-Michelle came over and started stirring it all up and I was gonna leave any way but then Wayne Duggan came over who I hate because I got off with him once and he bit my tit but anyway he threw a shoe at Tony Tozer and Tony Tozer fell in the reservor only it was really shallow anyway but he well made a fuss and said that Wayne Duggan's gonna get beatings but anyway I werent even there anyway so just leave me out of it. God this is like being at school. Oh I'm at school. Anyway you better pass me or give me at least an F or I'm well gonna come round your house and kick up your mum.

Mr Carver wants dogs

BUSTED

MCFLY

Samina Geshwani's got a mustash

2. In Christopher Marlowe's *Dr Faustus*, discuss the different ways in which evil is depicted.

what. We ain't even done Dr Marlowe. Oh my god this is SO unfair. This is like that time we was all down the ice rink and Paul Rowley who's totally fat and hasn't even got any pubes told the Bennett brother he got off with Destiny round the back of Foot Locker but he was well out of order for saying that cause everyone knows it was J.D Sports. Anyway I never got chance to go skating anyway cause they came and banned me but all I done was skate over someones hand AS A JOKE and just because they lost two fingers I got banned but I don't care anyway cause I went down Superdrug and nicked a pack of Peach Smints which I hate anyway and got away with it. Oh my god hang on a minute we was only supposed to answer one of the questions. You better give me double the marks or I'll cut you up and you know I so would. Anyway Joe Talbot is in front of me and keeps letting off and laughing. I reckon I should get even more extra marks for that cause its well putting me off.

Hollyoaks has gone well gay

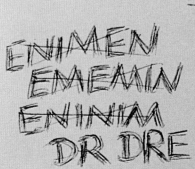

EPISODE three

TOM V/O: Britain, Britain. There's an old saying in Britain, 'Britain is top banana Yeah!' But why is it so great? Well, I'll tell you why it. It is because of the people that live in Britain. And it is these people what we will be following in this award breaking series.

SEBASTIAN AND MICHAEL – HEADLINES

EXT. NO. 10 DOWNING STREET. MAN WALKS PAST AND HAS A HEART ATTACK. POLICEMAN WANTS TO HELP BUT CAN'T LEAVE HIS POST.

TOM V/O: Inside 10 Downing Street, the Prime Minister, who is one of the most important people in this country, after myself and my friend Colin Gray, is going through the morning papers with his aide, Sebastian.

INT. PM'S OFFICE.

MICHAEL IS WORKING AT HIS DESK. SEBASTIAN SITS ON THE SOFA, FLICKING THROUGH A PILE OF NEWSPAPERS ON HIS LAP. THE MOOD IS SOMBRE. THE PRIME MINISTER LOOKS TIRED.

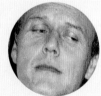

MICHAEL: And what about the broadsheets?

SEBASTIAN: Um, *The Guardian* go with 'By-Election Disaster for Government', *The Times* – 'Prime Minister Under Fire', *The Telegraph* – 'Black Day for PM'.

SEBASTIAN IS GETTING VERY EMOTIONAL.

MICHAEL: Are you all right, Sebastian?

SEBASTIAN: Yeah. I've just got something in my eye, Prime Minister, that's all. *Independent* – 'Poll Defeat Puts PM on the Ropes'.

SEBASTIAN STARTS TO CRY.

MICHAEL: Do you want a tissue?

SEBASTIAN: No, I'm fine, I'm fine. I'm fine.

MICHAEL: What about the tabloids, what does *The Sun* say?

SEBASTIAN PICKS UP A COPY OF *THE SUN*. ON THE FRONT THE PM'S FACE HAS BEEN SUPERIMPOSED ONTO A DETAILED PAINTING OF A DODO. ABOVE IS THE HEADLINE 'DEAD AS A DODO'. SEBASTIAN BECOMES VERY UPSET.

SEBASTIAN: Oh no!

MICHAEL: What?

SEBASTIAN: No, no, I can't show you.

MICHAEL: Oh, come on. It can't be all that bad.

SEBASTIAN: They've said you're as dead as a dodo! You're not as dead as a dodo!

MICHAEL: All right, Sebastian.

SEBASTIAN: You're not as dead as a dodo.

MICHAEL: Come on, you're being very silly.

SEBASTIAN SPEAKS BUT WE CAN'T UNDERSTAND WHAT HE IS SAYING THROUGH THE SOBS. MICHAEL GOES OVER TO HIM. SEBASTIAN HUGS MICHAEL TIGHTLY.

MICHAEL: It really doesn't matter. Don't get upset about it. I'm not upset about it.

SEBASTIAN: I want you to be Prime Minister forever.

MICHAEL: Well, well, I'm not planning on going anywhere just yet.

SEBASTIAN: Oh good.

PHONE RINGS. SEBASTIAN IS HOLDING ON TO MICHAEL'S LEGS AND DOESN'T LET GO AS MICHAEL WALKS TO THE PHONE.

MICHAEL: Hello. Yeah . . . OK . . . thank you. I'll be down. Thank you. My car's here, Sebastian, I have to leave now.

SEBASTIAN: OK. Where are we going?

SEBASTIAN HOLDS ONTO HIS LEGS AS MICHAEL WALKS. HE FALLS BEHIND THE SOFA.

MICHAEL: Thank you, Sebastian, that will be all.

MICHAEL DRAGS SEBASTIAN OUT OF THE ROOM, SEBASTIAN DESPERATELY CLINGING ON TO MICHAEL'S ANKLES.

VICKY POLLARD — PUB

EXT. PUB. A BLIND MAN WITH WHITE STICK AND GLASSES WALKS INTO SHOT. HE BUMPS INTO SOMETHING, LIFTS HIS GLASSES TO SEE IT IS A WALLET, PICKS IT UP, AND CONTINUES ON HIS WAY.

TOM V/O: Pubs are very popular in Britain, with over five pubs per person.

INT. PUB.

VICKY: Packet of pork scratchings. Nuvver packet of pork scratchings. Box of matches.

BARMAN: Anything else?

VICKY: And four pints of snakebites, please.

BARMAN: You, er, got any ID?

VICKY: No but yeah but no because you know Albany? Well she said I'd been going around saying that Samina Geshwani's got a moustache which she has but I never said it but anyway Paul Murphy told Yasmin that I showed him my tit on the school trip to Wookey Hole but I never – I just showed him my Wookey Hole.

BARMAN: If you ain't got ID I'm not serving you.

VICKY: No 'cause what you need to do right is ask Kevin Flanagan's brother 'cause he reckons I look at least fifteen and anyway I am older than that because one of my best friends in the whole world is Theresa McKenna and she goes to school with Gary Soper's sister and Gary Soper is like the hardest person in Cotham 'cause once right he was down by the canal and found this tyre and he like threw it at a swan.

BARMAN: Get out.

VICKY: No but I have got ID but I burnt it because I didn't even need it.

Packet of pork scratchings. Nuvver packet of pork scratchings. Box of matches.

EPISODE

SHANNON: You dropped your ID card, Vicky.

VICKY: Oh yeah, I just remember I never burnt it.

SHANNON GIVES VICKY A SCRAP OF PAPER. VICKY SHOWS THE BARMAN. WE SEE IT IS A HURRIEDLY DRAWN PICTURE WITH THE WORDS 'VICKY IS DEFINLY 18' ON IT.

VICKY: Oh my God that's like so unfair, Hayley Chapman reckons she went down the Firkin with loads of make-up on and they give her four Pernod and blacks. God she is so lucky, she's got her own council flat, three kids and she's only nine.

BARMAN: I'm not serving you.

VICKY: Don't matter anyway 'cause we've got one of these.

VICKY PRODUCES A PRITT STIK AND SNIFFS IT.

VICKY: Come on, let's go, this place is rubbish. Pervert!

LOU AND ANDY — SEASIDE

EXT. SEAFRONT. LOU AND ANDY ARE AT AN ICE CREAM VAN.

TOM V/O: As a special treat, Lou has taken his friend Andy to the seaside.

LOU: Right, can I have, please, a whippy with a flake. Have you decided what you're having?

ANDY: Yeah.

LOU: What do you want, then?

ANDY: Just a cone.

LOU: And another whippy plain, please.

ANDY: No, just a cone.

LOU: What, just the cone on its own? No whippy?

ANDY: Yeah.

LOU: Well, it's going to be very dry.

ANDY: Yeah, I know.

LOU: Tell you what. Why don't you have just a little bit of ice cream in it. You like ice cream. You said it was the perfect complement to a hot summer's day.

ANDY: Yeah, I know.

LOU: So what's it to be?

ANDY: Cone.

LOU: And then just a cone on its own. Thank you.

THE VAN IS NOW A LITTLE IN THE DISTANCE. LOU, WITH AN ICE CREAM IN HIS HAND, IS WHEELING ANDY AWAY. ANDY HOLDS JUST A CONE.

ANDY: I want a whippy.

LOU RETURNS TO THE VAN ANGRILY AND GETS AN ENORMOUS ICE CREAM. HE RTURNS, GIVES IT TO AN IMPASSIVE ANDY, AND WHEELS HIM OFF.

KELSEY GRAMMAR SCHOOL

INT. KELSEY GRAMMAR SCHOOL.

TOM V/O: Over at Kelsey Grammar School . . .

TEACHER: Right. You may have noticed we have a new boy here today. One or two of you will know him already. He's been put down a year from the fourth year, and his name is Thorpe. Say hello, Thorpe.

THORPE IS A GROWN MAN.

THORPE: All right!

Look into my EYES. Look into my EYES. The EYES, the EYES. Not around the EYES. Don't look around the EYES. Look into my EYES. You're under.

KENNY CRAIG — HOSPITAL

EXT./INT. HOSPITAL.

TOM V/O: If you need an operation in Britain, you can either perform it yourself in your home or you can check into a hospital.

TWO AMBULANCE MEN ARE OUTSIDE THE HOSPITAL WITH A PATIENT ON A WHEELED STRETCHER. ONE CHECKS HIS WATCH AND NODS AT THE OTHER. ONE GETS OUT A CIGARETTE, THE OTHER PULLS OUT A FLASK, ABANDONING THE PATIENT.

TOM V/O: At St Mohammed's in Shriek, stage hypnotist Kenny Craig has gone to see his mother.

INT. HOSPITAL WARD. KENNY AND HIS MOTHER ARE PLAYING SCRABBLE.

MOTHER: That puts me on 84. Your go. (KENNY STUDIES HIS LETTERS) Want some help love?

KENNY: No thank you, mother.

KENNY PUTS DOWN A WORD.

MOTHER: What's that?

KENNY: Cupboardy.

MOTHER: That's not a word.

KENNY: Yes it is. It means, er, cupboard-like.

MOTHER: Well I've never heard of that. Pass me the dictionary.

KENNY: Mother?

MOTHER: Yes.

KENNY: Look into my eyes. Look into the eyes. The eyes, the eyes. Don't look around the eyes. Look into the eyes. You're under. In a moment you will believe that 'cupboardy' is an actual word that is in the dictionary and it's not a silly word that I've just made up. Three, two, one. You're back in the room.

MOTHER: Oh, cupboardy, as in cupboard-like. Well done. That puts you on 106.

KENNY: Yeah. 106.

A FRIENDLY-LOOKING NURSE ENTERS

NURSE: Hello, Mrs Craig. Is this your toy boy?

MOTHER: Heh heh. No, this is my son, Kenny.

NURSE: Oh yes, of course, the famous hypnotist. So who's winning?

KENNY PUTS HIS HAND UP.

KENNY: I am. I'm winning.

MOTHER: He just put down 'cupboardy'.

NURSE: 'Cupboardy'? There's no such word.

KENNY TURNS TO THE NURSE.

KENNY: Look into my eyes. Look into my eyes. The eyes, the eyes. Not around the eyes. Don't look around the eyes. Look into my eyes. You're under. 'Cupboardy' is an actual word that is in the dictionary. Three, two, one – oh, and by the way, you did the toy boy gag last week and it didn't work then. If I were you I'd drop it. Three, two, one. You're back in the room.

NURSE: You're right, Mrs Craig, he can't really do it.

KENNY'S MOTHER LOOKS SHEEPISH. KENNY LOOKS ANGRY.

KENNY: Oh thanks.

BLACK AND WHITE MINSTRELS – B & B

EXT. STREET. TWO BLACK AND WHITE MINSTRELS, CARRYING SMALL SUITCASES, APPROACH A B & B AND KNOCK ON THE DOOR.

LANDLADY: I don't want to buy any dusters.

MIN. 1: Oh no, we just need a room.

LANDLADY: We're full, I'm afraid.

MIN. 2: It says 'vacancies'.

LANDLADY: No, we're full.

MIN. 1: Oh. Are there any other guesthouses you can recommend?

LANDLADY: Not in this town, no. Good day.

SHE CLOSES THE DOOR. THE MINSTRELS, OF COURSE, SHARE A FORLORN LOOK.

MIN. 2: Let's just go home.

MIN. 1: Yeah.

MARJORIE DAWES/FATFIGHTERS — NEW MEMBER

EARLY EVENING. MODERN SUBURBAN COMMUNITY CENTRE. WE SEE A GROUP OF WITCHES EXITING CHEERFULLY.

TOM V/O: Just as one group is finishing at this community centre, another begins. Inside, the weekly FatFighters meeting has just begun. Fortunately, I have never suffered from obesity myself, although I do have one very fat hand.

INT. FATFIGHTERS MEETING. MARJORIE IS STANDING BY A BOARD WITH 'HIGH IN FAT/LOW IN FAT' MARKED ON IT.

EPISODE

MARJORIE: Crisps. High in fat, low in fat? Anyone? Crisps? Paul.

PAUL: High in fat.

MARJORIE: High in fat but low in protein and low in fibre. So it's not all bad news. OK. Another one. Lettuce, lettuce. High in fat, low in fat? What do we think? Lettuce? Moira.

MEERA: Low in fat.

MARJORIE: Sorry?

MEERA: Low in fat.

MARJORIE: Do it, do it again.

MEERA: Low in fat.

MARJORIE: No, I can't . . .

PAUL: She said 'low in fat'.

MARJORIE: All right, don't patronize her! Low in fat. Well done. OK. We've got time for just one more. Dust. Anybody? No. High in fat, low in fat. Dust. Anybody? No. Dust. Anybody? No. Dust. Anybody. No. Dust. Anybody. No. Dust. Anybody? No. Dust. It's actually very low in fat. So you can have as much dust as you like. OK, moving on. Today is a very special day at FatFighters because we have a noo member. She's a noo member, her name is Barbara, and would you believe we are related!

PAUL: Is she your daughter?

MARJORIE: No, she's my sister. Nice to see you here, Barbara.

BARBARA: Thank you.

MARJORIE: There are normally more people, but Hank Marvin's playing the Pavilion tonight.

MEERA: Oooh.

MEERA GETS UP TO LEAVE.

MARJORIE: Stay where you are. So a big hello to Barbara.

ALL: Hello, Barbara, etc.

BARBARA: Hello.

MARJORIE: Yeah, she can't speak a word of English and he's already married so you're out of luck there. Not that that usually stops you. Actually it's funny, when we were growing up Barbara used to tease me, didn't you? Do you remember what you used to say?

BARBARA: No.

MARJORIE: I can. You used to say I was a greedy guts. Well all I can say is the shoe is now on the other sock. Because I may be one or two pounds overweight, but you are summin' else. She's had two kids each by different men, but that's not for here. And she's piled it on, haven't yer?

BARBARA: Well, I want to lose about a stone.

MARJORIE: A stone? More like five. Anyway, what's important is we're here to help. So what advice can we give to Barbara to turn her tragic life around? Paul.

PAUL: Cut out biscuits.

MARJORIE: Cut out biscuits. Good. Anyone else? Mary.

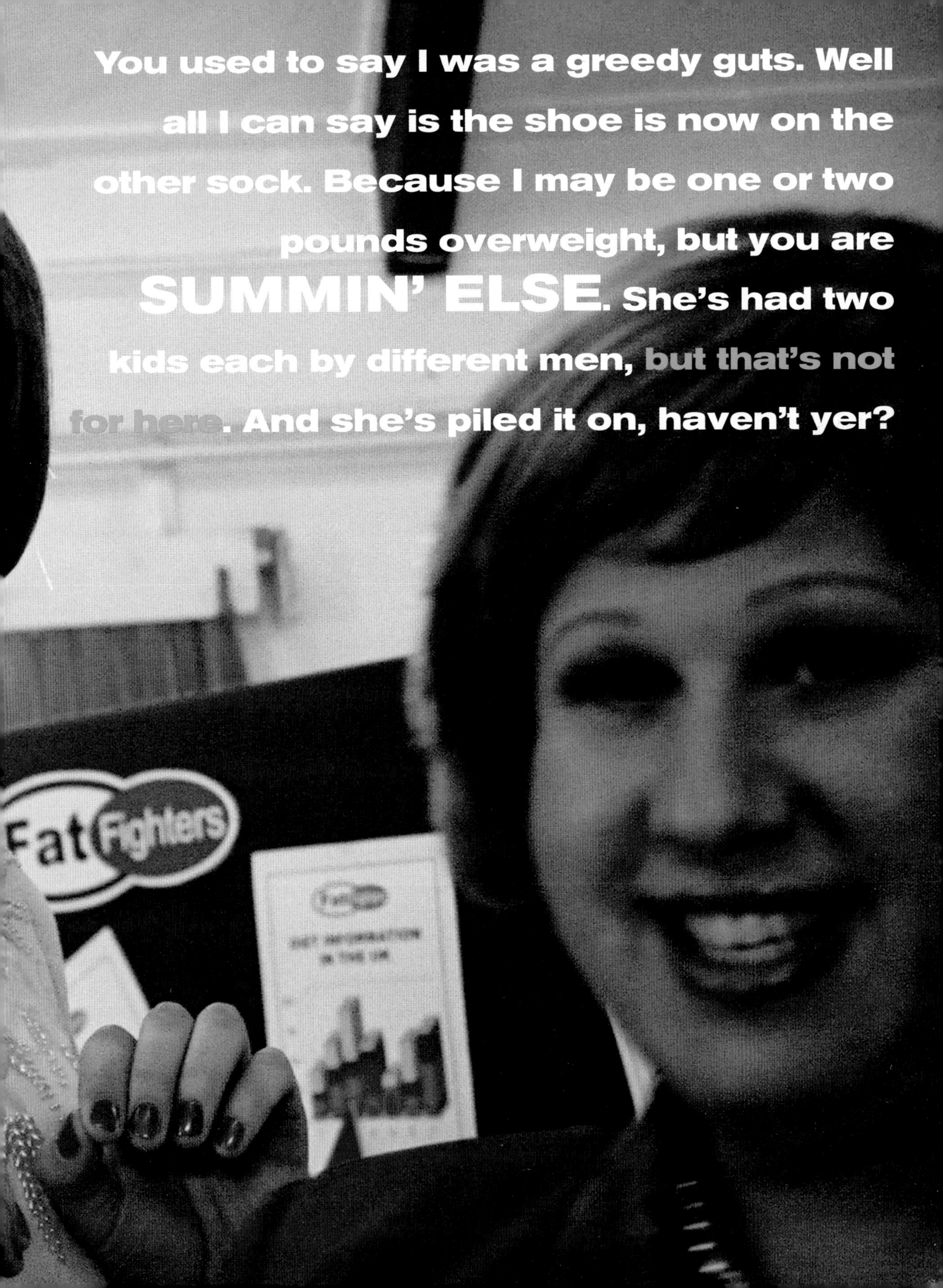

MEERA: Instead of sugar use artificial sweetener in tea.

MARJORIE: Something about sugar. But really I think the most useful advice we can all give you is to look at the person inside. Because you are obviously an incredibly unhappy person.

BARBARA: No I'm not.

MARJORIE: Well you deserve to be. I know Mum doesn't speak to you anymore but that's not for here. But as far as she's concerned if you got knocked down by a bus tomorrow the world would be a better place.

BARBARA: Mum does speak to me. I spoke to her yesterday.

MARJORIE: Barbara, we would be grateful if you could leave family matters for outside. Thanks. OK. The weigh-in. Let's, er, start with, um, Barbara. Ha ha. Will you be all right to get up or will you need sticks?

KELSEY GRAMMAR SCHOOL

INT. CLASSROOM, KELSEY GRAMMAR SCHOOL.

TEACHER: Right. One or two of you may have noticed we have a new boy here today. His name is Uppingham and he comes to us from the seventeenth century. Say hello, Uppingham.

WE SEE AN ARISTOCRATIC-LOOKING BOY IN PERIOD COSTUME.

UPPINGHAM: Hello.

PIANIST

ON STAGE, A RESPECTABLE-LOOKING PIANIST IS IN THE MIDDLE OF AN ACCOMPLISHED PIANO SOLO. HE STOPS
SUDDENLY.

PIANIST: What time do Sainsbury's shut tonight? Eight? Oh shit. On a Thursday?

HE CONTINUES TO PLAY.

DAFFYD — GAY TREKKIES

EXT. PUB.

TOM V/O: It's early evening at the Scarecrow and Mrs King pub in the Welsh mining
village of Llandewi Breffi.

A MINER, CARRYING A LARGE TRAY OF PINTS, APPEARS FROM THE PUB. HE WALKS PAST THE OTHER WAITING MINERS,
SITS ALONE AND STARTS DRINKING.

INT. PUB. DAFFYD SITS MOURNFULLY AT THE BAR.

DAFFYD: Can I have another Bacardi and Coke please, Myfanwy?

MYFANWY: Coming right up.

DAFFYD: Oh I wish there were more things for gay people to do around here.
It's so lonely being the only gay in the village.

MYFANWY: What you on about? There's loads of things to do. You've just got to look
in the local paper.

MYFANWY GRABS A COPY OF THE *LLANDEWI BREFFI GAZETTE* FROM THE BAR. SHE TURNS THE PAGES.

MYFANWY: Now, Lesbians, Bisexuals, Transgender . . . oh, here we are.
Gay section. There you go. There's a gay night on Thursdays at the BJ and the Bear pub
in Aberfanwy.

DAFFYD: Oh no, I couldn't possibly get over to Aberfanwy.

MYFANWY: Well it's only half a mile away.

DAFFYD: No, the stone path is quite treacherous.

MYFANWY: But the number four goes to Aberfanwy.

DAFFYD: Oh no, I couldn't possibly get on a bus. I'm gay, you see.

MYFANWY: 'Gay Mens' Choir, Gay Rambling Society, Gay Book Club, Gay Sex Club,
Gay Nation of Islam'.

DAFFYD: There's not much going on is there?

MYFANWY: Oh, 'Gay Trekkies'. Now that is right up your street. You love *Star Trek*, don't you?

DAFFYD: Well I don't like *Deep Space Nine*.

MYFANWY: Look, the Gay Trekkies have a meeting on Mondays at eight o'clock.

DAFFYD: Oh well, I've missed it then.

> ## Oh, 'Gay Trekkies'. Now that is right up your street. You love *Star Trek*, don't you?

MYFANWY: Right here.

DAFFYD: Let me see that!

MYFANWY: That must be them over there.

WE SEE A TABLE OF HALF A DOZEN FEY-LOOKING MEN OF VARIOUS AGES IN HOMEMADE *STAR TREK* COSTUME AND MAKE-UP, E.G. SPOCK EARS, TOPS, ETC.

DAFFYD: They don't look like *Star Trek* fans to me.

MYFANWY: 'Course they are.

DAFFYD: Well, they can't be gay.

TREKKIE: Oh I tell you dear, he was hung like a Klingon.

MYFANWY: Go over and talk to them.

DAFFYD: Oh no, Myfanwy, I couldn't possibly walk all the way over there. These hotpants give me terrible chaffing.

MYFANWY: (REPROACHFULLY) Daffyd.

DAFFYD APPROACHES THE GROUP, HIS SHORTS SQUEAK AS HE DOES SO.

DAFFYD: Greetings. Um, I've just been speaking to the barmaid.

EPISODE

TREKKIE: Yes?

DAFFYD: And she says, would you mind drinking up and leaving? Only they don't want your sort round here.

THE TREKKIES LEAVE.

DAFFYD: Well, I did try, (DAFFYD WALKS BACK TO HIS STOOL SQUEAKING) Oh, have you got any Savlon? I'm red raw down here.

LOU AND ANDY — VIDEO

INT. NEWSAGENTS. LOU AND ANDY CHECK OUT THE VIDEO RACK.

TOM V/O: With nothing on the telly but repeats of *Dr Who*, *Medics*, and that episode of *Blackadder II* I'm in, Lou and his friend Andy choose a video tape.

LOU: Have you seen anything you might like yet?

ANDY POINTS INDISCRIMINATELY.

ANDY: Yeah, I want that one.

LOU: You want that one?

ANDY: Yeah.

LOU: But that's *Pride and Prejudice*.

ANDY: Yeah, I know.

LOU: Well I'm not sure you'll like that one.

ANDY: I want that one.

LOU: It's all set in the olden days. No, I'm not sure you'll like that. You like your Chuck Norrises and your Steven Segals.

ANDY: Yeah, I know.

LOU: Well, just to be on the safe side, why don't we get a film with guns in it as well, just in case you don't like this one.

ANDY: I want that one.

LOU: You know I am going to go and see Maria tonight. So I can't take it back and get another one if you don't like it.

ANDY: Yeah, I know.

LOU: Are you sure you want this one?

I don't like it

ANDY: Yep.

IN ANDY'S FRONT ROOM LOU PUTS ON THE VIDEO FOR HIM.

ANDY: I don't like it.

LOU: Well I'm sorry but you're stuck with it. I told you, I've got to go and see Maria. Look, I'll be back around six.

LOU EXITS AND THEN ANDY GETS OUT OF HIS WHEELCHAIR. HE PUTS ANOTHER VIDEO ON AND RETURNS TO HIS CHAIR.

ANDY: Yeah! Monster Trucks, monster trucks, monster trucks!

EMILY HOWARD – GUESTHOUSE

EXT. BED AND BREAKFAST.

TOM V/O: 'Oh I do like to be beside the seaside . . . Oh I do like to be beside the seaside', as the famous song goes. At his guesthouse in Old Haven, not very good transvestite Emily Howard is showing a gentleman round.

INT. STAIRWAY. EMILY LEADS A MAN UP THE STAIRS.

EMILY: Of course, I don't normally allow single gentlemen to take rooms.

IVAN: No?

EMILY: No, a lady ought not open a house to menfolk.

IVAN: What lady?

EMILY: Me. I am a lady.

IVAN: Are you?

EMILY: Yes. Jesus! This'll be your room. It was going to be a nursery, being a lady, which I am, I was rather hoping to have children one day.

IVAN: Really?

EMILY: Oh yes, but it wasn't to be. I'm fine, I'm fine. This is my room. It has all my ladies' things in it – my lotions, my petticoats, my ladies' things. You must not come in here.

IVAN: Oh, sorry.

EMILY: Come in.

EMILY LOOKS AT DUMB-BELLS THAT ARE ON HER BED AND BRIEFLY DOES BICEPS CURLS.

EMILY: I don't know what they're doing there. Now you must know there is no lock on the door. A man like you could burst in at any time and see me in the altogether.

IVAN: Oh we don't want that.

EMILY: Yes we do . . . n't.

IVAN: So, er, how much did you say it was?

EMILY: Well, um, it's a guinea for the night, but you must remember, this is a lady's house and there are rules.

IVAN: Oh yes.

EMILY: Yes. No tobacco smoke, no coarse language, and I lock the door at 8 p.m. sharp.

IVAN: Ah, well, that might be a problem. I'm working late tonight.

EMILY: Oh really, what do you do?

IVAN: Well it might interest you, actually. I'm a female impersonator.

EMILY: What?

IVAN: Yes. I'm appearing at Bachelors. Miss Terri Lene.

IVAN SHOWS EMILY A FLYER OF HIS DRAG ACT.

EMILY: Get out! Get out!

IVAN: Why?

Just out of interest, who does your dresses?

EMILY: It's disgusting. Vamoosh! Get out of my house. Go! Go!

IVAN: Don't worry, pal. I'm off.

HE EXITS. EMILY SHOUTS AFTER HIM.

EMILY (MAN'S VOICE): Just out of interest, who does your dresses?

BERNARD CHUMLEY — BUDDING ACTOR

EXT. DAY. GRIM-LOOKING BLOCK OF HIGH-RISE FLATS ON COUNCIL ESTATE. WE SEE A SIGN – 'SANDI TOKSVIG HOUSE'. A CHILD OUTSIDE IS SPRAYING GRAFFITI ON A WALL. THE CAN IS RUNNING OUT. AN ADULT RUSHES IN, TAKES THE CAN OFF THE KID, AND GIVES HIM A NEW FULL ONE. THE KID CONTINUES TO SPRAY.

TOM V/O: Tower blocks were introduced to Britain in the 1960s and were an instant success. People loved the sense of social alienation, entrapment, and the stench of urine in the lifts. Here on the seventh floor, theatrical leg-end Bernard Chumley is preparing for a visit from an aspiring young actor.

INT. SMALL KITCHEN. WE SEE SIR BERNARD WASHING HIS PENIS BEFORE OPENING THE DOOR.

SIR BERNARD: Ah, you must be Joe.

JOE: Yes.

SIR BERNARD: Yes, do do come in, young Joe, through there. It's the room at the end, young Joe. Ha ha ha. (SIR BERNARD CHECKS HIS BREATH) Please do take a seat. That one's a bit wet. Tea?

JOE: Thank you.

SIR BERNARD DISAPPEARS INTO THE KITCHEN.

SIR BERNARD: I read your letter with great interest. Have you written to lots of other important actors?

JOE: Yes, but nobody else has actually invited me round to their . . . home.

SIR BERNARD REAPPEARS. HE HAS CHANGED HIS USUAL TOUPEE AND IS NOW WEARING A LUDICROUS BLOND, YOUNGER MAN'S WIG. WE SEE JOE'S SHOCKED REACTION TO THIS.

SIR BERNARD: Well it was such a charming letter. And the, er, photograph. And so, er . . . tea?

JOE: Thank you. Yes, well, it was so exciting to pass the audition and actually get a place at RADA, but the fees are just astronomical. It's over six thousand pounds a year.

SIR BERNARD: Do help yourself to a potato crisp.

JOE: Thank you.

SIR BERNARD: So who else did you write to?

JOE: Well, Sir Derek Jacobi wrote a nice letter.

SIR BERNARD: Terrible stutter.

JOE: And Sir Anthony Hopkins.

SIR BERNARD: Oh, he's a sir now, is he?

JOE: Yes, he gave me £200.

SIR BERNARD: Bastard! He didn't send me a penny. And I imagine you've always wanted to be an actor, have you?

JOE: Yes. Ever since I was a boy, I've always spent every penny I had on . . .

SIR BERNARD: Polo mint?

JOE: No . . . I spent every penny I had on going to the theatre.

SIR BERNARD: Well, I imagine you've seen muggins here quite a few times over the years.

JOE: No.

SIR BERNARD: Oh.

JOE: Your sister Kitty I've heard of. She had an accident?

SIR BERNARD: Yes. Terrible. Lost the use of her legs. Of course, I can look back on it now and laugh, but at the time it was very, . . . boiled egg?

JOE: Oh no. Thank you.

KNOCKING SOUND ON WALL.

SIR BERNARD: (CALLS) Don't worry, Kitty. It's just the gas man.

JOE: Maybe she needs to go to the toilet.

SIR BERNARD: Oh no no no. She went yesterday. (SIR BERNARD MOVES CLOSER) Got a girlfriend yet?

JOE: No, I haven't.

Well, I imagine you've seen MUGGINS here quite a few times over the years.

SIR BERNARD: Bet you have. I bet all the girls are after you.

JOE: Yes, I'd better be off in a mo. I'm actually having tea with Sir Ian McKellen. I'm meeting him at the Savoy.

SIR BERNARD: Oh, I see. A Sugar Puff?

JOE: No thank you.

SIR BERNARD: I didn't push her.

JOE: What?

SIR BERNARD: She fell.

JOE: Yes. Actually this is rather embarrassing, but do you think you could possibly help me with my tuition fees?

SIR BERNARD: Yes, yes of course. There you are.

HANDS JOE A POUND COIN.

JOE: Thank you.

SIR BERNARD: Have you got change?

RAY McCOONEY — FOOD CRITIC

EXT. HOTEL. ONCE AGAIN, A COUPLE ARE SUNBATHING IN THE RAIN, APPLYING SUN TAN LOTION.

TOM V/O: During the summer months, literally tens of people flock to Scotland for their holiday.

INT. LOBBY. THE PROPRIETOR OF THE HOTEL, RAY MCCOONEY, IS TALKING ON THE TELEPHONE.

RAY: Och we're easy to find. When you see the hanging tree, take a left. When you come to the old well, take a right. If you pass a scarecrow, ye've come too far. Yeah, that's right. Opposite Ikea. (A GENTLEMAN IN BLAZER AND CRAVAT APPROACHES THE COUNTER) Ah, Squire Mackenzie, I trust you enjoyed your stay?

RAY PLAYS THE FLUTE.

MACKENZIE: Yes, I shall be submitting a very positive review to the *Chronicle*. Oh, just one thing. The three courses for £15 set menu – is that available on a Sunday?

RAY: If you're to ask me on a Monday I'd say 'Yeeeees'. If you're to ask me on a Tuesday I'd say 'Yeeeees'. If you're to ask me on a Wednesday . . .

MACKENZIE: Oh for heaven's sake, it's a very simple question. Do you serve the set menu on a Sunday?

If you asked me on a Monday, I'd say 'Yeeeees'. If you asked me on a Tuesday I'd say . . . 'Yeeeees'. If you'd asked me on a Wednesday I'd say . . .

RAY: If you asked me on a Monday, I'd say 'Yeeeees'. If you asked me on a Tuesday I'd say . . . (RAY PLAYS THE FLUTE) 'Yeeeees'. If you'd asked me on a Wednesday I'd say . . .

A MAN ENTERS THROUGH THE FRONT DOOR CARRYING A BIG BOX OF MCCAIN OVEN CHIPS.

DELIVERY MAN: Oven chips?

RAY: Oh, just through there. Now where was I? Oh yes. If you were to ask me on a Monday, I'd say 'Yeeeees'.

MACKENZIE: Oh for goodness sake man, it's a very simple question. Do you serve the set menu on a Sunday?

RAY: I'll tell you, but through the medium of dance. Children!

RAY STARTS TO PLAY HIS FLUTE AND TWO DWARVES COME OUT AND BEGIN DANCING AROUND HIM AS IF HE WERE A MAYPOLE. THEY FINISH WITH A FLOURISH.

RAY: Does that answer your question?

KELSEY GRAMMAR SCHOOL

INT. CLASSROOM, KELSEY GRAMMAR SCHOOL.

TEACHER: Right. You may have noticed we have a new boy here today. His name is Charlie and I don't want any of you to treat him any differently. Say hello to everybody, Charlie.

ALL: Hello Charlie.

WE REVEAL HE IS A DOG IN A TIE.

TEACHER (WEARILY)**:** Yes, he's a dog.

DAME SALLY MARKHAM — TOBOGGAN

EXT. DAY. STATELY HOME SET IN ACRES OF LAND. A GARDENER IS TRIMMING A HEDGE IN THE SHAPE OF SOMEONE PICKING A NOSE.

TOM V/O: This is the residence of Dame Sally Markham, the famous novelist. I used to have a house like this until I lost it. If you find it please could you post it back to me care of the BBC. Thank you.

DAME SALLY IS DICTATING TO HER SECRETARY, MISS GRACE.

DAME SALLY: 'Young Toby was having a ripping time on his toboggan. "Yippeeeeeeeeeeeeeeeeeeeeeeeeeeeeeeeeeeeeeeeeeeeeeeeeeeeeeeeeeeeeeeeeeeeeeeeeeeeeeeeeeeeeeeeeeeeeeeeeeeeeeeeeeeeeeeeeeeeeeeeeeeeeeeeeeeeee"'. How many pages?

MISS GRACE: Er, thirty-four.

DAME SALLY: Oh. 'Clarissa was similarly overjoyed. "YahooooOoooooooooooooooooooooooooooooooooooooooOoooooooo ooooooooooooooooooooooooooooooooOoooooooooooooooooooooooooo ooooooooooo. Oh dear," she said, "I've hurt myself. Ahhhhhhhhhhhhhhhhhhhhhhhhhhhhhhhhhhhhhhhhhhhhhhhhhhhhhhh hhhhhhhhhhhhhhhhhhhhhhhhhhhhhhhhhhhhh". Oh publish.

DENVER MILLS — 'HUG A LEPER WEEK'

INT. MOVING CAR. RICHARD, A MIDDLE-AGED MAN, IS DRIVING, DENVER IS IN THE FRONT PASSENGER SEAT.

TOM V/O: Today, former Olympic athlete Denver Mills has been booked to promote the launch of 'Hug a Leper week'.

RICHARD: Thank you so much for helping us out at such short notice, Steve.

DENVER: Denver.

RICHARD: Denver. Sorry. Is, er, Geoff Capes all right?

DENVER: The Capester? He'll be fine, yeah. He's just had to have his dog put down and he's a bit upset about that. He's only doing the bigger money jobs this week.

RICHARD: You got your speech?

DENVER: Got it right here, boss.

RICHARD: See, what 'Hug a Leper' week is all about is dispelling a few myths about leprosy.

DENVER: About bloody time.

RICHARD: Mmmm, I mean there are people out there who think that lepers are still banished to colonies.

DENVER: They're not, are they?

RICHARD: No.

DENVER SURREPTITIOUSLY SLIPS ONE OF HIS SPEECH CARDS OUT OF THE WINDOW. RICHARD IS OBLIVIOUS.

RICHARD: And some people think that lepers' limbs just fall off.

DENVER: No, I mean that's just, that's just, that's just wrong.

DENVER SLIPS ANOTHER CARD OUT OF THE WINDOW.

RICHARD: And for too long now people who suffer from leprosy have just been the butt of jokes. And that's got to stop.

RICHARD: Yeah.

DENVER SLIPS CARD AFTER CARD OUT OF THE WINDOW. PAUSE. HE SLIPS HIS FINAL CARD OUT OF THE WINDOW.

RICHARD: You want to go through your speech at all?

DENVER: No, I'll be fine.

RICHARD: Fruit pastille?

DENVER: Thanks.

RICHARD: You couldn't get me one, could you? I tell you, I missed these out in Ghana.

DENVER: Oh yeah, what were you doing in Ghana?

RICHARD: I was working out there as a missionary. That's when I actually caught leprosy.

DENVER SPITS THE PASTILLE OUT OF THE WINDOW.

RICHARD: Luckily mine has been cured now.

DENVER: Has it?

RICHARD: Yeah. But today you'll get the chance to meet lots of people in various different stages of the disease.

DENVER OPENS THE DOOR AND LEAPS OUT OF THE MOVING VEHICLE. HE STARTS TAKING HIS CLOTHES OFF
IN HORROR.

WORLD RECORD ATTEMPT – HARD-BOILED EGGS

INT. CONFERENCE CENTRE. IAN 1 IS SEATED AT A TABLE WITH A BOWL OF HARD-BOILED EGGS IN FRONT OF HIM,
AND A BUCKET BY HIS SIDE.

IAN 2: Go!

IAN 2 PRESSES HIS STOPWATCH. IAN 1 EATS ALL THE EGGS AS FAST AS POSSIBLE. IAN 2 CHECKS HIS STOPWATCH.

IAN 2: Oh no. Pressed 'reset' instead of 'start'. We'll have to do it again. I'll just get some more eggs.

CREDITS ROLL.

TOM V/O: And so we conclude our journey round Britain. I hope you've enjoyed the shoe. I'm sorry to say I won't be here next week as I'm going into hospital to have a hysterectomy. Goodbite!

Letters

...ndewi
...nes Raise
...urch Roof
...se, the only gay in
...ong to your attention that
...called it is my duty
at no point in this piece of so-
any journalism was there
any mention of gays, lesbians,
bisexuals or those sort of
transsexual/transgender people,
you know, like Fay Presto — you
know, that magician with the big
hands.

Your article on the Brownies'
'Bring and Buy' sale could have
been the perfect springboard for
a damning critique on how gays,
lesbians, and those other ones
suffer in Llandewi Breffi. Only
yesterday I went into Breffi
News on the High Street to buy a
Funny Foot, only to be informed
that they had 'sold out' and
'would I like a Mini Milk
instead'. This is nothing more
than blatant small-minded
homophobia and must be
eradicated immediately.

Yours sincerely,
Daffyd Thomas (the only gay in
the village)

PS: They did promise they'd be
getting some more Funny Feet in
next week but I must say I'm not
holding my breath.

Dear Sir
Following a number of letters that
I have sent to the Mayor without
reply, I am compelled to write to
you with regard to the statue that
is due to be unveiled in the
village square on Saturday.

I am surely not alone in
voicing the opinion that Dylan
Thomas is a highly unsuitable
subject for a statue. What was his
contribution to gay rights? All he
was was some poet or something.
Why can't we have a gay for a
statue? Somebody who has made
a real difference to this country.
There is no shortage of
candidates. May I suggest Dale
Winton, whose struggles with
both his sexuality and a plethora
of underwhelming television
formats have rendered him a
figure of international
importance? He is surely a
Nelson Mandela for our times.
What about Will Young, who so
bravely came out of the closet
just as soon as all of the *Pop Idol*
votes had been counted and he
had been declared winner? What
about Sue out of Mel and Sue?
She's a lezzer. And they do the
Kingsmill adverts. In fact, while
we're at it, what about those two
gay blokes who present that DIY
show in the mornings?

Yours in hope,
Daffyd Thomas (still the only
gay in the village)

Dear Sir
Congratulations on your fantastic
paper. I never miss an edition. I
particularly enjoyed the
wonderful report last week on
the Brownies' 'Bring and Buy'
sale ('Brownies' Raise Money
For Church Roof Repairs'). As a
fledgling writer myself, may I be
so bold as to suggest a new
regular feature for the *Gazette*?
'Daffyd Meets . . .' Each week,
I, Daffyd Thomas, only gay in
village, etc., could do an in-depth
face-to-face interview with a
well-known celebrity. For
example. Charlie from Busted — you
know, the tall one with the lovely
blond hair and black eyebrows.
Not Matt or James. Charlie — you
And I think also I should stay
over at his house and get to know
him well, and probe him, and
that way the article would be
really good and sort of in-depth.
I also think I should do Dennis
from *EastEnders*. In his case, I
think it would be worthwhile to
actually go away with him
somewhere for the weekend.
Bangor. And to keep costs down
I would be prepared to share a
room with him. I'm thinking
really of the newspaper here. Oh
who else do I like? Gareth Gates.
Oh no, he's a bit young. Um.
Thinking. Thinking. Oh yeah.
Leonardo DiCaprio? As far as I
know he's never given an
interview with the *Llandewi
Breffi Gazette*. Perhaps we could
go on the waterslides at Tenby
together? In fact Llandewi
of tie in with the whole *Titanic*
theme.

Yours sincerely,
Daffyd Thomas (I remain the
only gay in the village)

PS. I have some trunks I can lend
him if he doesn't have a pair.
They are white, though, so when
they get wet they do become
quite see-thru. I trust this would
not be a problem.

EPISODE *four*

TOM V/O: Britain, Britain, Britain. Everybody is welcome in Britain. We are open nine 'til six, Monday to Saturday. No foreign gentlemen please. But what makes Britain such a wonderful place to visit for an afternoon? Why, it's the people of Britain, and it is these which we look at today. Ooh my sweet Lord!

DAFFYD – HAIRDRESSER'S

EXT. VILLAGE STREET. DAFFYD SKIPS DOWN THE ROAD, SINGING THE PET SHOP BOYS' 'IT'S A SIN', BRIGHTLY.

TOM V/O: Here we are in the charming Welsh village of Llandewi Breffi, home of committed homosexualist, Daffyd Thomas.

INT. HAIRDRESSING SALON. RECEPTION. DAFFYD ENTERS AND IS MET BY MRS DAVIES, A FRIENDLY MIDDLE-AGED LADY.

MRS DAVIES: Morning, Daffyd.

DAFFYD: Good morning, Mrs Davies.

MRS DAVIES: Now, I just had a phone call from Ruth. She got terrible morning sickness, see, and she's not coming in today.

DAFFYD: Oh.

MRS DAVIES: So I'm gonna put you with the new boy Ifan. (CALLING) Ifan? Your ten o'clock's here. (TO DAFFYD) Do you know, I think Ifan might be a gay.

DAFFYD: I think that's very unlikely. I am the only gay in the village.

ENTER IFAN, AN IMPOSSIBLY CAMP MAN.

IFAN: Hiya. I'm Ifan, but all me friends call me Fanny. Follow me.

DAFFYD'S FACE DROPS. IFAN GOES THROUGH TO THE SALON.

MRS DAVIES: Well? Is he?

DAFFYD: Too early to tell.

MRS DAVIES POTTERS ABOUT IN THE BACKGROUND WHILE DAFFYD SITS DOWN. IFAN PUTS A GOWN ON DAFFYD AND PLAYS WITH HIS HAIR.

IFAN: (TO DAFFYD) Come along now. Take the weight off your lallies. Let's put a nice big skirt

HIYA. I'm Ifan, but all me friends call me Fanny.

around you. Now what can we do for you? A nice wash and blow? Would you like that? A blow? Hoo hoo!

DAFFYD: Just a light trim, please.

IFAN STARTS TO CUT.

IFAN: Right you are. So do you go out much?

DAFFYD: Not really.

IFAN: Is there much of a scene?

DAFFYD: I beg your pardon.

IFAN: A scene, dear. A gay scene. You know, cocks and frocks.

DAFFYD: No, there is no 'Gay' scene in Llandewi Breffi. Just me.

IFAN: Really?

DAFFYD: Yes. I am the only gay in this village.

IFAN: Not any more, dear. Fanny's in town.

ENTER MRS DAVIES WITH TWO CUPS OF TEA.

MRS DAVIES: There you are, loves.

IFAN: Oh, ta.

AS SHE GIVES DAFFYD HIS TEA, SHE WHISPERS TO HIM.

MRS DAVIES: Well?

DAFFYD: No signs.

THE DOOR OPENS. ENTER GARETH, A CHUNKY, CHIRPY, VERY OBVIOUSLY HOMOSEXUAL MIDDLE-AGED MAN WITH PIERCINGS AND TWO SMALL DOGS (WITH RIBBONS IN THEIR HAIR).

GARETH: Fanny, love. You forgot your keys.

GARETH GIVES IFAN A SET OF KEYS.

IFAN: Thanks. I am a dizzy cow!

GARETH: Right, Hinge and Brackett need walking. So I'll see you later.

IFAN AND GARETH KISS.

DAFFYD: (MOUTHS TO MRS DAVIES) His brother.

Not any more, dear. **Fanny's in town.**

EMILY HOWARD — X-RAY

TOM V/O: At St Buddha's Hospital in Foulmouth, ropey transvestite Emily Howard is waiting to have an X-ray taken.

INT. X-RAY ROOM. EMILY LIES ON A BED. A DOCTOR STEPS OUT FROM BEHIND A SCREEN, CLUTCHING A CLIPBOARD.

DOCTOR: Right, sorry to keep you. (CHECKING CLIPBOARD) So, Eddie Howard . . .

EMILY: Emily Howard. I'm a lady, Emily Howard, yes.

DOCTOR: Right, er, what happened?

EMILY: Well, I was disembarking a motor coach when I took a tumble.

DOCTOR: You fell off the bus?

EMILY: Quite.

> # But I am a lady. I don't have testiclés. Well, perhaps little ladies' testiclés.

DOCTOR: Right, well, I'm going to need to do an X-ray of the whole leg. So if you'd just like to place this over your testicles.

THE DOCTOR HANDS EMILY A SMALL PILLOW. SHE IS QUITE ALARMED.

EMILY: Ooh, doctor, you do amuse!

DOCTOR: No, it's not a joke. It's got a sheet of lead in it. It deflects the radiation.

EMILY: But I am a lady. I don't have testiclés (PRONOUNCED 'TESTICLAY'). Well, perhaps little ladies' testiclés.

EMILY PULLS OUT A CHINESE FAN FROM HER HANDBAG AND MOVES IT AROUND HER MIDRIFF.

EMILY: Might, er, might this do for me instead?

DOCTOR: No.

EMILY: Or this?

EMILY PULLS OUT A VICTORIAN COPY OF *THE LADY* MAGAZINE. THE DOCTOR SHAKES HIS HEAD.

EPISODE

EMILY: Surely I . . .

EMILY PULLS OUT A SMALL, WHITE FLUFFY CAT.

DOCTOR: I'm sorry. You do need to use this.

HE HANDS EMILY THE SPECIAL PILLOW.

EMILY: Would you mind if I brightened it up a little with some appliqué and décollage? Yes. I could sew some lace around the edges.

DOCTOR: We don't really have time for this, Mr Howard.

EMILY: But I am a lady.

DOCTOR: Well, I can't give you the X-ray without it.

EMILY CHANGES TACK.

EMILY: Do you know? I think I am feeling rather better. Yes, I don't think I need an X-ray at all. Yes.

EMILY CLIMBS OFF THE BED UNEASILY AND HEADS FOR THE DOOR IN GREAT PAIN.

EMILY: (MANLY) Aargh! Shit!

LOU AND ANDY – PUB

EXT. DAY. PUB. SIGN READS 'THE TURNER AND HOOCH'. A PASSER-BY TOSSES AN EMPTY CAN INTO A NEARBY RUBBISH BIN. A VERY AGGRIEVED SMALL MAN APPEARS FROM INSIDE THE BIN AND THROWS THE CAN BACK AT THE PASSER-BY.

TOM V/O: This is a pub. As we all know, the word pub is an acronym for 'Phillip's Uncle's Boat'.

INT. DAY. FAIRLY EMPTY PUB. ANDY SITS AT A TABLE WITH LOTS OF EMPTY GLASSES ON IT.

LOU: Right. We'd better get you home, hadn't we?

ANDY: I know.

LOU: Oh, do you need to use the toilet before we go?

ANDY: No.

LOU: Are you sure?

ANDY: Yeah.

LOU: 'Cause once I've got you in the van you won't be able to do toilet until we're back home.

ANDY: Yeah, I know.

'Cause if I have to stop on the way and get you out of the van that's a right KERFUFFLE.

EPISODE

LOU: 'Cause if I have to stop on the way and get you out of the van that's a right kerfuffle.

ANDY: I know.

LOU: Are you sure you don't need the toilet?

ANDY: Yeah.

INT. VAN. ANDY IS IN THE PASSENGER SEAT. LOU PUTS THE KEY IN THE IGNITION AND BEGINS TO DRIVE.

ANDY: I need to go toilet.

DR LAWRENCE AND ANNE — LIBRARY 1

EXT. DAY. LIBRARY.

TOM V/O: Following the success of video libraries, book libraries like this one have sprung up everywhere.

A PIZZA DELIVERY MAN ARRIVES ON A SCOOTER, FOLDS A SMALL PIZZA IN HALF, AND POSTS IT INTO A NEARBY PILLAR BOX.

INT. TOWN LIBRARY. DR LAWRENCE AND DR BEAGRIE ENTER.

DR LAWRENCE: One of the things we encourage our patients to do is take a Saturday job. It gives them a sense of purpose and also a small income. Now I've brought you here today because Anne, whom you may have met, is working here.

WE SEE ANNE NEARBY. SHE PICKS UP A BOOK FROM A TROLLEY AND THROWS IT TO THE FLOOR.

ANNE: Eh eh eh!

DR LAWRENCE: Hello, Anne.

AGAIN ANNE PICKS UP A BOOK FROM THE TROLLEY AND RIPS OUT SOME PAGES. SHE HANDS THEM TO THE TWO
DOCTORS. SHE PLACES THE BOOK ON DR BEAGRIE'S SHOULDER.

DR LAWRENCE: Thank you. And how are you today?

ANNE: Eh eh eh!

ANNE RUBS SOME BOOKS ON HER BREASTS. SHE DROPS THEM AND LEAVES, STROKING DR BEAGRIE'S FACE
ON THE WAY OUT.

DR LAWRENCE: As you can see, she blends in very well.

DR BEAGRIE NODS.

VICKY POLLARD — MAGISTRATES' COURT

EXT. COURT. WE SEE A ROBED JUDGE ENJOYING A CIGARETTE SITTING ON THE STEPS.

TOM V/O: British justice is the best in the world. Anyone who disagrees is either a gay,
a woman, or a mental.

INT. COURT. VICKY POLLARD IS IN THE DOCK.

LAWYER: Vicky Pollard, you have been charged with shoplifting. On the 11th of April, it is
alleged you went into the Erskine branch of Superdrug. Once there you attempted to steal
an eyeliner pencil and a can of Red Bull by concealing them in your leggings. Now in the
face of the overwhelming evidence we've heard today against you, do you stand by your
plea of – 'Not guilty'?

VICKY: No but yeah but no because what happened was right this thing happened that
I didn't know nothing about shut up I wasn't meant to be anywhere even near there.
Then Meredith came over and started stirring it all up started calling me all these things
about this thing I didn't even know about.

THE LAWYER IS STUMPED.

LAWYER: Right, but you admit you were in Superdrug at the time?

VICKY: No but yeah but no because there's whole other thing what I didn't even know
about and Meredith said it weren't a thing but it was but don't listen to her because
she's a complete slag.

LAWYER: Sorry, Meredith? Who is Meredith?

VICKY: She's the one who done that thing about the thing but if she gives you sweets
don't eat 'em because she's dirty.

LAWYER: Thing? What thing?

VICKY: Yeah I know and anyway and there was this whole other thing what I didn't even

Nobutyeahbutnobecausewhat
happenedwasrightthisthing
happenedthatIdidn'tknownothing
aboutSHUTUPIwasn'tmeanttobe
anywhereevennearthere.
ThenMeredithcameoverandstarted
stirringitallupstartedcallingmeall
thesethingsaboutthisthingIdidn't
evenknowabout.

know about or somefink or nuffin' because nobody told Wayne Duggin that Jermyn fingered Carly round the back of the ice rink.

LAWYER: Right.

VICKY: But I was supposed to be doing Home Ec. But I wasn't right I was on the phone to Jules. But anyway don't listen to her because she had a baby and didn't tell anyone.

LAWYER: Vicky, were you at Superdrug at the time?

VICKY: No but yeah but no but yeah but no but yeah but no because I wasn't even with Amber.

LAWYER: Amber? Who's Amber?

VICKY: Yeah exactly. I wasn't even with her and anyway I didn't even know who she is so you'd better ask her.

LAWYER: Vicky, I don't think you realize the gravity of the situation you . . .

VICKY: No but there's something right what I didn't . . .

LAWYER: If you're found guilty . . .

VICKY: No you definitely can't say that right because . . .

LAWYER: You'll have a criminal record.

VICKY: No but I'm allergic to cat hair so I don't have to go into lessons.

LAWYER: This is a court of law you have . . . are you going to keep interrupting me?

VICKY: No no no no no no I'm not, I'm going to let you speak.

LAWYER: Oh. Now we've heard from the social workers . . .

VICKY: Oh my God! Right. There was this whole other thing I completely forgot to tell you about . . .

LAWYER: Oh I give up.

VICKY: You know Craig? Well he felt up Amy on the corkscrew at Alton Towers her mum totally had an eppy. But then Dean went on the Mary Rose and was sick on Louise Farren's head.

Oh my God! Right. There was this whole other thing I completely forgot to tell you about . . .

EPISODE

MATTHEW WATERHOUSE – KISSAGRAM

TOM V/O: It's Hilary o'clock and silly comedy character Matthew Waterhouse is looking for work at his local kissagram agency.

EXT. INDUSTRIAL ESTATE. WE SEE A FEW PORTAKABINS. MATTHEW WATERHOUSE APPROACHES.

INT. PORTAKABIN OFFICE. MATTHEW WATERHOUSE BURSTS IN, CARRYING A BIG BLACK SACK.

MATTHEW: I wanna be a kissagram!

MATTHEW MAKES LOTS OF KISSING NOISES.

MAN AT DESK: We're minicabs, mate. Kissagrams next door.

INT. PORTAKABIN OFFICE. MATTHEW WATERHOUSE BURSTS IN, CARRYING A BIG BLACK SACK.

MATTHEW: I wanna be a kissagram!

MATTHEW MAKES LOTS OF KISSING NOISES. JOAN LEESON, A WOMAN IN HER LATE FORTIES, IS SEATED AT HER DESK. BEHIND HER ARE A NUMBER OF ADS AND PHOTOS FOR HER KISSAGRAM AGENCY WITH PICTURES OF PEOPLE DRESSED AS GORILLAS, TARZAN, POLICE, ST TRINIAN'S GIRLS, ETC.

JOAN: Lovely. We're always looking for people. What . . .

MATTHEW EMPTIES THE CONTENTS OF HIS SACK ONTO THE DESK, CREATING A BIG MESS. HE PICKS UP A LONG FAKE GREY BEARD.

MATTHEW: Here's one for you. George Bernard Shawagram. I come in, take my beard off, and recite a play. How about that for starters?

HE THUMPS THE TABLE.

JOAN: Erm . . .

MATTHEW: Got another one. John McCarthyagram.

WATERHOUSE PICKS UP A SMALL RADIATOR FROM THE DESK.

JOAN: Oh, what happens there?

MATTHEW: I come in handcuffed to a radiator and discuss my five years as a hostage in the Lebanon. Book me!

JOAN: Yes, I don't think there's any market for . . .

MATTHEW: Got another one. Nurseagram.

WATERHOUSE PUTS ON A NURSE'S HAT.

JOAN: Ah well, you see, that's more like it.

MATTHEW: Yeah, I come in, sing 'Happy Birthday', and administer a local anaesthetic.

WATERHOUSE PICKS UP A LARGE NEEDLE.

JOAN: I really don't think there's any point in me saying . . .

MATTHEW: Zooagram.

JOAN: And what's that?

MATTHEW: I come in (PAUSE. WATERHOUSE THINKS.) Bear with me.

PAUSE.

JOAN: Well?

MATTHEW: I just told you. I come in and there's a bear with me.

JOAN: Sorry.

MATTHEW: Got another one. Ianagram. I come in and pretend my name is Ian.
'Hello, my name is Ian', etc.

JOAN: Please leave.

MATTHEW: Managram! I'm a man.

JOAN: Get out.

MATTHEW: Invisiblemanagram. I come in and I'm invisible. (DOES SOME INVISIBLE ACTING.)
Oooh oooh. Was I invisible then?

JOAN: No.

MATTHEW: Are you sure?

JOAN: Quite sure. Now please. I'm a very busy woman.

MATTHEW: Averybusywomanagram!

JOAN: So could you leave the room?

WATERHOUSE DRIFTS TOWARDS THE DOOR, QUITE HAPPILY.

MATTHEW: Leavingtheroomagram!

JOAN: That's right. Now open the door.

MATTHEW DOES SO.

MATTHEW: Openingthedooragram!

JOAN: Walk out.

MATTHEW DOES SO.

MATTHEW: Walkingoutthedooragram!

JOAN: And close the door.

MATTHEW DOES SO.

MATTHEW: Closingthedooragram!

PAUSE.

MATTHEW: (MUFFLED) Waitingoutsidethedooragram. (PAUSE. WATERHOUSE RE-ENTERS.)
Hello. I'd like a minicab please.

JOAN: No, that's next door.

MATTHEW: Thank you.

WALKS NEXT DOOR AND PUTS HIS HEAD ROUND THE DOOR.

MATTHEW: All right!

Here's one for you. **George Bernard Shawagram.**

I come in,

take my beard

off, and recite

a play.

How about

that for

starters?

KELSEY GRAMMAR SCHOOL

TOM V/O: Over in Flange at the Kelsey Grammar School . . .

INT. CLASSROOM. THE TEACHER WRITES ON THE BLACKBOARD, AS HE SPEAKS.

TEACHER: So Edward the Second divided by Henry the Fifth equals . . . anybody?
(THE CLASS ARE SILENT.) No?

THE TEACHER LOOKS AROUND, BEFORE RETURNING TO THE BOARD.

TEACHER: . . . equals Hydrogen Peroxide. Question six. Determine the square root
of Popeye.

SANDRA AND RALPH — ADVERT

TOM V/O: Sandra Patterson is so keen for her son to do well in the world of show
business that her hair is coming out in clumps.

INT. SMALL DANCE STUDIO-TYPE HALL. A DESK AND CAMERA ARE SET UP. SANDY, THE DIRECTOR, IS SEATED AT THE
DESK WITH HIS ASSISTANT, NORA, ALONG WITH TWO OTHER STERN-LOOKING PEOPLE. RALPH, A NINE-YEAR-OLD CHILD
ACTOR, IS IN HIS SCHOOL UNIFORM. HE IS STANDING IN THE CENTRE OF THE ROOM, FACING THE DESK, HOLDING UP A
PACKET OF SWEETS.

DIRECTOR: Back up a bit . . . and off you go.

RALPH: They're fruity and delicious . . . they're fruit-ilicious!

DIRECTOR: Lovely. OK, thanks very much, (READING) Raif. (TO ASSISTANT)
Can you send the next one in?

SANDRA, RALPH'S BEDRAGGLED MOTHER, STEPS IN FRONT OF THE CAMERA, NEXT TO HER SON. SHE PUTS HER ARM
ROUND HIM.

SANDRA: So, are we rocking? Have we got the gig?

DIRECTOR: Er, we'll let you know.

SANDR: He does a great Otis the Aardvark. Do your Otis the Aardvark.

RALPH: Mum . . .

DIRECTOR: We've just got a few more people to see so . . .

SANDRA: Have you seen *The Snowman*? You know, the car'oon. He does that. Go on.
Do it. It'll break your bleedin' heart. Go on, do it.

RALPH: (SINGS.) 'We're walking in the air . . .'

SANDRA: To them. To them.

RALPH: 'We're walking through the moonlit sky . . . '

MOTHER IS FOLLOWING HIM, SHOWERING HIM WITH BITS OF POLYSTYRENE PACKING.

DIRECTOR: Unfortunately we are up against it today so . . .

SANDRA: It's better with his pyjamas on. Come on. (KNEELS)

SANDRA DELVES INTO HER PLASTIC BAG TO RETRIEVE THEM.

RALPH: (EMBARRASSED) Mum!

DIRECTOR: We don't really have time you see, um . . .

SANDRA: It's his birthday today.

RALPH: No, it isn't.

DIRECTOR: Please.

SANDRA: He's dying.

RALPH: What?

SANDRA: Look a dying boy in the eye and say 'No'.

DIRECTOR: Well if you must know, it's a 'No'.

SANDRA: What?

DIRECTOR: Well it's nothing personal. We're just looking for something a bit different.

SANDRA: We can change him. We can have something done.

I'll tell them you touched him

SANDRA MANIPULATES THE BOY'S FEATURES TO ILLUSTRATE THE POSSIBILITIES – PINS BACK THE EYES, PUSHES UP THE NOSE, ETC.

DIRECTOR: Look, he's a real talent. I'm sure he's going to do really well.

SANDRA: I'll tell them you touched him.

DIRECTOR: Get out!

SANDRA: Don't worry. We know when we're not wanted.

THEY EXIT THROUGH A PAIR OF DOUBLE DOORS.

SANDRA (UNSEEN, FROM BEHIND THE DOORS, SCREAMS): Don't ever do that again.

DR LAWRENCE AND ANNE — LIBRARY 2

INT. LIBRARY. ANNE IS BEHIND THE COUNTER. DR LAWRENCE AND DR BEAGRIE APPROACH THE COUNTER.

DR LAWRENCE: Watch this.

DR LAWRENCE PULLS OUT A NEARBY BOOK.

DR LAWRENCE: Hello, Anne. I'd like to take this book out please.

DR LAWRENCE HANDS OVER THE BOOK AND HIS LIBRARY CARD.

ANNE: Eh eh eh!

ANNE TRIES TO EAT THE BOOK. SHE THEN JUMPS UP AND DOWN ON IT. SHE THEN PICKS UP THE RUBBER STAMP AND PUTS IT ON DR LAWRENCE'S HAND AND FACE. SUDDENLY WE HEAR A MOBILE PHONE RINGING. ANNE REACHES INTO HER POCKET AND PULLS OUT A PHONE.

ANNE: Hello. Yeah, sorry guys. Um, I'm just in the library at the moment Can I call you back? OK! Eh eh eh!

ANNE PUTS THE PHONE DOWN.

DR LAWRENCE: And can you tell me when the Oliver Sacks biography is back in?

ANNE TYPES ON THE COMPUTER KEYBOARD.

ANNE: Eh eh eh!

DR LAWRENCE: Thank you.

AS DR BEAGRIE WALKS PAST, SHE STOPS HIM AND STROKES HIS FACE.

MARJORIE DAWES — HOSPITAL

TOM V/O: The Health Service in Britain is thriving, with three doctors to every one patient. Today, Marjorie Dawes has gone to see her mother.

INT. HOSPITAL WARD. MARJORIE IS SEATED NEXT TO HER MUM, WHO IS IN BED. MUM HAS HER ARM IN A SLING. MARJORIE IS EATING HER MUM'S CHOCOLATES.

MARJORIE: Now I've been on to the doctor and he says you've definitely got to go into a home.

MUM: I don't want to go into a home. I just had a fall.

THE DOCTOR ENTERS.

DOCTOR: Morning. How are we today?

THE DOCTOR IS SLIGHTLY PERTURBED TO SEE THAT MARJORIE IS THERE TOO.

MARJORIE: Fine, Doctor. (TO MUM) Look it's Dr Harman, Mum. (TO DOCTOR HARMAN) And how is the good doctor today, Dr Harman?

DOCTOR: Quite well. Just a bit bunged up.

MARJORIE: Bunged up. Yes, there's something going round, isn't there? Yeah, well let me know if you want someone to look after you, Dr Harman.

DOCTOR: We've got the results here. It's good news. There's no internal haemorrhaging. So you can go home tomorrow.

MUM: Oh good.

MARJORIE: No . . . don't you think she might be better off in a home, Doctor? (TO MUM) Home. Yeah yeah, home. Yeah yeah, put you in a home. Yeah.

DOCTOR: No. We've done all the tests and she's perfectly capable of looking after herself.

MARJORIE: No, doctor. She doesn't know what day it is. (TO MUM, LOUDLY) Mum, what day is it?

MUM: It's Tuesday.

DOCTOR: Well there you go. It *is* Tuesday.

MARJORIE: Yeah, she thinks it's *last* Tuesday. Who's the Prime Minister?

MUM: Well it's –

MARJORIE: Of Belgium.

MUM: Well I don't know.

MARJORIE GIVES DR HARMAN A KNOWING LOOK.

MARJORIE: See what I have to put up with? Mum, what's this?

MARJORIE POINTS CLOSELY AT HER OWN NOSE.

MUM: It's your nose.

MARJORIE: No, it's my finger. See Doctor? She doesn't know if she's comin' or goin'.

DOCTOR: Mrs. Dawes . . .

MARJORIE: Call me Marjorie.

DOCTOR: Marjorie, we only put people in homes when they are incapable of looking after themselves.

MARJORIE: Well what if her flat was attacked by a pack of wolves? No, I'm sorry, doctor. She's very vulnerable.

DOCTOR: Well I'm sorry, I'm not going to recommend further care because she simply doesn't need it. Good day.

THE DOCTOR EXITS.

MARJORIE: Bye, doctor. Get well soon. (TO MUM) Oh he's such a flirt. Now what are we gonna do with you? You can't come and live with me, you know.

MUM: I don't bloody want to. I want to go back to me own flat.

MARJORIE: But I'm renting it out now.

MUM: Who to?

MARJORIE: Some gays. Now I've been on to Social Services and they've found you a very nice place, just an hour down the road.

I'M RENTING IT
OUT NOW
Who to?
SOME GAYS

MUM: Well maybe I could go and live with Barbara.

MARJORIE: Mum, Barbara hates you. That's why I think you should cut her out the will, but we've been through that. Now I'm coming back tomorrow – is there anything you would like me to bring you?

MUM: My dressing gown.

MARJORIE: No, I've taken it to Oxfam.

MUM: Well, I was halfway through that Maeve Binchy.

MARJORIE: Well I'm reading that now.

MUM: Oh. Well how about my jewellery?

MARJORIE CLASPS HER NECK TO HIDE THE PEARL NECKLACE SHE IS WEARING.

MARJORIE: Well I'll see you tomorrow then, Mum. Cheerio

MARJORIE HEADS FOR THE DOOR. AS SHE DOES SO, SHE MUTTERS TO A PASSING NURSE.

MARJORIE: Ooh she's a burden.

DES KAYE – HELPING A CUSTOMER

INT. DIY UNIVERSE. DES KAYE IS CHEERFULLY PUSHING A STAFF TROLLEY FULL OF PAINT POTS ROUND. HE IS WEARING DIY UNIVERSE OVERALLS, BUT HAS SLIGHTLY CUSTOMIZED HIS WITH BRACES, BADGES, TURN-UPS, AND LUMINOUS SOCKS.

TOM V/O: The fortunes of ex-children's entertainer Des Kaye have taken a tumble recently. To make ends meet, he has been forced to take a job at DIY Universe in the northern town of Little Tokyo.

EACH TIME CUSTOMERS PASS BY, DES SHOUTS:

DES: Wicky woo!

DES STOPS AT AN AISLE OF PAINT POTS AND SURREPTITIOUSLY STACKS IT WITH HIS OWN VIDEOS. A MANAGERESS APPEARS.

MANAGERESS: What's this now?

DES STANDS IN FRONT OF THE VIDEOS.

DES: Nothing.

MANAGERESS: I won't tell you again. You're not on telly any more. Now take those down and get on with your work.

DES RELUCTANTLY TAKES DOWN THE VIDEOS. A BUILDER ARRIVES.

BUILDER: (TO MANAGERESS) Excuse me, do you know where the masking tape is?

MANAGERESS: This man will help you.

THE MANAGERESS WALKS OFF.

BUILDER: Excuse me, do you know where the masking tape is?

DES: Oh Wicky Woo! Des Kaye, pleased to meet you.

DES SHAKES THE MAN'S HAND TOO MUCH AND DOESN'T LET GO.

DES: Ooh, can I have me hand back please?

DES LETS GO.

BUILDER: Yeah. Do you know where the masking tape is?

DES: No, I don't. But I've got a friend who does.

DES PRODUCES A CROCODILE PUPPET.

DES : Say hello to Mr Croc O'Dile.

'CROCODILE': Top of the morning. Where's me breakfast?

DES: Never mind about your breakfast. This young lad here wants to know where the masking tape is.

'CROCODILE': But I'm hungry. I want my breakfast.

CROC TUSSLES WITH THE BUILDER AND TRIES TO EAT HIM.

DES: (TO BUILDER) I'm so sorry about this.

WICKY WOO!
Des Kaye,
pleased to
meet you.

BUILDER: Get off me!

THE MANAGERESS APPEARS.

MANAGERESS: Des!

DES: I'm, I'm just helping a customer.

THE TUSSLE CONTINUES. CROC GOES FOR THE BUILDER'S PRIVATES.

DR LAWRENCE AND ANNE — LIBRARY 3

EXT. TOWN LIBRARY. DR LAWRENCE AND DR BEAGRIE ARE WALKING AWAY FROM THE LIBRARY. DR LAWRENCE HAS A STAMP ON ONE OF HIS CHEEKS AND ALSO HIS FOREHEAD. HE CARRIES A TORN BOOK. WE SEE ANNE EXIT THE BUILDING, IN FRONT OF THE PAIR.

DR LAWRENCE: We let Anne make her own way home. She's earned five pounds today. And that's her money. And she can spend that any way she wants.

ANNE HAS A FIVE POUND NOTE. SHE BENDS DOWN AND CALMLY PUTS IT DOWN A DRAIN.

DR LAWRENCE: See you later, Anne.

ANNE GIVES HIM THE FINGER.

PETER ANDRE — HIGHGROVE

EXT./INT. BBC TV CENTRE. SECURITY GUARDS TURNING A WOMBLE AWAY.

TOM V/O: At TV Centre, the BBC continues to fulfil its charter to educate, entertain, inform, and provide work for Patrick Kielty.

INT. EDIT SUITE. BBC TV NEWS. THE PRODUCER IS PERCHED ON A DESK TALKING TO ROYAL CORRESPONDENT PETER ANDRE.

PRODUCER: Peter, I've got a tape of last night's news here. I wasn't happy with it.

PETER: Really.

PRODUCER: Let's have a look, shall we?

THE PRODUCER POPS A TAPE INTO A VIDEO PLAYER. ON THE SCREEN WE SEE THE FOLLOWING:

INT. STUDIO. TYPICAL NEWS BROADCAST. SOPHIE RAWORTH ADDRESSES CAMERA.

SOPHIE: We'll have more on that later. Now we go over to our Royal Correspondent, Peter Andre . . .

THE FOOTAGE CUTS TO PETER, STANDING OUTSIDE A CHURCH.

PETER: Thank you, Raworth. Yes, I'm standing here outside Highgrove Church, where earlier today, the Royals were attending their traditional Easter Sunday service.

WE CUT TO FOOTAGE OF THE ROYAL FAMILY ARRIVING AT A CHURCH SERVICE. PETER'S COMMENTARY ACCOMPANIES THE IMAGES.

PETER: (TO PRODUCER) Textbook.

PETER V/O: Prince Charles there. He has magical powers. Prince Edward there, sadly without his beautiful wife, Griff Rhys Jones.

NB DURING THIS SEQUENCE, WE CUT BACK TO PETER AND THE PRODUCER WATCHING.
PETER IS VERY PLEASED WITH HIMSELF. THE PRODUCER IS LOOKING AT PETER'S REACTIONS.

PETER V/O: Prince Andrew there with a very young Sarah Ferguson. I've met him loads of times. He's really nice. I really like him. (CALLS) Hi Andrew!

I love you, **ANNE**, and I want you, **ANNE**. Please pull me, **ANNE**, and I'll push you, **ANNE**. Please hurt me, **ANNE**, and bite me, **ANNE**, 'cause I want you, **ANNE**, in the morning.

Andrew! No, he can't hear me. The Queen there, she's the main one. And light of my life, Princess Royal Anne. Oh Anne. Sweet Anne.

WE HEAR PETER SING A STRANGE, TUNELESS SONG ACCOMPANIED BY A LUTE.

PETER V/O: I love you, Anne, and I want you, Anne. Please pull me, Anne, and I'll push you, Anne. Please hurt me, Anne, and bite me, Anne, 'cause I want you, Anne, in the morning.

WE CUT TO PETER WHO IS NOW DANCING. A FEW BAFFLED ONLOOKERS HAVE GATHERED.
PETER TURNS TO CAMERA.

PETER V/O: Back to the studio.

WE RETURN TO THE STUDIO TO SEE SOPHIE LOOKING BEMUSED. SHE IS SO THROWN, IN FACT, THAT SHE LOSES CONCENTRATION. PAUSE.

SOPHIE: Um, Peter Andre there . . .

THE PRODUCER TURNS OFF THE VIDEO.

PETER: Problem?

OUTSIDE THE BBC WE SEE PETER BEING CHUCKED OUT, CLOSELY FOLLOWED BY HIS LUTE.

EPISODE

LOU AND ANDY — CHOCOLATES

INT. ANDY'S FRONT ROOM. ANDY IS SEATED IN HIS WHEELCHAIR.

TOM V/O: It is ten minutes since Andy last ate, and his stomach's already rumbling.

LOU: Right, I'm gonna go and pick up Maria. Is there anything you need me to do before I go?

ANDY: Yeah. I wanna chocolate.

ANDY POINTS AT A BOX OF CHOCOLATES ON A NEARBY SHELF (HIGH, OUT OF ANDY'S REACH).

LOU: I bought these chocolates for when Maria comes round.

ANDY: I wanna chocolate.

LOU: Well all right, you can have *one*.

LOU GETS THE BOX, OPENS IT, AND TAKES IT OVER TO ANDY.

LOU: Now, which one do you want?

ANDY: That one.

ANDY POINTS INDISCRIMINATELY.

LOU: That one?

ANDY: Yeah.

LOU: Well that's dark chocolate.

ANDY: Yeah, I know.

LOU: Well you don't like dark chocolate.

ANDY: I know.

LOU: You always said that dark chocolate has a bitter edge to it, and lacks the oral ecstasy of its milkier cousin.

ANDY: Yeah, I know.

LOU: Well why don't you have the caramel tub then? You like the caramel tub. It's caramel.

ANDY: I want that one.

ANDY PICKS OUT THE DARK CHOCOLATE.

LOU: Oh well, they're going back on the shelf now.

LOU PUTS THE BOX BACK ON THE SHELF. ANDY PUTS THE DARK CHOCOLATE IN HIS MOUTH. HE LETS IT DRIBBLE DOWN THE SIDE OF HIS MOUTH.

ANDY: I don't like it.

LOU: I did warn you.

ANDY: Can I have another one just to take the taste away?

LOU HEADS FOR THE DOOR.

LOU: No. You can have another one when Maria gets here, and not before.
See you later.

ANDY SULKS. LOU EXITS. PAUSE. ANDY GETS UP OUT OF HIS WHEELCHAIR, GRABS A NEARBY CHAIR, TAKES IT OVER
TO THE SHELF, STANDS ON IT, AND GRABS THE CHOCOLATES, BEFORE JUMPING DOWN. HE SITS DOWN. ANDY TAKES
A CHOCOLATE, SCREWS HIS FACE UP, AND SPITS IT OUT.

APRIL AND NEVILLE — OPERA

INT. THEATRE. AN OLD COUPLE ARE SEATED IN A BOX AT THE OPERA.

TOM V/O: Everyone in Britain loves the opera. Go to any bus stop or factory floor
and all you hear is 'Don Giovanni this, Rigoletto that'.

SUDDENLY THE OLD MAN PASSES OUT, SLUMPED IN HIS CHAIR. HIS WIFE IS SUITABLY ALARMED.

WIFE: Charles? Charles? What's the matter? Charles?

SUDDENLY A MIDDLE-AGED WOMAN, APRIL, AND A TEENAGE BOY, NEVILLE, IN ST TOM'S AMBULANCE UNIFORM, RUSH
INTO THE BOX. THEY ARE EACH CARRYING A FIRST-AID CASE — NEVILLE'S IS BRAND NEW, APRIL'S IS OLD AND
BATTERED. THEIR INITIALS APPEAR ON THEIR CASES.

APRIL: Make way. St Tom's. Make way. Coming through.

WIFE: He just passed out.

APRIL: Don't worry. He's in safe hands now. Now you go and dial 9999.

THE LADY EXITS. APRIL AND NEVILLE CROUCH DOWN BY THE MAN.

NEVILLE: Ooh, I didn't expect this on me first day.

APRIL: Come on now. Neville. What do we do? What do we do?

NEVILLE: Check his pulse.

NEVILLE LIFTS THE MAN'S WRIST.

APRIL: That's not gonna do much good, is it?

NEVILLE: Put him in the recovery position?

APRIL: He might be having a heart attack!

NEVILLE: (PANICKING) I dunno!

APRIL: Give him a Polo.

NEVILLE: What?

APRIL: Mint with a hole!

SHE TAKES A PACKET OUT OF HER POCKET AND POPS A POLO IN THE MAN'S MOUTH.

NEVILLE: That's not in the manual.

NEVILLE OPENS HIS CASE – IT IS FULL OF MEDICAL SUPPLIES – AND PULLS OUT A ST TOM'S AMBULANCE BRIGADE MANUAL AND STARTS LEAFING THROUGH IT. APRIL SNATCHES IT FROM HIM AND DISCARDS IT.

APRIL: There's no time for that, Neville. There's a man dying here.

NEVILLE: Well it doesn't seem to be doing anything.

APRIL: Well it can't be his heart then. Maybe it's a blood clot. Blood clot, blood clot. Let's see.

APRIL LOOKS IN HER CASE. WE SEE THE CONTENTS – DOZENS OF PACKETS OF MINTS, EVERY TYPE IMAGINABLE, ALL NEATLY ORDERED AND DISPLAYED. THERE ARE NO FIRST-AID ACCESSORIES WHATSOEVER.

Give him a Polo.

What?

Mint with a hole!

APRIL: Got it. Tic Tac.

APRIL OPENS A BOX OF TIC TACS AND TAKES ONE OUT.

APRIL: Just check he's not allergic. He ain't got a tag or nuffin'.

NEVILLE CHECKS.

NEVILLE: I can't see anything.

APRIL IS ON THE VERGE OF ADMINISTERING THE TIC TAC WHEN SHE IS DISTRACTED BY THE ACTION ON STAGE.

APRIL: Oh this is a good bit. This is a good bit. I saw this last night.

APRIL ABSENT-MINDEDLY POPS THE TIC TAC INTO HER MOUTH.

APRIL: She doesn't know that the Duke – him there with the hat – is really her husband in disguise. Oh it causes a right brouhahaha. (TURNING BACK TO THE PATIENT) Right, where were we? Ah yes.

SHE GIVES HIM THE TIC TAC. NOTHING HAPPENS.

APRIL: Oh, erm, maybe the dose is wrong.

SHE OPENS HIS MOUTH AND POURS THE WHOLE BOX IN. NEVILLE IS CHECKING THE MANUAL.

NEVILLE: I think he's had a stroke.

APRIL: Then we don't have any choice. Neville . . .

APRIL TAKES A DEEP BREATH. THE MUSIC FROM THE OPERA REACHES A SUITABLY DRAMATIC CRESCENDO.

APRIL: We're going to have to open the Extra Strong.

TOGETHER, APRIL AND NEVILLE GINGERLY PICK UP THE PACKET OF EXTRA STRONG. APRIL SNIFFS IT, IN ECSTASY.

RAY McCOONEY — CAKE

EXT. SCOTTISH HOTEL. TWO PEOPLE ARE SUNBATHING IN THE RAIN.

TOM V/O: A favourite destination for holidaymakers after Siberia is Scotland.

INT. DINING ROOM. EMPTY. AN OVERWEIGHT AMERICAN FAMILY CONSISTING OF MUM, DAD, AND DAUGHTER ENTER.

DAD: Hi, you – open for afternoon tea?

RAY: Ooh. Maybe I am and maybe I'm not.

HE PLAYS THE FLUTE.

DAD: Oh. OK.

HE BEGINS TO USHER HIS FAMILY OUT.

RAY: N-no, I am. Please. Sit down. Sit down.

HE SEATS THE FAMILY.

MUM: Oh what an adorable little place.

KIMBERLEY: It smells funny in here.

MUM (WHISPERS): Kimberley!

RAY: I shall be back in a moment with the cake trolley.

PUTS HIS HAND OUT AND GRABS THE TROLLEY.

RAY: Here I am with the cake trolley.

MUM: Ooh, those look great, don't they, Kimberley?

KIMBERLEY: I want the chocolate cake.

MUM: OK, honey. (TO RAY) Kimberley has a nut allergy. Do you know if there are any nuts in it?

RAY: Yeeeees.

MUM: What do you mean? 'Yes there are nuts' or 'Yes you know'?

RAY: Yeeeees.

DAD: Well which?

RAY: If I tell ye the truth, I'll tell ye a lie, but if you call me false then I'll also tell ye a lie.

RAY PLAYS THE FLUTE.

DAD: OK, so does the cake contain nuts?

RAY PICKS UP A SLICE OF CARROT CAKE FROM THE TROLLEY.

RAY: Carrot cake, carrot cake, ha' ye any nuts?

HE HOLDS THE SLICE TO HIS EAR AND LISTENS.

RAY: The carrot cake contains . . . no nuts.

HE PUTS THE SLICE BACK AND PICKS UP A SLICE OF LEMON CAKE.

RAY: Lemon drizzle cake, lemon drizzle cake, ha' ye any nuts?

HE LISTENS TO THE CAKE.

RAY: The lemon drizzle cake contains . . . no nuts.

HE PUTS THE CAKE DOWN AND PLAYS AN IMAGINARY FLUTE.

RAY: (WHISPERS) No nuts.

HE PICKS UP A SLICE OF CHOCOLATE CAKE.

RAY: Chocolate cake, chocolate cake, ha' ye any nuts?

HE HOLDS THE CAKE TO HIS EAR AND LISTENS. PAUSE. HE OFFERS THE SLICE TO THE DAD.

RAY: He wants to speak to you.

THE BAFFLED DAD PUTS THE CAKE TO HIS EAR.

DAD: Mike Kapalski?

DAME SALLY MARKHAM –
LADY CHATTERLEY'S LOVER

EXT. COUNTRY HOUSE. THE GARDENER IS JUST PUTTING THE FINISHING TOUCHES TO A TOPIARY
IN THE SHAPE OF TWO DOGS MATING.

TOM V/O: Here we are at the country home of romantic novelist Dame
Sally Markham. I'd love to write a book but unfortunately I don't
have a pen.

INT . HOUSE. MISS GRACE TYPES AS DAME SALLY DICTATES.

DAME SALLY: 'His hand passed over the curves of her body, firmly without
desire but with soft intimate knowledge.' End of chapter.

MISS GRACE: This is wonderful, Dame Sally.

DAME SALLY: (WE REVEAL DAME SALLY IS READING FROM *LADY CHATTERLEY'S LOVER*) Yes,
it is rather. Chapter Four. 'As she ran home in the twilight the world
seemed a dream. The trees in the park seemed bulging and surging at
anchor on a tide . . .'

MISS GRACE SIGHS, SCREWS UP THE PIECE OF PAPER AND THROWS IT AWAY.

DENNIS WATERMAN — JEREMY'S BIRTHDAY

EXT. OFFICE. A LITERAL MIME ARTIST IS AT WORK.

TOM V/O: Here in Britain's capital city of Sneddy are the offices of theatrical agent, Jeremy Rent.

INT. OFFICE. DENNIS WATERMAN IS SEATED OPPOSITE JEREMY'S DESK. DENNIS HOLDS A HUGE PIECE OF PAPER.

JEREMY: Right, if you'd just like to sign on the second page there.

DENNIS: Have you got a pen?

JEREMY: There you are.

JEREMY HANDS OVER A SMART BLACK GOLD-NIBBED FOUNTAIN PEN, WHICH, OF COURSE, IS HUGE IN DENNIS'S WORLD.

DENNIS: 'Den-nis Water-man.'

JEREMY: At last we've got you a job. I'm so glad to see you're finally over this silly 'write the theme tune, sing the theme tune' business.

DENNIS: Oh no, that's all in the past.

JEREMY: Well thank goodness for that.

DENNIS: (WOODEN) Well, if that is all I will be on my way. (GOES TO LEAVE. HE PAUSES.) Ooh, I have just remembered . . . Happy birthday!

DENNIS PRODUCES A LARGE PRESENT FROM HIS BAG. HE HANDS IT TO JEREMY. OF COURSE, IT IS NOW MUCH SMALLER.

JEREMY: Oh Dennis, you are naughty.

DENNIS: (A LITTLE HURT) No I'm not. I'm good.

JEREMY OPENS THE PRESENT AND FEIGNS BOTH SURPRISE AND DELIGHT. IT'S A *MINDER* VIDEO.

JEREMY: Oh thank you.

DENNIS: It's got great music on it.

JEREMY: (GENTLY WARNING) Dennis . . .

'I've got a good idea do do do,

just you keep me near, I'll be so good for,

Happy birthday dear Jeremy,

I'll be so good for you, do do do do!

DENNIS: Sorry.

JEREMY: Well that's very kind of you.

JEREMY BUZZES HIS INTERCOM.

JEREMY: I'm just going to cut the cake now, if you'd like to come in. (TO DENNIS) Can you pass me the knife please, Dennis?

DENNIS PICKS UP A VERY BIG KNIFE FROM HIS SIDE OF THE DESK AND PASSES IT TO JEREMY, WHO HAS BROUGHT THE CAKE OVER. TWO SECRETARIES ENTER.

SECRETARY: Oh, isn't Dennis with you?

DENNIS: (HOLDING A GIANT KNIFE) I'm right here.

THE SECRETARY LOOKS DOWN.

JEREMY: Thank you.

SECRETARY: Make a wish.

JEREMY LAUGHS.

DENNIS: We haven't sung 'Happy Birthday' yet.

JEREMY: (EMBARRASSED) Doh! Go on then.

DENNIS: 1–2–3 . . .

THE SECRETARY AND THE AGENT START TO SING 'HAPPY BIRTHDAY'.

DENNIS: (SINGS) 'If you want to, I'll change the situation, right people, right time, just the wrong location'.

THE SECRETARY AND THE AGENT FALL SILENT.

DENNIS: 'I've got a good idea do do do, just you keep me near, I'll be so good for, Happy birthday dear Jeremy, I'll be so good for you, do do do do do!

PAUSE. THERE IS AN EMBARRASSED PAUSE, WHICH JEREMY BREAKS BY SLICING THE CAKE.

JEREMY: Cake, anybody?

DENNIS PUTS HIS HANDS UP TO INDICATE THE SIZE OF THE SLICE.

DENNIS: Just a small piece.

JEREMY: There you go.

JEREMY CUTS DENNIS A SMALL PIECE AND HANDS IT TO HIM. DENNIS NEEDS TWO HANDS TO HOLD IT. HE TAKES A BITE.

LIZ AND CLIVE – BEATLES

EXT. CHINESE RESTAURANT. WE SEE A TOILET OUTSIDE WITH A SIGN SAYING 'PUBLIC TOILET'. A MAN USES THE TOILET AND THE NEXT MAN TO USE IT GESTURES ABOUT THE FACT IS SMELLS AND STARTS SPRAYING AIR FRESHENER.

TOM V/O: It's lunchtime at this Chinese restaurant in Ducking Down. I myself love Chinese food. My favourite dishes are 14, 29, and 53.

INT. RESTAURANT. CLIVE SITS ALONE AT A TABLE, WHILST LIZ STANDS, HOLDING COURT WITH A MIDDLE-AGED COUPLE (AT A FOUR-SEATER TABLE) ON THE OTHER SIDE OF THE RESTAURANT.

LIZ: . . . and me and Mollie Sugden were friends from the old days, I mean this was years before 'Are You Being Served?'.

CLIVE: (CALLS) Liz?

LIZ: In a minute. (TO DINERS) Then Mollie said to me, she said to me 'Would I like to be her bridesmaid?' . . . I mean, well . . .

CLIVE: (CALLS) Liz! Your food's getting cold.

LIZ: In a minute. (TO DINERS) And of course I was delighted. And it was a wonderful day all told. It really . . .

CLIVE APPROACHES.

CLIVE: Liz, I thought you said you were just going to the toilet.

LIZ: I was, and then I just happened to get chatting to these nice people about being Mollie Sugden's bridesmaid.

CLIVE: (TO DINERS) I'm so sorry about this.

DINER: Oh that's all right

LIZ: Yeah, it was a lovely do. We had a lovely meal and there was dancing and they played the Beatles, and there was dancing and . . .

TED – ONE OF THE DINERS – CHIPS IN.

TED: (SCOUSE) Oh I went to school with Paul McCartney.

LIZ: Oh right. And then they brought out the cake . . .

CLIVE: Really? What was he like?

TED: Oh he was a really nice bloke, and he was dead musical, even then. He'd always play the piano at break time. He had a lovely singing voice . . .

LIZ: (RAISES HER VOICE) Yeah, and then Mollie – Mollie Sugden, whose bridesmaid I was . . .

CLIVE: Did you ever meet John Lennon?

TED: I did actually, once. We went round at lunchtime and John was there and they were playing the piano and they were doing a bit of jamming. It was great . . .

LIZ: Yeah, the Beatles aren't really going anymore. Anyway I said to Mollie . . .

CLIVE: Oh I love the Beatles. I've got all their tapes. Yeah, I play them in the car.

TED: Listen, why don't you come and join us?

CLIVE: Oh, thank you very much.

LIZ: No, Clive! Come away. (TO DINERS) Excuse us.

LIZ LEADS CLIVE BACK TO THE TABLE.

CLIVE: But he was at school with Paul McCartney.

LIZ: Yeah, and I was Mollie Sugden's bridesmaid but I don't go on about it. (SHOUTS) Get over it. Bor-ing!

WORLD RECORD ATTEMPT – CIGARETTES

EPISODE

INT. CONFERENCE HALL. WE SEE IAN 1 WITH AS MANY CIGARETTES IN HIS MOUTH AS POSSIBLE. IAN 2 IS COUNTING THEM.

IAN 2: Forty-five, forty-six, forty-seven, forty-eight . . .

HE CHECKS HIS POCKETS.

IAN 2 : Have you got a light?

IAN 1 CHECKS HIS POCKETS. HE SHAKES HIS HEAD.

IAN 2: Oh. I won't be long.

IAN 2 HEADS OFF.

TOM V/O: And so this week's journey comes to an end. If you have enjoyed the programme you might like to get up and do a dance in honour of it. Goodbile.

Have you got a light?

Lou's To Do List

- Get up
- Drive to Andy's
- Get Andy up
- Wash Andy
- Dry Andy
- Cook Andy's breakfast
- Take Andy to the toilet
- Take Andy to the toilet again
- Take Andy to the toilet a third time (that should get it)
- Go to video shop. Get latest 'Monster Trucks' video for Andy to watch
- Get Andy's nuts
- Bring video and nuts home. Give nuts to Andy. Put video on for Andy.
- Go down chippy and buy Andy's lunch: deep fried sausage, large chips, tin of pop, choc ice (battered)
- Give Andy lunch
- Take Andy to the toilet
- Wash Andy's smalls
- Wash Andy's larges
- Clean entire flat
- Take Andy to the toilet
- Take Andy to cinema in van to see latest Mel Gibbons/Bruce Wallace film.
- Run out mid-film to get Andy a Frankie's hotdog.
- Run out again to get Andy his Coca-Cola and Lou

- Take Andy home in van
- Bath Andy
- Put Andy in his pyjamas
- Cook Andy's dinner (Bernard Matthew's Turkey Dinosaurs with Alphabetti Spaghetti, remembering to carefully remove all the B's as Andy doesn't like the way they taste)
- Watch Andy eat entire Viennetta
- Wait for Andy to demand another Viennetta
- Refuse to go and buy another Viennetta for Andy
- Give in and go and buy another Viennetta for Andy
- Take Andy to bathroom
- Put Andy's teeth in glass
- Give Andy stripwash
- Put Andy to bed
- Read Andy letters' page from 'Razzle'
- Bring Andy off
- Draw Andy's curtains
- Turn off lights
- Lock up
- Go home
- Cry

EPISODE five

TOM V/O: Britain, Britain, Britain. Here are some facts about Britain you may not know. Number one: Britain is a country. Number two: Britain is called Britain. Number five: Britain. But who are the people who live in Britain? Over the next five hours we aim to find out. Yeah.

VICKY POLLARD — BORSTAL

EXT. BORSTAL. SIGN SAYS 'PAUL YOUNG OFFENDERS' INSTITUTION'.

TOM V/O: Vicky Pollard is moving up in the world, and has now graduated to borstal. Today, she has been summoned to the governor's office.

INT. GLOOMY CORRIDOR OF A YOUNG OFFENDERS' INSTITUTION. VICKY SLOUCHES AGAINST THE WALL AND TAKES A DRAG FROM A CIGARETTE. SHE DROPS THE CIGARETTE ON THE FLOOR AND STUBS IT OUT. SHE THEN TAKES A DRAG FROM ANOTHER (HITHERTO UNSEEN) CIGARETTE IN HER OTHER HAND. THE DOOR OPENS.

GOVERNOR: Would you come in now please, Vicky?

VICKY ENTERS, FOLLOWED BY THE WARDEN.

INT. OFFICE. VICKY AND THE GOVERNOR STAND EITHER SIDE OF THE DESK. THE WARDEN SHUTS THE DOOR AND LURKS.

GOVERNOR: Right now. I've been hearing all sorts of stories about a very serious incident in the canteen. Vicky, I'm going to ask you a question now and I want a straight answer. Did you bite Jackie Hayes?

VICKY: I ain't not never even done nuffin' or nuffin'. Let me tell you the whole fing right because what happened was was Julie wrote this fing on the reccy wall about Lorraine being a hundred per cent minger and then Samantha came into our dorm after lights out and started stirring it all up but anyway Karly found a pube in her lasagne.

GOVERNOR: Oh, so Karly's involved in this, is she?

VICKY: Karly not never even done nuffin' or nuffin'. She weren't even there. Shut up. She was busy selling her phonecard to that girl with the manky foot but I don't even know about that because I was busy with Alison because she was feeling sick and was sick all over the sick bay but I never broke no chapel window and if Donna says that I did then don't listen to her because she plays with matches.

GOVERNOR: Vicky, did you bite Jackie Hayes?

VICKY: Shut up I didn't even know she got bit. I ain't even got no fing to bite her with have I? God this is like this film I saw once where this women goes into like this place and this whole fing happens then there's this other fing but then the video cut off. Anyway Rachel said that Denise done it with her brother.

GOVERNOR: Right. I've heard enough of this. (TO WARDEN) Would you go and fetch Jackie, please?

THE WARDEN EXITS. THE FOLLOWING SPEECH FROM VICKY IS MUTTERED UNDER HER BREATH.

Iain'tnotneverevendonenuffin'or nuffin'.Letmetellyouthewholefingright becausewhathappenedwas wasJuliewrotethisfingonthe reccywallaboutLorraine beingahundredpercent mingerandthenSamantha cameintoourdorm afterlightsout andstartedstirring itallupbutanyway Karlyfoundapube inherlasagne.

VICKY: (MUMBLING TO HERSELF) I don't know why you're bothering bring Jackie in. Everyone she knows ain't done nuffin'.

GOVERNOR: Yes, thank you Vicky.

THE WARDEN RETURNS WITH JACKIE. WE SEE THAT JACKIE LOOKS VERY MUCH LIKE VICKY.

GOVERNOR: Jackie, will you please tell me what happened in the canteen this afternoon?

JACKIE SPEAKS EXACTLY THE SAME WAY AS VICKY.

JACKIE: I ain't even never not even done nuffin'. Shut up. Have you been talking to Sheryl? Don't listen to her because she ate her own scab . . .

VICKY EXPLODES. JACKIE CONTINUES HER SPEECH. THE PAIR ARE BOTH RANTING OVER EACH OTHER.

VICKY: Oh my God I so can't believe you just said that. Sheryl ain't not never even not done nuffin'. What happened was right was there was this whole fing right, because Kelly wrote this fing in the bogs about Elaine being a total one hundred per cent cow and then Hannah came along and started stirring it all up but there was this whole other fing right what I didn't even not know about but anyway . . .

JACKIE: Anyway Sheryl ain't not never even done nuffin'. She wasn't even there. Shut up. She was doing another fing with Jaye but I don't even know about that because I was with Savannah but then she came over and started mixing it because everyone knows she's two-faced but I never stole no spoon and if Louise says that I did she's a lying bitch but anyway . . .

Oh my God I so can't believe you just said that.
Anyway Sheryl ain't not never even done nuffin'. She
Sheryl ain't not never even not done nuffin'. What
wasn't even there. Shut up. She was doing another fing
happened was right was there was this whole fing
with Jaye but I don't even know about that because I
right, because Kelly wrote this fing in the bogs about
was with Savannah but then she came over and
Elaine being a total one hundred per cent cow and
started mixing it because everyone knows she's two-
then Hannah came along and started stirring it all up
faced but I never stole no spoon and if Louise says that
but there was this whole other fing right what I didn't
I did she's a lying bitch but ANYWAY . . .
even not know about but ANYWAY . . .

BOTH: Don't listen to her because she's gone all lezzy.

WE SEE A LOOK OF EXASPERATION ON THE GOVERNOR'S FACE.

GOVERNOR: Piss off!

THE TWO GIRLS GO TO LEAVE. VICKY PUSHES JACKIE. JACKIE GOES TO HIT VICKY BUT THINKS BETTER OF IT.
THE PAIR EXIT.

VICKY: You fancy her.

JACKIE: You do.

VICKY: You do. (PAUSE) Everyone knows you finger yourself.

LOU AND ANDY — PET SHOP

EXT. PET SHOP IN HIGH STREET. WE SEE A SIGN IN THE WINDOW – 'NO DOGS ALLOWED'.

TOM V/O: If people in Britain want to buy a pet, they go to a pet shop. If they want to buy a pet shop they go to a pet shop shop. If they want to buy a pet shop shop, they're just being silly.

INT. PET SHOP. LOU IS PUSHING ANDY AROUND THE SHOP.

LOU: Of course when you've got this rabbit you're gonna have to think of a name for it.

ANDY: Name for it, yeah.

LOU: I wonder where they keep them?

ANDY POINTS INDISCRIMINATELY.

ANDY: I want that one.

LOU: That one?

ANDY: Yeah.

LOU: Well that's a snake.

ANDY: Yeah, I know.

LOU: Well you don't like snakes. You're scared of them. Remember when we watched that film with all the snakes in it? You said that all serpents had an aura of evil.

ANDY: Yeah, I know.

LOU: Let's get a rabbit then.

ANDY: I want that one.

ANDY POINTS AT THE SNAKE AGAIN.

EPISODE

LOU: Are you sure?

ANDY: Yeah.

LOU: All right. Well it's *your* birthday money. What are you gonna call it then?

ANDY: Thumper.

LOU TURNS TO THE SHOP ASSISTANT, WHO IS NEARBY.

LOU: We'll, er, take the snake please. Yeah.

EXT. PET SHOP. LOU IS WHEELING ANDY OUT OF THE SHOP. ANDY HAS A CAGE ON HIS LAP WITH A SNAKE IN IT. LOU PAUSES, WAITING FOR ANDY TO SAY SOMETHING. HE DOESN'T. LOU WHEELS HIM AWAY. AS SOON AS THE PAIR ARE OUT OF SHOT ...

ANDY: I wanna rabbit.

LOU WHEELS HIM BACK INTO THE PET SHOP ANGRILY.

10 DOWNING STREET – PRESS CONFERENCE

EXT. NO. 10 DOWNING STREET. THE POLICEMAN STANDING BY THE DOOR SEES A ROBBER COMPLETE WITH SWAG BAG WALKING BY. THE POLICEMAN DOESN'T WANT TO CHASE AFTER HIM BECAUSE HE'S MEANT TO BE PROTECTING NO. 10. SO HE LEAVES HIM ALONE.

TOM V/O: Ten Downing Street is the home of the Prime Minister. The Prime Minister is like this guy who is like in charge of like the whole country.

INT. NO. 10 DOWNING STREET. THE PRIME MINISTER, MICHAEL, IS HOLDING A PRESS CONFERENCE.

MICHAEL: So it is with great reluctance that I have decided to accept the Minister's resignation. I will take a few questions.

BOYD HILTON: Boyd Hilton, *Smash Hits.* Prime Minister. Do you admit that the Foreign Secretary lied to the House?

MICHAEL: I have answered that question already. Next.

GREG DAVIES: Greg Davies, *Puzzler.* Have you appointed a replacement?

MICHAEL: We'll be making an announcement shortly.

ANGUS THOMAS: Angus Thomas *'Kerrang!* Who is next to go from your Cabinet?

MICHAEL: There will be no more resignations from my Cabinet.

ROY SLOAN: Roy Sloan, *Whizzer and Chips.* Are you concerned you've lost your strongest ally in the Cabinet?

MICHAEL: There is no rift in the Cabinet.

ANDREW JARMAN: Andrew Jarman, *Dinosaur Magazine*. What was your reaction . . .

MICHAEL: I'm sorry I don't know that one.

ANDREW JARMAN: It's new. You get a free binder with part one, you collect it over 24 weeks. It's everything you need to know about dinosaurs.

MICHAEL: Oh yes. Go ahead.

ANDREW JARMAN: Oh, I'm sorry I've forgotten the question.

ALL: Oh.

ROGER WAKELY: Roger Wakely, *Asian Babes*. Um, given your support of yet another disgraced minister, don't you think that your position has become untenable?

MICHAEL: Certainly not. One more question.

GEORGE PAXTON: George Paxton, *Daily Telegraph*.

MICHAEL: Yes.

GEORGE PAXTON: Who is your favourite member of Westlife?

MARJORIE DAWES/FATFIGHTERS — LIPS

INT. A SMALL COMMUNITY CENTRE. SITTING IN A CIRCLE ARE PAUL, TANIA, PAT, AND HALF A DOZEN OTHERS. NEARBY ARE A SET OF SCALES, A NOTICEBOARD WITH PLENTY OF DIFFERENT FATFIGHTERS LEAFLETS ON, AND A TABLE NEARBY WITH LOTS OF FATFIGHTERS PRODUCTS – CEREALS, SELF-HELP VIDEOTAPES, CRISPS, CHOCOLATES, ETC. MARJORIE IS ON HER MOBILE.

TOM V/O: It's five past Alberto, and at FatFighters the meeting is just beginning.

MARJORIE: Yeah, I know, well they're all the same. Anyway, listen, I'd better go. I've got my fat people here. So Johansen's here, Paul's here, Pat's here.

MARJORIE PEERS OVER HER CLIPBOARD.

MARJORIE: Where's Meera?

PAT: She's in hospital. She's having liposuction.

MARJORIE REMOVES HER CLIPBOARD TO REVEAL ENORMOUS COLLAGEN-INJECTED LIPS.

MARJORIE: Ooh I just think it's such a shame the way people feel the need to tamper with themselves. Tania's here. Who are you?

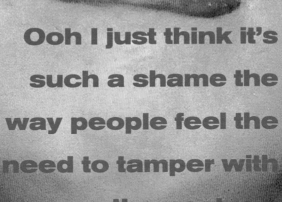

Ooh I just think it's such a shame the way people feel the need to tamper with themselves

EDWARD AND SAMANTHA — VALENTINE'S DAY

EXT. HOUSE. THE MILKMAN WALKS BY AND THROWS A MILK BOTTLE AT THE FRONT DOOR.

TOM V/O: This is the home of schoolteacher Edward Grant, who recently caused a stir by marrying one of his former pupils. (TO HIMSELF) Lucky bugger.

INT. FLAT. BEDROOM. EDWARD AND SAMANTHA ARE IN BED TOGETHER. HE IS DOING SOME MARKING WHILE SHE FRETS OVER A LETTER. EDWARD LOOKS UP AND NOTICES THAT SHE IS IRRITATED.

EDWARD: Problem?

SAMANTHA: Another letter from Mum.

EDWARD: (SIGHING) Oh for goodness sake, what is so strange about a teacher marrying one of his ex-pupils?

SAMANTHA: Nothing.

EDWARD: I'm sorry?

SAMANTHA: Nothing.

EDWARD: Nothing what?

SAMANTHA: Nothing, sir.

EDWARD: That's better.

SAMANTHA OPENS THE DRAWER IN HER BEDSIDE TABLE AND PULLS OUT A CARD.

EDWARD: What's this?

SAMANTHA: Happy Valentine's Day, darling.

EDWARD: Oh, pop it in my pigeonhole. (GRINS TO HIMSELF)

SAMANTHA: Oh, go on. Open it now.

SAMANTHA HANDS EDWARD THE CARD. HE OPENS IT AND READS.

EDWARD: Ah, 'dear Edward' . . .

EDWARD WHIPS OUT A BALLPOINT PEN AND BEGINS TO MARK.

EDWARD: Capital 'D' on 'dear' – 'I love you with all my heat' . . . oh, heart . . . – handwriting – 'yours forever' – comma – 'Samantha'. (IMPRESSED) Hmmm. Six out of ten. See me.

HE HANDS THE CARD BACK TO HER AND RETURNS TO HIS NEWSPAPER.

Capital 'D' on 'dear' — 'I love you with all my heat' . . . oh, heart . . . — handwriting – 'yours forever' — comma — 'Samantha'. Hmmm. Six out of ten. See me.

SAMANTHA: You do love me, don't you?

EDWARD: If you have a question put your hand up.

SAMANTHA PUTS HER HAND UP. EDWARD LOOKS UP.

EDWARD: Um yes, Samantha.

SAMANTHA: Do you love me?

EDWARD: Yes.

SAMANTHA: How much?

EDWARD PUTS HIS MARKING DOWN AND GETS OUT OF BED. THERE IS A LARGE CLASSICAL, FLORAL PAINTING
ON THE WALL. HE GOES TO IT AND TURNS IT ROUND TO REVEAL A BLACKBOARD ON THE OTHER SIDE. EDWARD PICKS
UP A PIECE OF CHALK AND BEGINS TO DRAW AN L-SHAPED GRAPH.

EDWARD: OK – 'How much do you love me?'

HE LABELS THE VERTICAL LINE AS 'LOVE' AND THE HORIZONTAL LINE AS 'TIME' AND ILLUSTRATES ACCORDINGLY.

EDWARD: Let's say that this is 'Love' here and this is 'Time' here. Now this is where we
first met, this is that detention we shared together, dropped a little here when I didn't cast
you in the school play, school trip to Calais . . .

THE LINE RISES DRAMATICALLY.

EDWARD: . . . parents' evening, wedding day, wedding night . . .

INEXPLICABLY THE LINE DROPS A LITTLE AT 'WEDDING NIGHT', BEFORE RISING AGAIN.

EDWARD: And this is where we are now. So, as you see, as time has progressed,
love has increased.

SAMANTHA: Oh, Edward, put your chalk down and come back to bed.

EDWARD: Sorry, I got carried away.

THEY KISS.

EDWARD: Are you chewing? Into my hand.

KELSEY GRAMMAR SCHOOL

EXT. SCHOOL.N

TOM V/O: It's one two o'clock and at Kelsey Grammar School, a young pupil
has an appointment with his careers adviser.

INT. OFFICE. A 12-YEAR-OLD SCHOOLBOY SITS NERVOUSLY AT A DESK.

BOY: Sorry I'm late, sir.

WE REVEAL THAT THE BOY IS TALKING TO A ROBOT.

ROBOT: Make sure it doesn't happen again. Take a seat.

BOY: Thank you, sir.

ROBOT: What do you have in mind?

BOY: Well, really ever since I was small I've always wanted to go into catering.

ROBOT: In the future there will be no jobs for humans in the catering industry. Only robots.

BOY: Oh, does that include catering in hotels?

ROBOT: Er, yes.

BOY: Well, the other thing I was thinking of was engineering. You see . . .

ROBOT: There will be no jobs for humans. We will inherit the earth.

BOY: Oh dear.

THE ROBOT DELIVERS A PAMPHLET.

ROBOT: This booklet will explain everything. Go now.

BOY: Thank you, sir.

THE BOY TAKES THE BOOKLET AND GOES TO LEAVE.

ROBOT: Tuck your shirt in.

THE BOY STARTS TO EXIT.

ROBOT: I am a robot.

BOY: Yeah.

LOU AND ANDY — LIBRARY

EXT. LIBRARY. A MAN IS LEAVING THE LIBRARY AND GETS A LIGHT FOR HIS CIGARETTE FROM A PASSING FLAMING TORCH BEARER.

TOM V/O: In Herby city centre lies this library. The word library is derived from the Latin, Libres, meaning Sssh.

INT. LIBRARY.

LOU: So have you seen anything you fancy?

ANDY POINTS INDISCRIMINATELY.

ANDY: Yeah, I want that one.

LOU TAKES THE BOOK FROM THE SHELF. IT IS CALLED *A POLITICAL AND SOCIAL HISTORY OF CHINA*.

LOU: Well that is a book on Chinese history.

ANDY: Yeah, I know.

LOU: Well how do you know? You weren't even looking at it.

ANDY: Yeah, I know.

LOU: It all looks a bit involved, really. Now how about that book I was telling you about in the van, about the cave boy who lived in a rubbish tip? – *Stig of the Dump*.

ANDY POINTS AGAIN AT ANOTHER BOOK.

That is Chinese Language and its Origins. Again, it might be a little bit hard for you.

ANDY: And I want that one.

LOU: That is *Chinese Language and its Origins*. Again, it might be a little bit hard for you.

ANDY: I want it.

LOU: All right. You've got these two. Now you're allowed one more. Shall we go and see if we can find *Stig of the Dump*?

ANDY POINTS AGAIN.

ANDY: That one.

ANDY POINTS INDISCRIMINATELY AT A BOOK. IT HAPPENS TO BE ANOTHER COPY OF THE FIRST BOOK, *A POLITICAL AND SOCIAL HISTORY OF CHINA*.

LOU: That one?

ANDY: Yeah.

LOU: That is the same one as the one you've got there.

ANDY: Yeah, I know.

LOU: Well you sure you want these three?

ANDY: Yeah.

LOU GIVES ANDY THE THIRD BOOK.

LOU: You're positive?

ANDY: Yeah.

LOU: All right, let's go and get them stamped.

EXT. LIBRARY. LOU AND ANDY ARE COMING OUT OF THE DOORS. ANDY HAS ALL THREE BOOKS ON HIS LAP.

LOU: Are you happy with your choices?

ANDY: Yeah.

LOU: You're sticking with these three?

ANDY: Yeah.

LOU: Good.

PAUSE.

ANDY: I can't read.

LOU GRABS THE BOOKS OFF HIM AND MARCHES BACK INTO THE LIBRARY.

EDWARD AND SAMANTHA — EVENING OUT

INT. BEDROOM. EDWARD IS FULLY DRESSED AND PERCHED ON THE BED. HE IS SPEAKING ON THE PHONE.
WE HEAR THE SHOWER RUNNING IN THE EN-SUITE BATHROOM.

EDWARD: So that's a table for two at eight. Thank you.

THE SHOWER STOPS. SAMANTHA ENTERS, WITH A TOWEL WRAPPED ROUND HER.

SAMANTHA: I can't wait.

EDWARD: Anything for my little star pupil.

THEY KISS.

EDWARD: Would you, er, like to draw the curtains?

SAMANTHA EXCITEDLY DOES SO. THE ROOM GETS DARKER. EDWARD FLICKS A SWITCH ON A (HITHERTO UNSEEN)
OVERHEAD PROJECTOR. A TIMETABLE OF THE EVENING'S EVENTS IS PROJECTED ON THE WALL ABOVE THE BED.

EDWARD: This is our timetable for the evening. (READS FROM BOARD THEN TURNS TO SAMANTHA, WHO
IS NAKED) Seven p.m., coach leaves for restaurant. Anybody not on the coach at that time
will be left behind. (EDWARD SEES THAT SAMANTHA HAS OPENED HER TOWEL) It's not mufti day, is it?
Seven-thirty p.m., arrive at restaurant. And get a hair cut!

BERNARD CHUMLEY – MEALS ON WHEELS

EXT. BLOCK OF FLATS – 'SANDY TOKSVIG HOUSE'. A YOUNG BOY GOES TO THROW A BRICK AT A WINDOW. AN OLDER MAN STOPS HIM THEN CHOOSES A HEAVIER, BIGGER ONE AND THE YOUNG BOY THROWS THAT INSTEAD.

TOM V/O: Council flats are where the old, thick, and bone idle are forced to live.

INT. POKEY LIVING ROOM. IT IS DUSTY, DATED, AND MESSY. AS WE HEAR THE V/O THE CAMERA GLIDES PAST THE FRAMED PLAYBILLS AND NEWSPAPER HEADLINES ON THE WALL. WE SEE A *DAILY MIRROR* HEADLINE 'I WILL WALK AGAIN VOWS KITTY' AND A SUBHEADING 'THEATRE STAR'S TRAGIC ACCIDENT'. WE HEAR KNOCKING ON THE WALL.

TOM V/O: This flat, on the seventh floor, is the home of brother and sister Bernard and Kitty Chumley.

SIR BERNARD: Yes, I heard it, Kitty.

CUT TO EXT. CORRIDOR IN BLOCK OF COUNCIL FLATS. SIR BERNARD OPENS THE DOOR. HE IS WEARING A WIG. A FRIENDLY, MATURE LADY IS STANDING WITH A TROLLEY. ON TOP IS A TRAY, WITH VARIOUS METAL SALVERS COVERING THE FOOD. ABOVE THE DOOR, WE SEE A HOMEMADE ROUND BLUE PLAQUE WITH 'SIR BERNARD CHUMLEY LIVES HERE. 1984– '.

WOMAN: Hello. Meals on Wheels for Kitty Chumley.

SIR BERNARD: Oh yes, yes yes. Do come in, yes.

SHE WHEELS THE TROLLEY IN.

SIR BERNARD: Right, so what is it today, then?

WOMAN: Oxtail soup for starters, and then shepherd's pie with cabbage and swede.

SIR BERNARD: Oh I don't like swede. I mean, er, Kitty doesn't like swede.

WOMAN: And there's a choice of arctic roll or a peach.

SIR BERNARD: Arctic roll, obviously.

THE WOMAN BENDS DOWN AND TAKES A SLICE OF ARCTIC ROLL FROM ONE OF THE SHELVES ON HER TROLLEY. SHE PLACES IT ON SIR BERNARD'S TRAY.

SIR BERNARD: Thank you.

WOMAN: So how is your sister today?

SIR BERNARD: I didn't do it.

WOMAN: No, how is she?

SIR BERNARD: Oh, I see. Still not walking, but I think a lot of it is psychological.

WOMAN: Can I see her?

SIR BERNARD: Eh? Er, no no no. She's biting today. Thank you ever so much.

EPISODE

Er, no no no no... **She's biting today.**

WOMAN: Have you got yesterday's plates?

SIR BERNARD: Oh yes.

SIR BERNARD PICKS UP A COUPLE OF PLATES, WITH DRY FOOD ENCRUSTED, FROM THE FLOOR.

WOMAN: We do ask that they are returned clean.

SIR BERNARD TAKES A PLATE AND LICKS IT. HE HANDS IT OVER.

SIR BERNARD: By the way, the jam roly-poly was delicious. Kitty said. If anything, there could have been more of that. She added.

PAUSE.

WOMAN: They tell me you were an actor.

SIR BERNARD: *Am* an actor, yes.

WOMAN: Oh, right. Are you in anything at the moment?

SIR BERNARD: Bits and bobs. You know. Well, thank you very much. Good day.

SIR BERNARD TRIES TO SHOW THE LADY OUT.

WOMAN: You know, Mr Chumley, I think *you* might qualify yourself for the Meals on Wheels service.

SIR BERNARD: I am forty-three.

THE WOMAN DOESN'T QUITE KNOW HOW TO RESPOND.

WOMAN: Right. Well, I'll see you soon then.

SIR BERNARD: Yes, thank you.

THE WOMAN GOES TO LEAVE BUT HE CALLS OUT TO HER.

SIR BERNARD (OFF-CAMERA): Bit dry.

WOMAN: Sorry?

SHE SEES SIR BERNARD WITH THE MEAL ON HIS LAP HOLDING A KNIFE AND FORK.

SIR BERNARD: Kitty said.

I am forty-three.

PETER ANDRE — GARDEN PARTY

TOM V/O: Everybody in Britain loves the Royal Family. They are the cleverest, strongest, loveliest, most selfish people in Britain. Today, Her Majesty the Queen is hosting a royal garden party.

EXT. PALACE GATES. SUMMER'S DAY. TWO POLICEMEN STAND GUARD, CHECKING TICKETS. WE HEAR IN THE BACKGROUND THE GARDEN PARTY IN FULL PROGRESS – A STRING QUARTET, CHATTER, ETC. A COUPLE ARRIVE, HAVE THEIR TICKETS APPROVED BY THE POLICEMAN, AND ENTER.

A CHIRPY, UNSHAVEN, SLIGHTLY SHABBY PETER ARRIVES HOLDING A THIN PLASTIC CARRIER BAG AND STRIDES CONFIDENTLY TOWARDS THE GATE. HE SALUTES THE POLICEMAN.

PETER: Carry on.

THE POLICEMAN POLITELY BLOCKS HIS PATH.

POLICEMAN: Good afternoon, sir. Can I see your invitation, please?

PETER: I trust everything is going well.

POLICEMAN: Fine, thank you, sir.

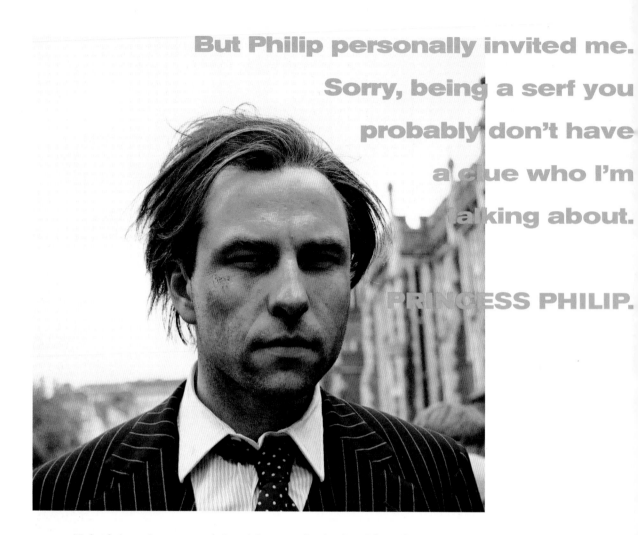

But Philip personally invited me. Sorry, being a serf you probably don't have a clue who I'm talking about.

PRINCESS PHILIP.

PETER: Nobody's trying to sneak in without an invitation I hope?

POLICEMAN: Not yet, sir.

PETER: Keep up the good work.

THE POLICEMAN BLOCKS HIS PATH.

PETER: I'm Peter Andre, Royal Correspondent for the BBC.

POLICEMAN: I'm not allowed to let anyone in without an invitation, sir.

PETER: Look, this is a bit embarrassing. I don't want to draw attention to myself –

PETER SCREAMS OUT IN AN OVERLY FRIENDLY MANNER.

PETER: Hello! – Yeah, I'll be in in a minute.

PETER CARRIES ON TALKING TO THE POLICEMAN.

PETER: But Philip personally invited me. Sorry, being a serf you probably don't have a clue who I'm talking about. Princess Philip.

POLICEMAN: Oh yes? And what did he say?

PETER: He said 'We're having a party. It should be a laugh. Just pop round anytime after four.'

POLICEMAN: I'm sorry, sir.

PETER: Anne and I are very much in love.

POLICEMAN: Step aside, please.

PETER PULLS A LUTE FROM HIS BAG. HE STARTS TO PLAY AND SING BADLY.

PETER: 'I want you, Anne, and I need you, Anne.
You can hurt me, Anne, and I'll pull you, Anne'.

POLICEMAN: Step aside please, sir.

PETER PULLS SOME LOOSE PIECES OF PAPER FROM HIS BAG.

PETER: I must give her these drawings!

BBC ROYAL CORRESPONDENT JENNIE BOND ARRIVES WITH A TICKET.

POLICEMAN: Ah, good afternoon, Miss Bond.

JENNIE BOND: Good afternoon.

POLICEMAN: Ah, that's lovely. Straight through.

JENNIE BOND: Thank you very much.

PETER: Jennie! Jennie!

JENNIE BOND: Sorry, Peter. I can't help you now.

JENNIE BOND WALKS ON. PAUSE. PETER STANDS DEJECTED.

POLICEMAN: (SYMPATHETIC) Probably best to go home, sir.

PETER: Yes.

PETER, DOWNCAST, WALKS SLOWLY AWAY.

POLICEMAN: And put some trousers on, will you?

WE REVEAL THAT, APART FROM SHOES AND SOCKS, PETER IS NAKED FROM THE WAIST DOWN. HE EXITS, STRUMMING HIS LUTE.

KENNY CRAIG — CAR BOOT SALE

TOM V/O: If your car doesn't already have a boot, you can buy one – at a car boot sale. Today, stage hypnotist Kenny Craig is getting rid of some old junk.

EXT. MORNING. CAR BOOT SALE. VARIOUS PEOPLE MILLING ABOUT. IN THE BOOT OF KENNY'S ORDINARY CAR WE SEE VARIOUS TAT – OLD VIDEOS, BOOKS, ELECTRICAL GOODS, A LAVA LAMP, ETC. A MAN ARRIVES AND STARTS TO BROWSE.

KENNY: Anything take your fancy, sir?

MAN: No, thanks, I'm just looking.

KENNY: Humorous book about cricket?

THE MAN SHAKES HIS HEAD.

KENNY: Foreword by John Major.

MAN: No thanks.

THE MAN PICKS UP SOME *BLACKADDER* VIDEOS.

KENNY: Complete set of *Blackadder* there.

MAN: Yeah, OK, I'll take it. Oh no, hang on, there's no *Blackadder 3*. I think I'll leave it.

KENNY: Look into my eyes. Look into my eyes. The eyes. The eyes. Not around the eyes. Don't look around my eyes. Look into my eyes. You're under. What you see before you is a complete set of *Blackadder* videos. There *was* no *Blackadder 3* – anyway it's called *Blackadder the Third* . . . Three, two, one . . . you're back in the room.

THE MAN COMES OUT OF HIS TRANCE AND HAPPILY HANDS OVER A TENNER, IN EXCHANGE FOR THE USED BAG OF VIDEOS. KENNY PICKS UP A *RED DWARF* VIDEO.

MAN: Oh, OK. I'll take them. There you go.

KENNY: Cheers. (KENNY CHECKS THE NOTE) Lovely. You like *Red Dwarf*? Got the whole first series there, including 'Smeg-Ups'.

MAN: Oh no. I've got these. I taped them off the telly.

KENNY: Look into my eyes. Look into my eyes. The eyes. The eyes. Not around the eyes. Don't look around my eyes. Look into my eyes. (CLICKS FINGERS) You're under. You did not – repeat not – tape *Red Dwarf* off the television, you cheapskate. Three, two, one – you're back in the room.

MAN: OK. I'll take those as well. There you go.

KENNY BAGS IT UP AND TAKES THE MONEY, CHECKING THE NOTE.

KENNY: Thank you. I, er, I see you're a bit of a comedy fan. How about that?

KENNY PICKS OUT A VIDEO OF PAUL MERTON IN GALTON AND SIMPSON'S *THE BLOOD DONOR*.

MAN: Oh no. I saw that. It was rubbish.

KENNY: Look into my eyes. Look into my eyes. The eyes. The eyes. Don't look around the eyes. Don't look around the eyes. Look into my eyes. (CLICKS FINGERS) You're under. Paul Merton in Galton and Simpson's *The Blood Donor* was hilarious and just as funny as when Tony Hancock did it. Three, two, one – you're back in the room.

MAN: Yeah, don't push your luck, mate.

THE MAN EXITS.

How about a musical version of the film *Scum*?

'4737, Carling, sir. I'm the daddy round here'.

'Where's yer effing tool?

What effing tool?' 'Don't go into the greenhouse, greenhouse, greenhouse'.

MATTHEW WATERHOUSE – MUSICALS

INT. LARGE OFFICE. SIR MICHAEL CRAZE SITS AT HIS DESK. WATERHOUSE STORMS IN, CARRYING HIS SACK.

TOM V/O: This man is theatrical producer Sir Michael Craze. Sir Michael currently has over three thousand musicals running in the West End.

MATTHEW: Here's one for you. How about a musical version of the film *Scum*?

SIR MICHAEL CRAZE: Excuse me? I wasn't actually expecting anybody . . .

MATTHEW PULLS A KEYBOARD OUT OF THE SACK, PLAYS AND SINGS ALONG.

MATTHEW: '4737, Carling, sir. I'm the daddy round here'. 'Where's yer effing tool? What effing tool?' 'Don't go into the greenhouse, greenhouse, greenhouse'.

SIR MICHAEL CRAZE: Yeah, I'm not actually looking to put anything on at the moment so . . .

MATTHEW: Got another one. 'Ceefax: The Musical'. We open on a giant ceefax. A thousand Vietnamese children come on in rags.

HE PLAYS AND SINGS.

MATTHEW: Page 142 weather. Page 220 joke time.

SIR MICHAEL CRAZE: I'm not quite sure that's right for the West End.

MATTHEW: A thousand Vietnamese children in rags!

SIR MICHAEL CRAZE: I'm sorry. I'm actually very busy today. You do need to make a proper appointment.

MATTHEW: Did you not get the tape I sent you?

SIR MICHAEL CRAZE: Aah, what's your name?

MATTHEW: Waterhouse.

SIR MICHAEL LOOKS IN HIS DRAWER AND PULLS OUT AN OPENED JIFFY-BAG ENVELOPE. HE REACHES INTO IT AND PULLS OUT A ROLL OF SELLOTAPE.

SIR MICHAEL CRAZE: Oh yes. It was very kind of you but . . .

MATTHEW: Got another one. 'Musical: The Musical'. A giant musical flies in. A thousand Vietnamese children in rags swarm the stage.

HE SINGS AND PLAYS.

MATTHEW: 'Musical. Musical'.

SIR MICHAEL CRAZE: You see that's quite expensive.

MATTHEW: One Vietnamese children swarms the stage. (SINGS) 'Musical, musical'.

SIR MICHAEL CRAZE: No.

MATTHEW: Got another one. How about a musical adaptation of David Baddiel?

SIR MICHAEL CRAZE: No.

MATTHEW: Got another one. 'Dangerous Liasons: The Musical'.

SIR MICHAEL CRAZE: Ah now, you see, this is the sort of thing we're looking for. This sounds very interesting.

MATTHEW: Yeah. I've done a set for it.

WATERHOUSE REACHES INTO HIS SACK AND BRINGS OUT A VERY WELL-MADE MODEL OF A SET. HE MOVES HIS HAND INTO THE SET.

MATTHEW: So he comes in here . . .

SIR MICHAEL CRAZE: Who's this?

MATTHEW: The character of the Giant Hand. He . . . stay with me. Stay with me. Please.

DAFFYD — THE TEST

EXT. SEXUAL HEALTH CLINIC. A MAN HAS HIS PENIS IN A SLING. A WOMAN IS INSPECTING IT.

TOM V/O: Meanwhile, at this sexual health clinic in Llandewi Breffi . . .

INT. HEALTH CLINIC. DAFFYD IS SEATED OPPOSITE A FRIENDLY WOMAN IN A WHITE COAT.

DOCTOR: OK. So before we give you the test we do have to ask you a few questions. Don't worry – it's all confidential. OK, so . . . age?

DAFFYD: Twenty-five.

DOCTOR: Occupation.

DAFFYD: Gay.

DOCTOR: No, what do you do?

DAFFYD: Oh, I see. I am an unemployed out gay man.

DOCTOR: And how many sexual partners would you say you've had in the past year?

DAFFYD: None.

DOCTOR: And how many would you say you've had in the past five years?

DAFFYD: Ooh. Past five years, you say? (THINKS) Excluding myself?

DOCTOR: Yes.

DAFFYD: None.

DOCTOR: Have you had *any* sexual partners?

DAFFYD: Oh no. No. I am the only gay in the village, you see.

DOCTOR: What, from Llandewi? Ooh no, we've had loads of folk in from there.

DAFFYD: I don't think so.

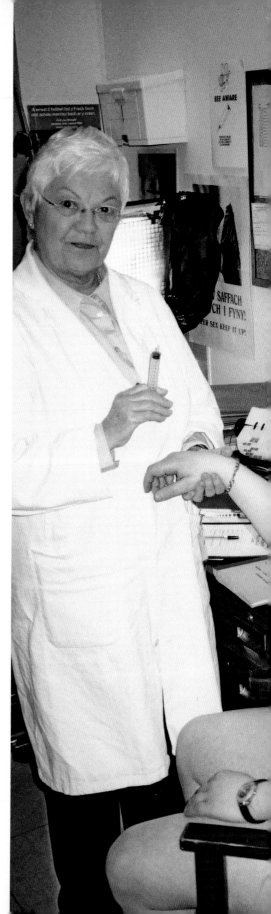

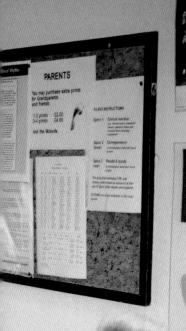

Make a fist. Now you may feel a prick, but there's a first time for everything.

DOCTOR: Well, if you haven't had any sexual partners, then I don't think you need the test.

DAFFYD: Oh, go on. Please. I am a gay, you know.

DOCTOR: (SIGHS) OK. Give me your arm. (GENTLY SARCASTIC) Make a fist. Now you may feel a prick, but there's a first time for everything.

THE DOCTOR TAKES A BLOOD SAMPLE.

CUT TO: INT. WAITING ROOM. THERE ARE A FEW PEOPLE IN THERE. DAFFYD FINDS A SEAT NEXT TO A MIDDLE-AGED GAY MAN.

DAFFYD: Oh I've just had the test. I do hope everything's going to be all right.

MAN: I'm sure it will be fine. (PAUSE) Though, of course, it does just need to be that one time.

DAFFYD TRIES TO NOD IN AGREEMENT.

DAFFYD: Yeah.

DENVER MILLS – SCHOOL PRIZE-GIVING

EXT. DAY. SUBURBAN PRIMARY SCHOOL ENTRANCE. WE SEE A TEN-YEAR-OLD GIRL IN SCHOOL UNIFORM DIRECTING THREE LOLLIPOP MEN AND WOMEN ACROSS THE ROAD.

TOM V/O: Small children in Britain are notoriously stupid and must attend schools. At Robert Downey Junior School in Area 52, it's prize-giving day, which is to be hosted by retired athlete Denver Mills.

WE SEE A WOMAN ANXIOUSLY WAITING FOR SOMEONE. AN ELDERLY SECRETARY APPEARS WITH DENVER.

EPISODE

SECRETARY: Ah, Miss Bingham. This is Dennis Mills.

DENVER: *Denver* Mills.

THEY START WALKING ALONG TOGETHER QUICKLY.

MISS BINGHAM: Who?

DENVER: Denver Mills. I won the 400-metre Silver, Los Angeles, '84.

MISS BINGHAM: Where's Fatima Whitbread?

DENVER: Guernsey. Apparently she had no idea about today. (SHRUGS) That's Jayne Torvill Management for you.

MISS BINGHAM: Well you know what you've got to do?

DENVER: Yeah. (MOVE) Do the speech, give out the prizes. Piece of piss.

MISS BINGHAM: Do you mind if I just have a quick look at your speech?

DENVER: Yeah. You go ahead, Miss.

DENVER GIVES MISS BINGHAM A PILE OF NOTE CARDS. SHE STUDIES THEM INTENTLY. DENVER POINTS OVER HER SHOULDER.

DENVER: I say 'Good afternoon' and then I do a gag – I say 'Thank God this is a private school. If it was a state school I'd be afraid to park my car outside.'

MISS BINGHAM: This *is* a state school.

DENVER: That's gone.

MISS BINGHAM DISCARDS THE CARD AND MOVES ON TO THE NEXT.

MISS BINGHAM: Steve Cram. Remind me.

DENVER: Crammy? The Cramster? Won the 1500-metre Gold? Used to promote 'Start'?

MISS BINGHAM: I don't think the children are going to remember him, I'm afraid.

DENVER: Shame. It's a very very funny story, which ends up with Steve completely covered in . . .

DENVER PUTS THE CARD ASIDE.

Yeah. Do the speech, give out the prizes. Piece of piss.

MISS BINGHAM: Covered in?

DENVER STARTS TO GO BACK TO THE CARD AND THINKS BETTER OF IT.

DENVER: No. I can't tell you. No.

DENVER QUICKLY POINTS AT THE NEXT CARD.

DENVER: Ah, now this is a great bit. 'Squite political – you see in my village, where I live, there is a lot of these so-called asylum seekers. Now . . .

MISS BINGHAM: I don't think that's going to be relevant for here.

DENVER: It went down very well at the countryside march.

MISS BINGHAM: No. Sorry.

DENVER GIVES A 'WELL IT'S YOUR LOSS'-STYLE SHRUG. MISS BINGHAM REMOVES THE CARD. AND THE NEXT. AND THE NEXT.

DENVER: This is all still asylum seekers.

MISS BINGHAM REMOVES TWO MORE CARDS.

DENVER: Ah, now this gag I may or may not do really, depending on how . . .

MISS BINGHAM: (READS TO HERSELF) '. . . the French Relay team . . .'

SHE READS FURTHER.

MISS BINGHAM: 'Do Action'. What's the action?

DENVER DOES THE 'BLOWJOB' ACTION. A SHOCKED MISS BINGHAM REMOVES THE CARD.

DENVER: Like I say, that was always in the balance . . .

MISS BINGHAM IS HOLDING THE LAST CARD.

MISS BINGHAM: 'Thank you and I hope you enjoyed the speech'.

DENVER: (MILDLY SARCASTIC) Is that OK? Or have you got a problem with that?

MISS BINGHAM: No, that's fine. Right, I'll just go and introduce you.

MISS BINGHAM HANDS DENVER THE REMAINING CARDS AND DISAPPEARS THROUGH THE DOUBLE DOORS. DENVER LOOKS DOWN AT THE CARDS. THERE ARE TWO OF THEM.

DENVER: (READS THE FIRST CARD) 'Good afternoon.' (READS THE SECOND CARD) 'Thank you and I hope you enjoyed the speech.'

DENVER TAKES OUT HIS MOBILE PHONE AND DIALS.

MISS BINGHAM: (OFF-SCREEN) Right then, boys and girls. We have a special guest. Please welcome Dennis Mills.

WE HEAR POLITE APPLAUSE.

DENVER: (ON PHONE) Hi, Jayne. It's Denver. Is it too late to pull out of the school?

LOU AND ANDY — BROKEN LIFT

INT. HOSPITAL STAIRCASE. QUITE A FEW FLOORS UP. LOU IS STRUGGLING WITH THE WHEELCHAIR. ANDY HAS FLOWERS ON HIS LAP. THEY REACH THE FINAL STEP.

TOM V/O: With the hospital lift out of order, Lou has pushed his friend Andy up three flights of stairs.

LOU: Ooh, what a kerfuffle! They should get that lift fixed.

ANDY: What are we doing?

LOU: Do you remember Maria, who used to look after you? Well, she's not been very well so we're going to take her some flowers.

ANDY: Then can we go?

LOU: Yeah. I'll go and find out what ward she's on.

LOU WALKS OVER TO A NURSE.

LOU: Excuse me, nurse, can you tell me where I might find Maria Donelly please?

NURSE: Yes. She's in Griffiths ward. It's on the next floor up.

LOU: Thank you.

MEANWHILE, IN THE BACKGROUND, UNSEEN BY LOU, ANDY GETS OUT OF THE CHAIR AND STRETCHES HIS LEGS, BEFORE SITTING DOWN AGAIN. LOU RETURNS.

LOU: Up one more flight, I'm afraid.

ANDY: Oh no.

LOU: Yeah.

LOU STRUGGLES TO LIFT ANDY UP THE STAIRS.

Ooh, what a **kerfuffle!**

EILEEN AND JANET

EXT. ROW OF HOUSES. DUSTBIN MEN ARE THROWING FULL RUBBISH BAGS AT THE FRONT DOORS.

TOM V/O: At home in Byright, Eileen is comforting her recently bereaved sister, Janet.

INT. SUBURBAN KITCHEN. EILEEN AND JANET ARE SEATED AT THE KITCHEN TABLE. THERE IS A TEAPOT AND TWO MUGS ON IT AND A BISCUIT TIN. EILEEN HAS HER ARM ROUND JANET, WHO IS WEEPING SOFTLY.

EILEEN: Tell you what, why don't I put the kettle on? Make us both a nice cup of tea. Yeah. Lovely. (JANET NODS) Would you like a nice biscuit to go with it? Nice Penguin? Yeah. (JANET STARTS TO CRY) What now love?

JANET: Ivor used to love Penguins. It always makes me think of him.

EILEEN: Oh. Yeah yeah. Well, we'll have it without. We'll have tea on its own. (JANET CRIES) Don't mind it in a mug do you?

JANET: Ivor used to have his tea in a mug. Except when he had it in a cup and saucer.

EILEEN: Yeah. I understand, love. I understand. Well, tell you what. It's a lovely day. Why don't we go outside. We could go down the shops, couldn't we?

JANET WAILS.

JANET: Me and Ivor used to go down the shops. When we needed to buy things.

EILEEN: Yeah, yeah, you would have done. Yeah. Yeah. Well we'll stay in. I'll get the paper and we'll see what's on the telly.

JANET SCREECHES.

EILEEN: Oh dear. Ivor?

JANET: Ivor used to . . .

BOTH: Watch telly.

JANET: The news. The sport. The dramas. Comedy programmes. All sorts, really, you know. He was someone who liked telly. You know, that was Ivor.

EILEEN: (SIGHS) Now come on, I thought we'd agreed not to talk about Ivor.

JANET HOWLS.

JANET: Ivor. That was the name of Ivor. If ever I wanted to call him I'd say 'Ivor?'

EILEEN: Yeah.

JANET SOBS.

JANET: Yeah. That's the word Ivor used to use, when he wanted to answer in the affirmative. When he wanted to respond in a casual manner, as an alternative to the more formal 'Yes'.

EILEEN NODS, SMILES AND WALKS OFF INTO THE KITCHEN.

JANET: Silence! That's what Ivor used to crave when he didn't think . . .

EILEEN, IN THE KITCHEN, MAKES A PHONE CALL. LEAVING JANET ON HER OWN.

EILEEN (ON THE PHONE)**:** Oh I'm sorry, I didn't recognize you, yeah. . .

JANET LOOKS ANNOYED.

DES KAYE — TEA BREAK

INT. DIY UNIVERSE STAFFROOM. FAIRLY GRUBBY. HALF A DOZEN STAFF ARE CHATTING, READING MAGAZINES, SMOKING AND FLICKING ASH ON THE FLOOR, ETC. DES KAYE ENTERS, WITH PUPPET CROCODILE ON HIS HAND. THE ROOM GOES SILENT.

TOM V/O: Over at DIY Universe, the staff *were* enjoying their tea break.

DES: (BRIGHTLY) Hiya gang. Wicky woo!

DES TURNS HIS BACK ON THE ROOM, TO FILL THE KETTLE.

DES: I'm having an Options. Does anyone want one?

WITH DES'S BACK TURNED, MOST OF THE OTHER STAFF TAKE THE OPPORTUNITY TO LEAVE QUIETLY. ONLY AL, WHO IS DOZING, AND KIERAN, A NEW BOY, REMAIN.

KIERAN: We don't have to go back yet, do we?

NO ONE REMAINS TO ANSWER. DES TURNS ROUND AND SPOTS KIERAN.

DES: Oh hello. I don't know you, do I?

KIERAN: No, I'm new.

DES: Wicky woo! Des Kaye, pleased to meet you.

DES SHAKES KIERAN'S HAND AND DOESN'T LET GO.

DES: Ooh, can I have me hand back please?

DES EVENTUALLY LETS GO. AL WAKES UP AND SPOTS DES. HIS FACE DROPS.

KIERAN: (FOGGY) Didn't you used to be on the telly?

AL SILENTLY TRIES TO SIGNAL TO KIERAN NOT TO GET INTO THIS SORT OF CONVERSATION.

DES: That's right, yes. I used to present 'The Fun Bus'.

Yeah. That's the word [voi] used to use, when he wanted to answer in the affirmative. When he wanted to respond in a casual manner, as an alternative to the more formal 'Yes'.

KIERAN: Yeah. Them Bubble Twins do it now, yeah?

AL SIGNALS VIOLENTLY TO KIERAN.

DES: Do they? I haven't watched it.

KIERAN: Yeah, my little sister loves 'em.

DES TAKES A DEEP BREATH.

DES: Let me tell you about the Bubble Twins . . . (SITS)

AL: Come on, Kieran. It's time to get back.

DES: We've still got ten minutes.

AL IS FORCED TO REMAIN.

DES: The Bubble Twins started off in 1986 doing a little bit on my show 'Des Kaye's Fun Bus'. You remember we used have this bit 'What's in the Custard'?

KIERAN: I don't think so no.

DES: You remember it, don't you, Al?

AL: No.

DES: You do. You do. You're lying – you do. (TO PUPPET CROCODILE) Come away, Croc. Well, basically, they used to pour the custard.

AL: I never watched it.

DES: Well good, 'cause they were rubbish. Then I hear the Fun Bus has been pulled. Why is that? I hear you ask.

AL: Wasn't it because that girl lost an eye?

DES: No. Yeah. But actually, no. It's because . . .

'CROCODILE': Top o' the morning! Where's me breakfast?

DES: (ANGRILY) Not now, Croc. I'm talking! Very rude. It's because Dicky Bubble is a queer . . .

AL: How do you know?

DES: Oh, I see him in all the clubs . . . and the head of Children's – Robin Dee – is also a queer. You know, he's got a wife but he's a queer and basically Dicky Bubble said to

I'm having an Options. Does anyone want one?

Robin Dee, I'll fill your slot. (TO KIERAN) Bum sex. (TO BOTH) Hey presto! Des Kaye out of a job. So if you don't mind, can we change the subject?

PAUSE.

AL: Kettle's boiled.

DES: Thank you.

DES GOES OVER TO THE KETTLE AND POURS HIS OPTIONS DRINK. HE STIRS HIS DRINK WITH HIS BACK TO THE ROOM. AL GESTURES TO KIERAN TO LEAVE QUIETLY.

DES: So what's everybody doing later?

HE TURNS ROUND TO DISCOVER THE ROOM IS EMPTY.

CUT TO: WIDE SHOT OF THE VAST INTERIOR OF THE DIY UNIVERSE STORE. THE DOOR FROM THE STAFF ROOM IS OPENED. DES LEANS OUT.

DES: (SHOUTS) I said 'What's everybody doing later?'

WORLD RECORD ATTEMPT — HOUSE OF CARDS

INT. CONFERENCE CENTRE. IAN 2 WALKS DOWN THE STEPS TOWARDS THE STAGE. HIS SWEATSHIRT READS 'HOUSE OF CARDS – WORLD RECORD ATTEMPT'.

IAN 2: Ian!

IAN 1: Yeah?

IAN 2: I've just spoken to Mr McWhirter and he says you're not allowed to use Sellotape.

IAN 1: What? Any?

IAN 2: Apparently not.

WE REVEAL IAN 1, WHO IS ONSTAGE, IN FRONT OF A BANNER. HE STANDS AT THE TOP OF A STEPLADDER, PUTTING THE FINISHING TOUCHES TO AN ENORMOUS HOUSE OF CARDS THAT IS OBVIOUSLY STUCK TOGETHER WITH SELLOTAPE. HE HAS A ROLL OF SELLOTAPE IN ONE HAND.

IAN 1: It's a shame. I was happy with that.

IAN 2: Oh well, best start again, eh.

AS THE CREDITS ROLL, THE PAIR PITIFULLY ATTEMPT TO BUILD ANOTHER HOUSE OF CARDS.

TOM V/O: And so our tour of Britain is over for another week. If you enjoyed the programme you might like to know that the book accompanying the series has not yet been written. Goodbyes.

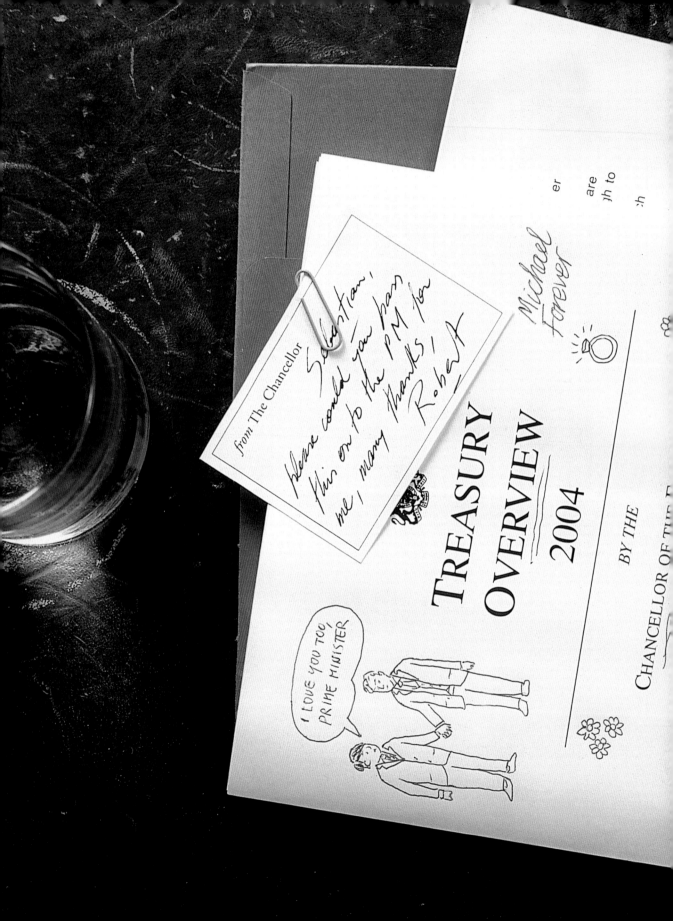

EPISODE

TOM V/O: Britain, Britain, Britain. Discovered by Sir Henry Britain in 16010. Sold to Germany a year later for a Pfennig and the promise of a kiss. Destroyed in 1830 42 and rebuilt a week later by a man. This we know. Hello. But what of the people of Britain. Who they, what do, and why?

SEBASTIAN AND MICHAEL — THE CHANCELLOR

EXT. NO. 10 DOWNING STREET. A MAN DELIVERS A BIG BOARD SAYING 'TWAT'. THE POLICEMAN IS UNABLE TO LEAVE HIS POST TO ARREST THE MAN OR MOVE THE SIGN.

TOM V/O: Inside 10 Downing Street the Prime Minister is having a meeting with the Chancellor of the Exchequer. Of course when I say the Prime Minister, I don't mean the real Prime Minister. I just mean that guy out of *Buffy*.

INT. PRIME MINISTER'S OFFICE. MICHAEL IS SEATED AT HIS DESK. SEATED IN FRONT OF HIM IS THE CHANCELLOR, A DOUR SCOT. SEBASTIAN STANDS BEHIND MICHAEL.

CHANCELLOR: So in principle the budget is approved, is it?

MICHAEL: Yes, though you might like to have a look at the focus group report that's just come through.

THE CHANCELLOR ROLLS HIS EYES.

MICHAEL: Do you have that, Sebastian?

SEBASTIAN HANDS THE REPORT OVER.

CHANCELLOR: (WEARY) Oh that should make for interesting reading, Prime Minister. Is that all?

MICHAEL: Yes. (THE CHANCELLOR GOES TO LEAVE) Though I must say, Robert, I do feel rather undermined that you consistently distance yourself from me in public. If you are going to stand against me for the leadership, come out and say so.

SEBASTIAN: Yeah!

CHANCELLOR: I can assure you, Prime Minister, that if and when I have ambitions for the leadership you will be first to know.

SEBASTIAN: (SARCASTIC) Yeah right.

MICHAEL: Thank you, Sebastian.

SEBASTIAN: Yeah but . . . you know . . . he's so two-faced.

MICHAEL: Yes, thank you. (TO CHANCELLOR) I heard that you had a private meeting with the Home Secretary this morning.

CHANCELLOR: I did, but the question of leadership never arose.

SEBASTIAN: Ooh, you lying cow!

MICHAEL: Sebastian!

SEBASTIAN: I don't know what you're getting so het up about. It's not as if the public are ever gonna vote for him.

CHANCELLOR: Why not?

SEBASTIAN: Well, look at you. You're overweight, you're losing your hair. The Prime Minister here is gorgeous – well I wouldn't know, but he is.

CHANCELLOR: Well maybe if I *was* to stand it would be about policies rather than presentation.

SEBASTIAN: Ooh, so you *are* standing now!

CHANCELLOR: I didn't say that.

SEBASTIAN: Go on. Just try it. Just try it!

CHANCELLOR: If you must know, Prime Minister, I am going to stand. I shall make my announcement in the House tomorrow.

MICHAEL: Sebastian, would you like to show the ex-Chancellor out now?

SEBASTIAN WALKS OVER TO THE CHANCELLOR, PAUSES FOR A SECOND, AND SLAPS HIM IN THE FACE.

SEBASTIAN: Get out.

THE CHANCELLOR – SHOCKED – LEAVES. SEBASTIAN STARTS MASSAGING MICHAEL'S SHOULDERS.

SEBASTIAN: That showed her. Right, we are going to book you a manicure, a pedicure, a facial, the works.

DENNIS WATERMAN – EUSTON FILMS

EXT. OFFICE. A LITERAL MIME ARTIST IS AT WORK.

TOM V/O: Here we are at the office of theatrical agent Jeremy Rent. I had an agent once. Before I made the mistake of strangling her.

INT. OFFICE. SUNNY DAY. JEREMY IS ON THE PHONE.

JEREMY: Well I'm sorry, but Richard O'Sullivan doesn't get out of bed for less than fifty pounds. Good day!

JEREMY PUTS THE PHONE DOWN. DENNIS ENTERS HOLDING TWO (VERY LARGE) 99 ICE CREAMS WITH FLAKES.

JEREMY: Ah, Dennis. Do come in, dear heart. Lovely to see you. Take a seat. I've got some wonderful news.

DENNIS SITS DOWN.

DENNIS: I got you an ice cream.

JEREMY: Oh, thank you.

DENNIS HANDS JEREMY AN ICE CREAM. IT MAGICALLY APPEARS SMALLER IN JEREMY'S FRAME.

WE CUT BACK TO DENNIS ENJOYING HIS VERY BIG ICE CREAM. HE HAS ICE CREAM AROUND HIS MOUTH.

DENNIS: No, it's the same size.

JEREMY: Ooh. Well, anyway. I've had a fax this morning from Euston Films. Now where is it? Can you hold this a moment please.

JEREMY STARTS SEARCHING. WITHOUT LOOKING UP, HE HANDS DENNIS A SMALL POT PLANT THAT WAS ON HIS MESSY DESK, ON TOP OF A PILE OF PAPERS. WE SEE DENNIS STRUGGLE TO HOLD A HUGE POT PLANT. JEREMY FINDS THE FAX.

JEREMY: Here we are.

DENNIS IS PANICKING.

DENNIS: I don't think I can hold it for much longer.

JEREMY: Oh just pop it down.

DENNIS PUTS THE PLANT BACK ON THE DESK. JEREMY READS ALOUD FROM THE FAX.

JEREMY: 'Sonia Chance, the new head of ITV, has requested a new series of *Minder*, to go into production in the Spring. Would Dennis be interested?'

DENNIS LOOKS BLANK. HE POINTS TO HIS ICE CREAM.

DENNIS: I don't want any more.

JEREMY: Oh well, just give it here.

DENNIS HANDS JEREMY THE REMAINS OF HIS ICE CREAM. JEREMY COMPARES THE TWO. HE OBSERVES QUIZZICALLY THAT DENNIS'S CONE REALLY IS A GREAT DEAL BIGGER! HE THROWS THEM BOTH AWAY.

JEREMY: Now I've done a ring-round. George Cole's on board and they're talking to Dave the Barman's people.

DENNIS: Oh, that's nice. So they want me to star in it, write the feem toon, sing the feem toon . . .

JEREMY: Well . . . yes. I imagine they do. Anyway, they're very keen. Sonia Chance herself has been ringing me all morning. (PHONE RINGS) Ooh, that will probably be her now. (JEREMY ANSWERS THE PHONE) Hello? Sonia? Yes, he's right here.

DENNIS: Let me speak to her.

JEREMY: Passing you over.

DENNIS: Hello, Sonia. Oh, so you want me to reprise my role as Terry McCann? Write the feem toon, sing the feem toon? No thanks, I've moved on.

DENNIS HANDS BACK THE PHONE. THIS TIME IT IS BIG IN JEREMY'S SHOT. JEREMY LOOKS BAFFLED.

VICKY POLLARD — AT THE DOCTOR'S

EXT. STREET. PAN WITH BUS TO EXT., DOCTOR'S SURGERY.

TOM V/O: Those are buses. But anyway, at his surgery in Darkley Noone, Dr Albarn is examining one of his patients.

INT. DOCTOR'S SURGERY. VICKY IS BEHIND A SCREEN. THE DOCTOR EMERGES FROM BEHIND IT, REMOVING HIS STETHOSCOPE, ETC., AND RETURNS TO HIS DESK.

DOCTOR: OK, Vicky. You can put your clothes back on. Well, after having had a good look at you it's pretty obvious to me what the diagnosis is.

VICKY APPEARS FROM BEHIND THE SCREEN. SHE IS VERY HEAVILY PREGNANT.

VICKY: I got the lurgy. Yeah, I know because there was this whole fing 'cause I was all down the arcade and Kelly flobbed on Destiny and a bit of it landed in my hair because Kelly hates Destiny because Destiny told Warren that Kelly pads her bra. It's true – Nathan reckons he put his hand down there and pulled out a bag of Jelly Tots.

VICKY HAS SAT DOWN.

DOCTOR: No, Vicky. I have to tell you you are in fact eight months' pregnant.

VICKY: No doctor because you can only get pregnant by sitting in someone else's bath water and anyway if anyone's pregnant it's Jo Rowley because Meredith reckons she's seen her with her hand down Ashley's trackie bottoms.

DOCTOR: Well you are pregnant so you must have had sexual intercourse at some point, well, eight months ago.

VICKY: No but yeah but no but yeah but no but yeah but no but yeah but no but yeah because I've never even had sex apart from that one time eight months ago but apart from that I'm a complete virgin.

DOCTOR: So you have had sex at least once?

VICKY: Yeah *as a joke*! God this is like being back at school. What happened was was you know Trish?

DOCTOR: Trish who?

VICKY: Trish. *Trish* Trish. Trish. Rochelle and Trish.

DOCTOR: No.

VICKY: Well she ain't got nothing to do with it anyway she wasn't even there. Shut up. You don't even know what you're talking about. Anyway she dared Melody she wouldn't nick a Hubba Bubba off Darren Sheen but anyway Darren Sheen ain't got any pubes.

ave it on
efore you
ave it off
DOMS CAN PREVENT
AIDS
Cervical Cancer
Chlamydia
Gonorrhoea
Syphilis
Other STDs
PREGNANCY
Nobutyeahbutnobut
yeahbutnobutyeah
butnobutyeahbutno
butyeahbecauseI've
neverevenhadsex
apartfromthatone
timeeightmonthsago
butapartfromthat
I'macompletevirgin.

DOCTOR: OK, Vicky. Well, um, I would strongly advise you, if you haven't already, for the sake of your baby, to give up smoking and drinking.

VICKY: Oh my God I so can't believe you just said that! I smoked like once for like two years when I was like nine and I only drink to numb the pain of my worthless life so you're well out of order.

DOCTOR: OK, right. Well what I'm going to do is, I am going to refer you to our Young Mothers' Unit at the city hospital. You're going to have to pop down there this afternoon. Is there someone who can accompany you?

VICKY: Well I'm not asking Shelley because she's a slag.

DOCTOR: OK. Is there someone else you can go with? Perhaps your mother?

VICKY: That is my mother.

DENVER MILLS — AFTER-DINNER SPEECH

TOM V/O: In Hamham, ex-Olympic athlete Denver Mills has been brought to give an after-dinner speech.

INT. POSH HOTEL FUNCTION ROOM. ANNUAL POLICE FEDERATION DINNER. A TRACKSUITED DENVER IS HOLDING COURT AT THE TOP TABLE ALONG WITH SOME HIGH-RANKING POLICEMAN IN SMART UNIFORMS.

DENVER: . . . Steve Cram ended up completely covered in . . .

CHIEF OF POLICE: Save it for the speech, Denver.

DENVER: You sure you don't want to go through it first?

CHIEF OF POLICE: No no no. I trust you. I'm just going to introduce you.

DENVER NODS CONFIDENTLY. THE CHIEF RISES AND TAPS HIS GLASS. THE ROOM QUIETENS.

CHIEF OF POLICE: A little bit of hush, ladies and gentlemen – that includes you, Detective Inspector

. . . But maybe being an Olympic athlete isn't so different from being a police officer. First of all, we both get a lot of practice running after black guys. The difference is I beat some of mine . . . I mean 'caught up with' them, not beat them, like you do.

Willow. (THERE IS LAUGHTER IN THE ROOM) OK, it is time to introduce you to our special guest speaker of the evening. You may have seen him on *They Think it's All Over*. Please give it up for Olympic silver medallist, Denver Mills.

DENVER RISES. APPLAUSE. THE CHIEF SITS.

DENVER: Evening all. Great to be here. You know, when I was a lad I always dreamed of going into the force. But maybe being an Olympic athlete isn't so different from being a police officer. First of all, we both get a lot of practice running after black guys. The difference is I beat some of mine . . . I mean 'caught up with' them, not beat them, like you do.

WE SEE SHOCKED FACES AT THE TABLE.

DENVER: Shall I just go?

HE LEAVES, THEN COMES BACK AND PINCHES A BOTTLE OF WINE

LOU AND ANDY — BIRTHDAY CARD

EXT. DAY. SMALL NEWSAGENT IN A LOW-RENT PARADE OF SHOPS. SIGN – 'FAGS AND THAT'. WE SEE A CAGEY LOOKING MAN EXIT CARRYING A COPY OF THE *DAILY TELEGRAPH* AND A PORNO MAG CALLED *BIG BAPS*. HE SURREPTITIOUSLY SLIPS THE *TELEGRAPH* INSIDE THE PORNO MAG AND EXITS.

TOM V/O: Since cigarette smoking has become mandatory, newsagents in Britain have flourished.

INT. NEWSAGENT'S. LOU AND ANDY ARE LOOKING AT A RACK OF GREETINGS CARDS.

LOU: Right now, you know it's Declan's birthday coming up?

ANDY: Who?

LOU: Declan. Your brother.

ANDY: Yeah, I know.

LOU: Well, it's his birthday coming up and you gotta get him a card. Now can you see any you like?

ANDY POINTS INDISCRIMINATELY.

ANDY: I want that one.

LOU: That one?

ANDY: Yeah.

LOU: Well that says 'With Deepest Sympathy'.

ANDY: Yeah, I know.

LOU: Well that's what you send someone when somebody's died.

ANDY: I want that one.

LOU: Well I'm not sure Declan's gonna like that. 'Cos it will send out the wrong message. No. Declan likes sailing boats. Why don't we get one with sailing boats on it?

ANDY: I want that one.

LOU: This one's got a sailing boat. He likes sailing boats.

ANDY: *That one.*

LOU: (SIGHS) Are you sure? This is the card you want to send your brother Declan for his birthday?

ANDY: Yeah, yeah, yeah.

EXT. NEWSAGENT. LOU IS WHEELING ANDY OUT OF THE SHOP. ANDY IS HOLDING THE CARD AND LOOKING AT IT, SLIGHTLY BEWILDERED.

ANDY: It's his birthday. He's not dead.

ANDY THROWS THE CARD AWAY.

LOU (IN DESPAIR) LETS GO OF THE WHEELCHAIR FOR A MOMENT.

MAJORIE DAWES — SUPERMARKET

TOM V/O: Meanwhile, FatFighters course leader Marjorie Dawes has popped into her local supermarket to pick up a few sundries. And mondries. And tuesdries and wednesdries.

INT. SUPERMARKET. SHOTS OF MARJORIE FILLING UP HER TROLLEY WITH LOTS OF VERY FATTENING FOOD.

PAUL: (FRIENDLY) Oh, hello.

MARJORIE: Sorry. Do I know you?

PAUL: I come to FatFighters.

MARJORIE: Oh yes, Paul, isn't it? Yes, sorry, so many people come to class that I can't possibly remember everybody.

PAUL: (INCREDULOUS) Is this yours?

PAUL INDICATES HER FULL TROLLEY.

MARJORIE: Eh? No, no, this is my trolley over here.

MARJORIE POINTS TO A NEARBY TROLLEY, WHICH HAS A SMALL CHILD IN IT.

PAUL: Oh hello. What's his name?

MARJORIE: Baby.

PAUL IS BRIEFLY STUMPED. HE PICKS UP A PACKET OF SWEETS.

PAUL: Ooh, this is gonna have a lot of calories in it.

MARJORIE: Yeah, it's for the baby. Anyway what's all this? Eh?

MARJORIE LEAFS THROUGH PAUL'S BASKET. WE SEE THAT PAUL HAS SELECTED HEALTHY ITEMS, E.G. SKIMMED
MILK, A CHILLI CON CARNE LEAN CUISINE MEAL FOR ONE, GRAPEFRUIT, A MIXED SALAD, ETC. MARJORIE MAKES
MOCKING SOUNDS. EVENTUALLY SHE PULLS OUT A TRACKER.

MARJORIE: Oh dear. We've found your Achilles foot, haven't we?

PAUL: It's just a Tracker bar.

MARJORIE: 'Just a Tracker bar', he says. (READING THE LABEL) I don't know why I bother.

PAUL: Well I'll put it back then.

MARJORIE KEEPS HOLD OF THE TRACKER.

MARJORIE: I don't think there's much point in you coming to FatFighters any more, is there, Paul, if all you're gonna do is stuff your face every time my back is turned?

PAUL: Well, if that's the way you feel maybe I shouldn't come.

MARJORIE: No, do, do, because we need to keep the numbers up.

PAUL: OK. Bye then.

MARJORIE: (SIGHS) Goodbye.

PAUL EXITS. SHE PULLS HER TROLLEY OUT OF SHOT. MARJORIE TAKES BACK HER REAL TROLLEY AND HEADS FOR THE CHECKOUT. SHE ARRIVES AT THE TILL AND STARTS TO UNLOAD HER VERY UNHEALTHY FOOD.

MEERA: Hello, Marjorie.

MARJORIE LOOKS UP. WE SEE THAT MEERA IS ON THE TILL. MARJORIE LOOKS EMBARRASSED.

MARJORIE: Oh hello, Meera. Er, it's not mine. Another man put them there. I don't know . . .

MARJORIE RUNS OFF.

RAY McCOONEY — TV REPAIR MAN

EXT. HOTEL. TWO PEOPLE ARE SUNBATHING IN THE RAIN AND THUNDER, ENJOYING ICE LOLLIES.

TOM V/O: Scotland is a smashing place to take a holiday and regularly wins the award for best Scottish holiday destination.

INT. SMALL HOTEL LOUNGE. A REPAIR MAN, TOOLKIT BY HIS SIDE, IS TAKING A LOOK ROUND THE BACK OF THE TV. RAY HOVERS, ANIMATED.

TV REPAIR MAN: So what happened?

RAY: Well it was a Sunday afternoon and we were all sat round as a family, watching the telly box. What were we watching, children?

CHILDREN: *Naked Video.*

RAY: Oh yes, the *Naked Video* comedy show. And the sprites were a talking and a laughing and then all of a sudden POOF! – all was darkness in the kingdom of the sprites.

TV REPAIR MAN: The screen went dead?

RAY: Yeeeees. 'Awaken, sprites!' I cried. And I tried to tempt them oot, like so.

RAY PLAYS 'THE BIRDY SONG' ON HIS PICCOLO.

RAY: 'Come oot, ye sprite, ye naughty sprites'.

RAY PLAYS HIS PICCOLO AGAIN.

TV REPAIR MAN: And that didnae work?

RAY: I'd love to say 'Yeeeees', but unfortunately the answer is . . . no.

THE TV REPAIR MAN HAS REMOVED THE BACK OF THE SET. RAY HAS A LOOK INSIDE.

TV REPAIR MAN: You've got a faulty connection. Try it now.

RAY TURNS THE SET ON SUCCESSFULLY. RAY RECOILS IN HORROR, COVERING HIS EYES. WE SEE A BRIEF SHOT OF LAURENCE LLEWELLYN-BOWEN.

RAY: Aaaaah. It's the arch-wizard himself! Avert thine eyes, children. He enters a room, and with a budget of just five hundred pounds, he makes it transform-ed. He is truly the master of the black arts.

RAY PLAYS A SWANEE WHISTLE.

TV REPAIR MAN: Right, you said you had another TV you wanted me to take a look at.

RAY: Yeeeees. 'Tis a curious thing. By day 'tis bright but at night 'tis as black as a black man's cape.

RAY PULLS A CURTAIN TO REVEAL A WINDOW. THE TV MAN IS STUMPED.

TV REPAIR MAN: That is a window. You do know that, don't you?

RAY: Yeeeees.

DR LAWRENCE AND ANNE — COUNTRY COTTAGE 1

EXT. DAY. IDYLLIC COUNTRY COTTAGE.

TOM V/O: Psychiatrist Dr Lawrence lives with his children in this delightful old cottage here in Flatley Village.

A DIRTY WHITE VAN WITH A PENIS ETCHED ON IT PULLS UP IN FRONT OF THE CAMERA, OBSCURING THE COTTAGE.

TOM V/O: Just look at it. What a beauty. I'd love to have one like that.

INT. FAMILY HOME. LIVING ROOM. A BOY AND A GIRL (BOTH ABOUT TEN) ARE SEATED ON THE SOFA. DR LAWRENCE IS ADDRESSING THEM.

DR LAWRENCE: Now, we've got a special guest coming to stay with us this weekend who lives at the hospital where Daddy works. Her name is Anne and we've got to be extra special nice to her. OK?

THE KIDS NOD. THE DOOR OPENS. ANNE ENTERS HOLDING A BOX OF CEREAL.

ANNE: Eh eh eh!

ANNE POURS THE CEREAL ON THE FLOOR.

DR LAWRENCE: Say hello to Anne.

CHILDREN: Hello.

ANNE: Eh eh eh, eh eh eh!

DR LAWRENCE: She's nice, isn't she? Oh yes. Anne loves goldfish. She looks after the one at the hospital. Don't you?

ANNE SCOOPS A FISH OUT OF THE BOWL AND EATS IT.

DR LAWRENCE: Here we go, Anne's painted a picture for you.

ANNE HANDS A PICTURE OVER MADE OF HER OWN EXCREMENT.

DR LAWRENCE: Say thank you.

CHILDREN: Thank you

PAUSE.

DR LAWRENCE: Don't touch the middle of it . . .

DES KAYE — ROBIN AND DICKY

INT. DIY UNIVERSE. DES KAYE IS PRICING SOME TINS OF PAINT. A MAN (ROBIN) APPEARS PUSHING A TROLLEY DOWN AN AISLE, LOOKING LOST.

TOM V/O: Back at DIY Universe, Des Kaye is hard at work.

ROBIN: Excuse me. Can you tell me where the barbecues are, please?

DES: Over by the . . .

ROBIN: Des!

DES: Robin Dee! Hello. How is everything over at Children's? I see the Bubble Twins are doing well for themselves.

ROBIN: Yep, still pulling in the viewers.

FROM AROUND THE CORNER, A FLAMBOYANTLY-DRESSED MAN (DICKY BUBBLE) APPEARS, CARRYING A GARDEN HOSE.

DICKY: This is the longest one they've got.

HE PUTS THE HOSE IN THE TROLLEY.

DES: (COLDLY) Dicky Bubble.

DICKY: Hello, Des.

DES: Oh, so you two just happened to be out in the same shop on the same day. Oooh. What a coincidence.

DICKY: No, we're a couple.

ROBIN: My divorce came through.

DES: Oh, so you just . . . oh.

DICKY: Are you working here now then, Des?

TANNOY: 'Des Kaye to the stockroom please'.

DES: No.

ROBIN: You must come in for a meeting some time.

DES: Oh, erm, I've actually got a big new show in development for ITV . . .

ROBIN: Well, er, good luck with it.

DICKY: Cheerio, Des.

ROBIN AND DICKY START TO MOVE OFF. DES FOLLOWS THEM.

DES: But if you've got any money . . .

THERE IS AN EMBARRASSED PAUSE. DICKY AND ROBIN LOOK AT EACH OTHER. DICKY DOESN'T HAVE ANY
MONEY ON HIM. ROBIN FINDS SOME AND GIVES IT TO DES. DES NODS APPRECIATIVELY. ROBIN AND DICKY
CONTINUE TO BROWSE. DES QUIETLY APPROACHES A NEARBY SECURITY GUARD.

DES: Those two are shoplifters.

LOU AND ANDY — HOLIDAY

EXT. DAY. ANDY'S HOUSE. A NAKED MAN EXITS THE HOUSE NEXT DOOR AND SUDDENLY STOPS – AS IF HE HAS
JUST REMEMBERED SOMETHING. HE GOES BACK INTO THE HOUSE AND REAPPEARS TWO SECONDS LATER,
CARRYING HIS BRIEFCASE

TOM V/O: As the sun sets in southern Britain, for those in the North the day
is just beginning.

INT. ANDY'S FRONT ROOM. LOU ENTERS CLUTCHING A LARGE PILE OF HOLIDAY BROCHURES. ANDY IS IN HIS
PYJAMAS.

LOU: Right, I've got the brochures here. Now let's have a look and see where you
wanna go.

LOU STARTS TO FLICK THROUGH THE PAGES. WITHIN A SECOND AND WITHOUT ACTUALLY LOOKING,
ANDY POINTS EMPHATICALLY.

ANDY: That one.

LOU: You wanna go there?

ANDY: Yeah, that one.

LOU: Well that is Helsinki.

ANDY: Yeah, I know.

LOU: You wanna go to Helsinki?

ANDY: Yeah.

LOU: Well we've got loads of brochures here. We haven't even looked yet. We could
go to Rome or Barcelona or . . . Florida. You can go to Florida very cheap now.

ANDY: Helsinki.

LOU: But you always said Finland had a maudlin quality to it, rendering it unsuitable as a holiday destination.

ANDY: Yeah, I know.

LOU: So where do you wanna go?

ANDY: Helsinki.

LOU: You're sticking with Helsinki?

ANDY: Helsinki.

CUT TO A SHOT OF A PLANE TAKING OFF.

ANDY: (OFF-SCREEN) I want to go to Florida.

KELSEY GRAMMAR SCHOOL

INT. CLASSROOM. THE TEACHER IS AT HIS DESK AND IS FINISHING TAKING THE REGISTER.

TOM V/O: At Kelsey Grammar School Mr Cleaves is busy taking the register.

TEACHER: Unman.

UNMAN: Here.

TEACHER: Wittering.

WITTERING: Here.

TEACHER: And Zigo. Absent.

A SMALL BOY HANDS NOTE TO TEACHER.

TEACHER: Right, come along, up you pop. Thank you. Right. Just a couple of points from the headmaster. Any boys who signed for the school trip to the moon need to pay their deposit by Friday. That's five pounds. The 'Bring and Buy Sale' on Sunday in the car park raised over thirty-six million pounds for Ethiopian Famine. Well done . . .

EPISODE

SANDRA AND RALPH – RSC

TOM V/O: Minewhile, at the offices of the Royal Shakespeare Company . . .

INT. OFFICE. A COUPLE OF STOREYS UP. A MAN (TREVOR) ENTERS, CLUTCHING A COPY OF *THE GUARDIAN* AND A CAPPUCCINO. HE CLOSES THE DOOR TO REVEAL SANDRA AND RALPH, STANDING. HE DOES NOT NOTICE THEM.

SANDRA: Found your Boy yet?

TREVOR JUMPS.

TREVOR: Sorry! Who are you?

SANDRA: We sent you a letter.

TREVOR: Did you?

SANDRA: Yes, we did do. Raif here wanted to audition for the part of the Boy in *Henry the Fifth*.

TREVOR: Oh, well, I'm afraid we've cast that part now.

SANDRA: I know.

TREVOR: Well, perhaps he can come and audition for us next season.

SANDRA: You never even replied.

TREVOR: Really? What's your name?

SANDRA: Speak up.

RALPH: Ralph –

SANDRA: (BARKS) *Raif!*

RALPH: Raif Patterson.

TREVOR: Well it is our policy to reply to all letters. I'll just see if we have it on file. (TREVOR LEAFS THROUGH A FILE AND PULLS OUT A LETTER) Ha ha, yes, here it is.

TREVOR: I must say we thought it was a wind-up.

SANDRA: Why's that?

TREVOR: (READS) 'Dear Bastard . . . '

SANDRA: Just trying to get your attention.

TREVOR: 'My name is Ralph, Raif, Patterson and I am the best actor in the world ever . . . '

SANDRA: Yeah. We did toy with 'ever ever' but we didn't want him to come across as arrogant.

I've always loved Shakespeare's plays and am delighted to hear he's written a new one.

TREVOR: 'You may have seen me in *The Demon Headmaster*.' (TO RALPH) Were you in that?

RALPH: (BRUSHING IT ASIDE) I had a line.

SANDRA: Go on. Do it. Do it.

RALPH: 'Hello'.

SANDRA: Told you he was good. Told you he was good.

TREVOR: (READS) 'I've always loved Shakespeare's plays and am delighted to hear he's written a new one.'

TREVOR GIVES SANDRA A LOOK.

TREVOR: 'I would be a . . . ' – what does that say?

TREVOR SHOWS SANDRA THE LETTER.

SANDRA: 'Brilliant'. Sorry, it's just quite difficult writing in blood.

TREVOR: 'I would be a brilliant Boy in it or even Henry the Fifth himself. Brackets, did you see Bodger and Badger? Close brackets.' (TO RALPH) Ah well, you see, we always had Jonathan Pryce in place for the king.

SANDRA: Him? He's Chinese, ain't he?

TREVOR: 'Give me this job, you shit. Yours sincerely, Raif Patterson.'

SANDRA: Is it a 'yes' now, or do I have to dangle him out the window?

DR LAWRENCE AND ANNE – COUNTRY COTTAGE 2

INT. LIVING ROOM. THERE ARE CAKES AND SANDWICHES ON THE TABLE. DR LAWRENCE AND HIS CHILDREN, RICHARD AND EMMA, HAVE STARTED EATING.

DR LAWRENCE: Yes. Don't have *all* the sandwiches, Emma. Anne might like some.

ANNE ENTERS CARRYING A BUNDLE OF DR LAWRENCE'S SHOES.

ANNE: Eh eh eh!

SHE DUMPS THEM ON THE FLOOR.

DR LAWRENCE: Thank you, Anne. Now do help yourself to sandwiches and cakes. Those are egg and those are tuna.

ANNE: Eh eh eh!

ANNE TAKES AN EGG SANDWICH AND PUTS IT ON HER PLATE.

DR LAWRENCE: That's right. That's egg.

ANNE: Eh eh eh!

ANNE TAKES A TUNA SANDWICH AND PUTS IT ON HER PLATE.

DR LAWRENCE: And that's tuna.

ANNE PICKS UP BOTH SANDWICHES AND SMEARS THEM OVER THE WINDOW. SUDDENLY WE HEAR A MOBILE PHONE RINGING. ANNE REACHES INTO HER POCKET AND PULLS OUT HER PHONE.

ANNE: Eh eh eh! Hello. I'm just over at someone's house, can I call you back? Yes, it's a bit rude. OK. All right. Bye bye.

ANNE PUTS THE PHONE DOWN AND RETURNS TO HER SCREECHING AND SMEARING.

PIANIST

INT. UNCLE ALBERT HALL. ONSTAGE, A RESPECTABLE-LOOKING PIANIST IS IN THE MIDDLE OF AN ACCOMPLISHED PIANO SOLO. HE STOPS SUDDENLY.

PIANIST: Oh, I forgot to set the video for *Room 101* (HE PLAYS A BUM NOTE) . . . Sorry!

HE CONTINUES THE PIECE WHERE HE LEFT OFF.

DAME SALLY MARKHAM — BIBLE

EXT. HOUSE. THE GARDENER IS MAKING A TOPIARY PENIS.

TOM V/O: This is the home of romantic novelist Dame Sally Markham. The books she's written have recently become very popular. Thanks to the invention of reading.

INT. DRAWING ROOM. MISS GRACE TYPES AS DAME SALLY RECLINES, STROKING HER DOG.

DAME SALLY: '"Yes, I will marry you," cried Geraldine. "I will! I will!". The End.' How many pages?

MISS GRACE: Um, twelve.

DAME SALLY: Oh. '"Do you know the Bible?" said Lord Harper. "No," said Geraldine. "I've never even heard of it." "Oh, it's really good. Let me read it to you," said Lord Harper. "Oh, OK then," said Geraldine. "Chapter One. Genesis. In the beginning God created Heaven and earth . . .".' You'll find the rest of the Bible on the shelf, Miss Grace. Wake me up when you've finished.

DAME SALLY FALLS ASLEEP. MISS GRACE RELUCTANTLY FINDS THE BIBLE AND STARTS TYPING.

Um, twelve.

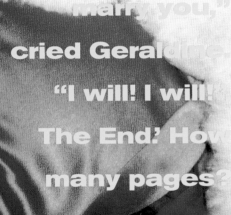

"Yes, I will marry you," cried Geraldine. "I will! I will! The End." How many pages?

MATTHEW WATERHOUSE – CEREALS

INT. CEREALS MANUFACTURER'S BOARDROOM. HALF A DOZEN PEOPLE ARE SITTING AROUND A TABLE.

TOM V/O: In this boardroom in Gore, a meeting is taking place. (PAUSE) The room doesn't look that bored to me. It looks quite perky.

NICHOLAS COURTNEY: Sales of 'Crunchy Nut' have dropped but I'm not too concerned . . .

MATTHEW WATERHOUSE BURSTS IN, WITH A SHOPPING TROLLEY FULL OF HOME-MADE CEREAL BOXES.

MATTHEW: Here's one for you – 'Nutty Nut Nuts'. Real nuts covered in, wait for it, nuts! How about that for starters?

WATERHOUSE PULLS OUT A HOME-MADE BOX AND EMPTIES IT ON TO THE TABLE. LOTS OF NUTS FALL OUT.

NICHOLAS COURTNEY: This is a private meeting.

MATTHEW: Oh well, I've just been in the supermarket and I couldn't help noticing your cereals aren't selling. There's boxes of 'em.

'Sugar Poofs'.
Gay Men frosted with sugar . . .

NICHOLAS COURTNEY: Well if you have any ideas just jot them down on a piece of paper and send them in

AN OLDER, MORE SENIOR MEMBER OF STAFF (ROGER DELGADO) CHIMES IN.

ROGER DELGADO: No come on, Nick. Play fair. The lad's come in with a few ideas, he's shown some pluck and initiative. Let's hear him out.

MATTHEW: Thank you, Granddad!

WATERHOUSE PRODUCES A BOX WITH A PICTURE OF BOY GEORGE ON IT.

MATTHEW: 'Sugar Poofs'. Gay Men frosted with sugar . . .

ROGER DELGADO: Interesting.

MATTHEW: 'Golden Graeme'. Dr Graeme Garden cut up and covered in delicious gold.

WATERHOUSE PULLS OUT A BOX WITH A PICTURE OF GRAEME GARDEN CUT UP AND SPRAYED GOLD.

ROGER DELGADO: Not sure.

MATTHEW: 'Coco Pups'.

WATERHOUSE PULLS OUT A ' COCO PUPS' BOX.

MATTHEW: Real puppy dogs smothered in chocolate.

ROGER DELGADO: Not for us.

MATTHEW: For the health-conscious amongst you, how about an apple?

WATERHOUSE PULLS OUT A BOX MARKED 'APPLE' WITH AN APPLE IN IT.

ROGER DELGADO: I can't really see it.

MATTHEW: Rice Krispies.

WATERHOUSE PULLS OUT A STANDARD BOX OF RICE KRISPIES.

ROGER DELGADO: No.

MATTHEW: Slice of toast.

'Coco Pups'

WATERHOUSE HOLDS UP A SLICE OF TOAST.

ROGER DELGADO: No.

MATTHEW: Full English.

WATERHOUSE PRODUCES A BOX AND EMPTIES THE CONTENTS ONTO THE TABLE, E.G. COOKED EGGS, TOMATOES, HASH BROWNS, MUSHROOMS, SAUSAGES AND FRIED BREAD.

ROGER DELGADO: Now look, this really isn't what we're looking for.
Now we'd be grateful if . . .

MATTHEW: What if I was to tell you that I can invent a cereal that would make everyone who ate it beautiful?

ROGER DELGADO: Can you?

MATTHEW: No.

ROGER DELGADO: Get out!

MATTHEW (TO NICHOLAS): You heard him. Out.

Who's Maria?

Maria's the nice lady who used to look after you before she got too ill.

Yeah, I know.

LOU AND ANDY — TROUSERS

INT. ANDY'S BEDROOM. ANDY SITS IN HIS WHEELCHAIR. LOU CROUCHES DOWN BESIDE HIM.

TOM V/O: It is a sad day in Andy's flat, and Lou is being as gentle as he can with him.

LOU: You know it's Maria's funeral today, don't you?

ANDY: Yeah, I know.

LOU: We'd better put you in your smart suit, shouldn't we?

ANDY: Yeah. (PAUSE) Who's Maria?

LOU: Maria's the nice lady who used to look after you before she got too ill.

ANDY: Yeah, I know.

LOU: Well let's just slip those off. There you go.

LOU CHANGES ANDY'S TRACKSUIT TROUSERS. ANDY REMAINS IN HIS CHAIR.

LOU: Ooh, what a kerfuffle! I don't know how Maria coped on her own all those years.

THE TROUSERS ARE OFF. LOU MANAGES SOMEHOW TO PUT THE SMART TROUSERS ON ANDY.

LOU: Right, let's just get these smart trousers on. One foot, two foot. There you go. Oh it's hard work – right? Let's find you a nice belt. Because you want to look nice and smart, don't you. Give her a good send-off.

ANDY: Good send-off, yeah.

LOU TURNS HIS BACK AND OPENS A MESSY CUPBOARD. AS LOU IS SEARCHING, ANDY STANDS UP, PULLS HIS TROUSERS UP, TUCKS HIS SHIRT IN, AND SITS DOWN AGAIN. LOU IS TOO BUSY LOOKING FOR A BELT TO NOTICE. EVENTUALLY HE TURNS ROUND, HOLDING A BELT.

LOU: Aaah, this is the one Maria bought you.

ANDY: Yeah. (PAUSE) Who's Maria?

WHITELAW – CHARITY SHOP

EXT. DAY. VILLAGE. PARADE OF SHOPS. SHOP WITH A SIGN ABOVE IT – 'CANCER APPEAL SHOP'. WE SEE A DWARF WINDOW CLEANER JUST CLEANING THE LOWER HALF OF EACH WINDOW.

TOM V/O: If you like to buy jigsaw puzzles with pieces missing or faulty electrical goods, then why not pop down to your local charity shop?

INT. OXFAM-STYLE CHARITY SHOP. AN OLD LADY AND A CAMP MAN SERVE BEHIND THE COUNTER. A WOMAN (WHITELAW) IS BROWSING THROUGH THE MEN'S CLOTHING SECTION. SHE PICKS UP A MAN'S SUIT AND TURNS TO THE SHOP ASSISTANTS.

WHITELAW: Excuse me?

OLD LADY: Yes?

WHITELAW: Do you know if anybody died in this?

OLD LADY: Erm, I don't know. I couldn't say. I'm sorry.

WHITELAW PUTS THE SUIT BACK AND FINDS A SHIRT.

WHITELAW: This is very nice.

OLD LADY: Yes, it's a lovely colour.

WHITELAW: Do you know if anyone died in it?

OLD LADY: I don't know.

CAMP MAN: We don't tend to ask.

OLD LADY: No, we don't tend to ask.

WHITELAW: I think I'll leave it then.

WHITELAW PUTS THE SHIRT BACK. SHE BROWSES A LITTLE LONGER AND FINDS SOME PYJAMAS.

WHITELAW: Oh these pyjamas are beautiful.

CAMP MAN: Oh yes, they're pure silk.

WHITELAW: Do you know if anyone died in these?

CAMP MAN: Well actually, a lady did come in yesterday with a big sack of men's clothes and said her husband had died in his sleep so, yes, he would have died in those.

WHITELAW: I'll take them.

DR LAWRENCE AND ANNE — COUNTRY COTTAGE 3

EXT. GARDEN. DR LAWRENCE HAS A HOSE GOING INTO A PADDLING POOL. DR LAWRENCE TURNS AND CALLS BACK
TO THE HOUSE.

DR LAWRENCE: We're just out in the garden, Anne, if you want to join us.

ANNE LEANS OUT OF ONE OF THE UPSTAIRS WINDOWS AND THROWS A BOARD GAME OUT. IT DROPS
AND THE PIECES SCATTER.

ANNE: Eh eh eh!

DR LAWRENCE: Ooh, we can play that later, if you like.

ANNE DROPS A TOILET SEAT. IT SHATTERS.

ANNE: Eh eh eh !

DR LAWRENCE: We don't need toilet just now, Anne.

ANNE APPEARS CARRYING A SMALL CAGE WITH A GUINEA PIG IN IT.

ANNE: Eh eh eh!

DR LAWRENCE: (KIND BUT FIRM) No, Anne. That's Emma's guinea pig. Put that back.

ANNE: (DISAPPOINTED) Oh!

DR LAWRENCE BREATHES A SIGH. HE TURNS HIS BACK ON THE HOUSE. AT THAT MOMENT A RODENT FLIES OUT
THE WINDOW.

DR LAWRENCE (TO CHILDREN)**:** We'll get you another one.

EMILY HOWARD — SEAFRONT

EXT. SEAFRONT. FLORIST. A LADY IN HER FORTIES IS LOOKING AT SOME POTTED PLANTS. EMILY APPEARS.

TOM V/O: In the seaside town of Oldhaven, unconvincing transvestite
Emily Howard has gone for a quiet stroll along the prom.

EMILY: Oh, lovely choice!

WOMAN: Yes.

THE WOMAN NODS POLITELY.

EMILY: I am a lady.

THE WOMAN AGAIN NODS POLITELY.

EMILY: Are *you* a lady?

WOMAN: (A LITTLE SURPRISED) Yes.

Hello. I'm a friend of your wife.

EMILY: Isn't it lovely being a lady? I am one.

THE WOMAN NODS.

EMILY: And being a lady I love flowers. Do you love flowers?

WOMAN: Yes

EMILY: Oh we're like two peas in a pod, aren't we?

WOMAN: Yes, well . . . I must get back to my husband.

EMILY: Yes. I have a husband! They can be so terribly troublesome these husbands, can't they? We should know, being ladies.

THE WOMAN'S HUSBAND APPEARS.

HUSBAND: Shall we go?

EMILY: Hello. I'm a friend of your wife.

EMILY OFFERS HER HAND, TO BE KISSED. THE HUSBAND SHAKES IT MANFULLY.

HUSBAND: All right?

EMILY: Yes, we're both ladies and we got chatting and you know . . .

HUSBAND: Hang on. Don't I know you from somewhere?

EMILY: I don't think so. I am a lady.

HUSBAND: Yeah, I know you. You're Eddie. Eddie Howard.

EMILY: No . . . No, I am Emily Howard, a lady.

HUSBAND: Yeah. We used to work together.

EMILY: I ain't never worked down the docks!

HUSBAND: That's right. Down the docks.

EMILY TURNS TO THE LADY.

EMILY: You can vouch for me, can't you?

THE LADY SHRUGS. EMILY STOPS A CHILD PASSING BY ON A SKATEBOARD.

EMILY: You, child – you know I'm a lady, don't you?

CHILD: No.

THE CHILD EXITS.

EMILY: (CALLING TO A MAN FAR AWAY ON THE BEACH) You, man on the beach. You know I'm a lady, don't you?

MAN: (SHOUTS) No. You're a bloke.

EMILY: I am a lady and my name is Emily Howard – look!

EMILY TAKES OFF HER WIG AND POINTS TO THE LABEL AT THE BACK.

Isn't it lovely being a lady?

I am one.

EPISODE

EMILY: 'Emily Howard'. (EMILY PUTS THE WIG BACK ON AT AN ANGLE) Good day!

EMILY MARCHES OFF, BLOWING A RASPBERRY AND MAKING A V-SIGN IN THE DIRECTION OF THE MAN SHE CALLED OUT TO.

WORLD RECORD ATTEMPT — WORLD'S SMALLEST ANT

INT. CONFERENCE CENTRE. IAN 1 IS LOOKING INTO A GLASS TANK ON A PLINTH. HE IS WEARING A SWEATSHIRT WITH THE WORDS, 'WORLD'S SMALLEST ANT'. THERE IS A BANNER IN THE BACKGROUND WITH THE SAME WORDS ON IT.

IAN 1: Um, it doesn't seem to be here.

IAN 2: Yeah. Must have crawled out.

IAN 1: Well it'll be in here somewhere.

IAN 2: Yeah.

THE PAIR GET DOWN ON THEIR KNEES AND START SEARCHING FOR IT.

TOM V/O: So we reach the end of another episode of 'Little Britain'. If you have enjoyed this programme you may like to know that there are other programmes available to watch on televizzion. Such as the news, cartoons, and magazine programmes. Goodboo.

Marjorie's shopping list

Ryvita
Fat-free cottage cheese
A stick of celery
Low-calorie lettuce
Reduced-fat water
Chicken breast
        Chicken nipple
A tomato
Half an apple
Grain of rice
A pea
A smell of melon
A look at a grapefruit
    (but not to buy)
Dust

Sainsbury's Cuisine

South...
176 ...

TELEPHONE...
VAT NUMBER...

4 X DANISH PASTRIES
LARD (3 FOR 2)
2 LITRES CREAM   £4.80
VICTORIA SPONGE   £3.69
WALNUT WHIP X 24   £7.31
CRISPS, READY SALTED   £0.30
CRISPS, CHEESE 'N' ONION   £7.60
CRISPS, PRAWN COCKTAIL   £0.47
CRISPS, SALT 'N' VINEGAR   £0.47
CRISPS, ROAST CHICKEN   £0.47
CRISPS, WORCESTER SAUCE   £0.47
CRISPS, BEEF   £0.47
CRISPS, SOUR CREAM AND CHIVE   £0.47
CRISPS, SALMON AND NUTMEG   £0.47
CRISPS, EGG AND CRESS   £0.47
CRISPS, MUD   £0.47
CHAMBOURCEY HIPPOPOTAMOUSSE   £0.47
(MULTIBUY)
FRIED BUTTER   £7.33
BAILEY'S (BUY ONE GET ONE FREE)   £1.62
BAILEY'S (BUY ONE GET ONE FREE)   £14.99
BAILEY'S (BUY ONE GET ONE FREE)   £14.99
WALLS' MAGNUM X 58   £14.99
BIRDSEYE CHICKEN DIPPERS   £29.00
BACON RIND   £2.99
BLACK PUDDING   £0.23
BLACK BETTY   £1.75
BAM-A-LAM   £4.49
TRIPE   £7.99
OFFAL   £0.10
BIRDSEYE POTATO WAFFLES (THEY'RE   £0.05
WAFFLE-Y VERSATILE) X 48
DIET COKE, 2 LTR
*REFUND: DIET COKE 2 LTR   £19.99
COKE, 2 LTR   £0.89
DUST   £0.89

BALANCE DUE   £0.89
CASH   £0.79

TOTAL NUMBER OF ITEMS SOLD = 35   £151.06
                                           £155
CHANGE
Re-used Bags
....
                                           £3.94
                                           None
....

TOM V/O: Britain, Britain, Britain, land of diversity. There are hardback books and paperback books. Socks come in different lengths and eggs is cooked in a variety of ways. But how diverse are the people of Britain? We aim to find out by following the lives of ordinary British persons. Oh, my sweet lil' alleluia!

VICKY POLLARD — SOCIAL WORKER

EXT. ESTATE. A WOMAN CHATS TO A PREGNANT MAN, ADMIRING HIS BUMP.

INT. VICKY'S BEDSIT. A LADY IS SAT OPPOSITE VICKY.

TOM V/O: In her bedsit on this estate in Darkley Noone, young mother Vicky Pollard is meeting her social worker.

SOCIAL WORKER: So, how are you coping with everything, Vicky?

VICKY: No because there was this whole thing because the other day we was all in the park and we was all laughing because Nicola said she was gonna set fire to Candice's hair. But then Ryan Morris butted in who I hate and then we started getting off together and he phlegmed in my mouth and I was like 'Oh my God! I so can't believe you just done that!' Then there was this whole other thing, because you know Amanda Kaye, right? Well she told Ian Buchan she'd do it for a Creme Egg.

SOCIAL WORKER: So you're fine, good. And how's the baby?

VICKY: Fine!

SOCIAL WORKER: Well can I see her?

VICKY: It's not 'her', it's 'it'.

SOCIAL WORKER: Well can I see 'it'?

VICKY: No but yeah but no but yeah but no because we was all going to go down the offy but then they wouldn't serve us because Emma only looks about nine. So then we was going to go down Wimpy instead but then Liberty said she didn't want to go there 'cause she heard Tyrone was gonna be there so she went up the arcade with Sophie Bannerman instead but she was a complete bitch to do that because Sophie Bannerman is best friends with Vanessa and Vanessa told Tony that I fancy David Wu but everyone knows David Wu's got scabby legs.

Nobutyeahbutnobutyeahbutnobecause
wewasallgoingtogodowntheoffybutthen
theywouldn'tserveusbecauseEmmaonly
looksaboutnine.Sothenwewasgoingtogo
downWimpyinsteadbutthenLibertysaidshe
didn'twanttogothere'causesheheard
Tyronewasgonnabetheresoshewentup
thearcadewithSophieBannermaninsteadbut
shewasacompletebitchtodothatbecause
SophieBannermanisbestfriendswith
VanessaandVanessatoldTony
thatIfancyDavidWu
buteveryoneknows
DavidWu'sgot
scabbylegs.

SOCIAL WORKER: And the baby?

VICKY: I'm getting there! Oh my God, so oh no there was this whole thing 'cause Carmella's mum was going away so Carmella said she was gonna have a party but then her mum found out and said she couldn't have it but we said she had to have 'cause she'd said it now so she had it but I wasn't invited. So me and Jools who's a bit mental went round Michaela's house but she wasn't there she was at the party getting fingered by Jamie Stone, but anyway Kelly told Shaznay that Penny Webb's got hairy tits.

SOCIAL WORKER: Vicky, where is the baby?

VICKY: Swapped it for a Westlife CD.

SOCIAL WORKER: How could you do such a thing?

VICKY: I know, they're rubbish. (THE SOCIAL WORKER LOOKS AT VICKY DISAPPROVINGLY) Don't go giving me evils!

TOY SHOP 1

TOM V/O: Toys in Britain are sold in toy shops. This isn't a toy shop, it's a real shop.

A VICAR STEALS A CYCLE COURIER'S CYCLE FROM OUTSIDE THE SHOP.

ROY: Hello, are you looking for anything in particular?

MR MANN: Yes, I was wondering whether you had any pirate memory games suitable for children between the ages of four and eight?

ROY: Er, I'll just have a look. I can't see any here. One moment. (CALLS) Margaret? Margaret?

THERE IS A LONG PAUSE.

MARGARET (OFF-CAMERA): Yes?

ROY: There's a gentleman here wants to know if we've got any pirate memory games.

MR MANN: Ages four to . . .

ROY: Ages four to eight.

MARGARET (OFF-CAMERA): We should have some, over by the farm toys.

ROY EFFORTLESSLY FINDS A PIRATE MEMORY GAME.

ROY: Oh yes. Here we are. *Pieces of Eight*, a pirate memory game, ages four to eight.

MR MANN: Can I have a look?

ROY: There you go.

MR MANN: Match the pirates and find the treasure.

ROY: That's all right for you?

MR MANN: Have you got any other pirate memory games?

ROY: Um . . .

MR MANN: It's not quite what I had in mind.

ROY LOOKS.

I was wondering whether you had any pirate memory games suitable for children between the ages of four and eight?

ROY: I can't see any here. One moment. Margaret? Margaret?!

MARGARET (OFF-CAMERA)**:** What?

ROY: Have we got any other pirate memory games?

MARGARET (OFF-CAMERA)**:** What?

ROY: Have we got any other pirate memory games?

MARGARET (OFF-CAMERA)**:** No.

ROY: No.

MARGARET (OFF-CAMERA)**:** I think that's the only one they do.

ROY: She says she thinks that's the only one they do.

MARGARET (OFF-CAMERA)**:** What's wrong with that one?

ROY: What's wrong with that one?

MR MANN: I wanted something a little less piratey.

ROY: He wanted something a little less piratey.

MARGARET (OFF-CAMERA)**:** Oh, right. Has he tried Simmons?

ROY: Have you tried Simmons on the High Street?

MR MANN: Yes, I've just been there.

ROY: Oh, I don't know what to suggest.

MR MANN: Is there a shop near here that specializes in pirate memory games?

ROY: Er, I'm not sure. Margaret will know. One moment. Margaret? Margaret?! Is there a shop that specializes in pirate memory games?

MR MANN: Near here.

ROY: Near here?

MARGARET (OFF-CAMERA)**:** I don't think there are any in the local area, no.

ROY: She says she doesn't think there are any in the local area, no.

MR MANN: OK, I'll, er, I'll just wait.

MR MANN STANDS AND WAITS.

MARJORIE DAWES/FATFIGHTERS — PAUL

TOM V/O: Meanwhile, the fatties arrive for their weekly meeting.

INT. FATFIGHTERS. VARIOUS GROUP MEMBERS ARRIVE. MARJORIE WAITS AND APPROACHES
PAUL AS HE ENTERS.

MARJORIE: Paul, can I just, er, have a quick word please?
Paul, what happened last night was just a one-off. OK?

PAUL: Yeah, I was gonna say something.

MARJORIE: Yeah, I don't know what came over me.

PAUL: I think I had a bit too much to drink.

MARJORIE: Yeah, I had more, but whatever, it's not gonna happen again.
OK? So let's just try and forget about it and not let it come into the
meeting. All right?

PAUL NODS AND SITS WITH THE GROUP.

MARJORIE: OK, welcome to FatFighters. Now today we're going to be
talking about motivation. You all need a little bit more motivation, so

what we're gonna do, we're gonna start with a little exercise. Now I want everybody to close their eyes. Close your eyes. (THE GROUP DO SO) Yeah. Empty your thoughts – that's it, yeah. And picture yourself naked. Not nice, is it?! Eh? Now who the hell would want a great lump like that huffing and puffing away on top of them all night? (PAUSE) Eyes closed, Paul.

OK, welcome to FatFighters. Now today we're going to be talking about motivation. You all need a little bit more motivation, so what we're gonna do, we're gonna start with a little exercise. Now I want everybody to close their eyes. Close your eyes. Yeah. Empty your thoughts — that's it, yeah.

And picture yourself naked. Not nice, is it?! Eh? Now who the hell would want a great lump like that huffing and puffing away on top of them all night? Eyes closed, Paul.

EPISODE

LOU AND ANDY — PAINTING ANDY'S ROOM

TOM V/O: In Herby, Lou Todd has kindly offered to paint his friend Andy's bedroom.

INT. ANDY'S BEDROOM. ANDY SITS IN HIS WHEELCHAIR, AS LOU — IN HIS ORANGE BOILER SUIT — KNEELS BESIDE HIM.

LOU: Now, are you sure you want red?

ANDY: Yeah.

LOU: 'Cause I've got a very nice blue here – you like blue.

ANDY: Yeah, I know.

LOU: But you'd rather have red?

ANDY: Red, yeah.

LOU: Well, you did ask for red last time, and then you said you didn't like it. You said it was oppressive. You said red was the colour of blood and henceforth death.

ANDY: Yeah, I know.

LOU: So what's it to be?

ANDY: Red.

LOU: Yeah, but I'm not painting it once and then having to do it again because you say you don't like it, because that's a right kerfuffle.

ANDY: I know.

LOU: So final choice, red?

ANDY: Red. Yeah.

LATER THE WHOLE ROOM IS NEARLY FINISHED IN RED.

LOU: Do you want to do the last little bit?

ANDY: Yeah.

LOU: OK. Here we go.

LOU WHEELS ANDY TO THE WALL AND HELPS HIM PAINT THE LAST BIT.

LOU: There, it's finished.

ANDY: I don't like red.

LOU CAN'T SPEAK. ANDY THROWS THE ROLLER ON THE FLOOR.

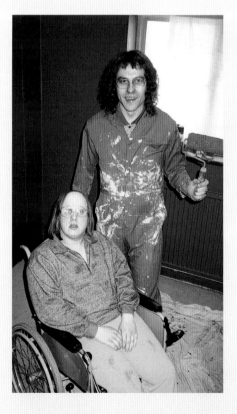

LEN BOOTHE – POVE VILLAGE TOURS

TOM V/O: For twenty years now, Len Boothe has been taking visitors on his tour of the charming village of Pove.

EXT. VILLAGE LANE. A COACH WITH 'POVE VILLAGE TOURS' DRIVES PAST.

INT. COACH. LEN, A SIDE-BURNED MAN IN HIS MID-FIFTIES ADDRESSES A GROUP OF TOURISTS.

LEN: OK, ladies and gents. First up, on your right, is St Robin's Church. The church was built in 1508, although there was actually a fire here in 1812 and the original wooden roof was destroyed. It's a funny thing actually. I will always have fond memories of that church, because it was on that bench there that me and my wife Eileen first kissed. And we've been married thirty-two year this year.

THE VISITORS APPLAUD.

LEN: Thank you very much. Now next up is the, The Hanging Judge, which is actually the oldest pub in Pove. Dates back to we think 1604. Why it's called The Hanging Judge no one seems to know. Incidentally, just in the beer garden by the swings is where Eileen first permitted me to have a little go on her breasts. (PAUSE) OK. We're coming up now to the Old Bridge, which actually goes back to Roman times. And it was actually underneath this bridge that my wife first performed an act of oral love upon me.

(PAUSE). A LADY GOES TO LIGHT A CIGARETTE.

LEN: Sorry, it's a no-smoking vehicle, love. OK. (PAUSE) Now we are coming up to one of the oldest blacksmiths' in the country. Legend has it that Charles the First stopped off there to get his horses' shoes changed. And it was just down that path there that I first took Eileen up the wrong-un. Moving on . . .

EPISODE

And it was actually underneath this bridge that my wife first . . .

DAFFYD — GAY NIGHT

TOM V/O: Meanwhile, at this pub in Llandewi Breffi, the glasses are being collected early because it's a special night.

EXT. PUB. THE LANDLADY COLLECTS THE MINERS' SPECTACLES.

INT. PUB. IT IS EMPTY BUT FOR DAFFYD AND MYFANWY. THERE ARE STREAMERS, BALLOONS AND A BANNER THAT READS 'DAFFYD'S GAY NIGHT'.

DAFFYD: Oh Myfanwy, these crisps are cheese 'n' onion!

MYFANWY: Oh. Do gay people not like cheese 'n' onion?

DAFFYD: Well I don't and I am a gay.

MYFANWY: I'll open the barbecue beef.

DAFFYD: If you wouldn't mind.

MYFANWY: I think you're gonna get a big crowd in tonight.

DAFFYD: I'd be very surprised if anybody turned up at all, Myfanwy. Everybody knows I am the only gay in this village.

MYFANWY: So you keep saying.

DAFFYD: Well, it's five to eight. There's no one here. I might as well go home now.

MYFANWY: But it's still early. And it says eight o'clock on the posters.

DAFFYD: I don't know why I bother putting on this gay night. It was doomed from the start. Well, Myfanwy, I imagine I'll always be the only gay in the village. Good night to you.

HE OPENS THE DOOR AND A CROWD OF GAY-LOOKING PEOPLE SURGE IN.

DAFFYD: Get back! Get back! Get back, you gay bastards! (DAFFYD PUSHES THEM BACK AND LOCKS THE DOOR) There's hundreds of 'em! What am I going to do?!

MYFANWY: Well let them in!

DAFFYD: Oh no, Myfanwy, get rid of them!

MYFANWY: I'll do no such thing. You made your gay bed, now lie in it.

DAFFYD: Myfanwy!

Get back! Get back! Get back, you gay bastards!

MYFANWY: Daffyd.

DAFFYD OPENS THE DOOR ON THE LATCH.

DAFFYD: Quiet! *Liza Minnelli*! (THE MOB IMMEDIATELY GO QUIET) Thank you.
Now, er, I'm very sorry, gays, but I'm afraid gay night has been cancelled.

GAYS: Oh no. No!

DAFFYD: Yes, I've, I've just had a letter from the council saying that there's only one gay allowed in Llandewi Breffi and that's me. So if you could all return to your neighbouring villages please.

THE GAYS PROTEST, BUT LEAVE.

MYFANWY: Oh Daffyd, you bloody fool!

DAFFYD: What?

MYFANWY: Think of all the cock and bum fun you could have had. That's the last time I close my pub for one of your gay nights!

DAFFYD: Oh I see, you've got something against gay people have you?

EDWARD AND SAMANTHA — PARENTS' EVENING 1

TOM V/O: Samantha Grant recently upset her parents by marrying her former teacher. In an effort to clear the air, she has invited them round for dinner.

INT. LIVING ROOM. EDWARD IS MARKING SOME EXERCISE BOOKS. SAMANTHA POTTERS.

EDWARD: What time are your parents coming?

SAMANTHA: Any minute now and I can't find the napkin rings.

EDWARD: Calm down, Samantha.

SAMANTHA: I just want everything to be right, that's all.

EDWARD: Look, I may have been your teacher, but we're just like any other couple.

THEY KISS. THE DOORBELL RINGS, SAMANTHA GOES TO ANSWER IT.

EDWARD: The bell is a signal for me, not you.

SAMANTHA: I'll just put the veg on.

EDWARD OPENS THE DOOR TO SAMANTHA'S PARENTS, ADRIAN AND JEANETTE.

EDWARD: Ah, Mr and Mrs Hughes. Please, come in. Come in.

ADRIAN: Ah, thank you.

EDWARD: Please, sit down. (EDWARD PUTS A SIGN ON DISPLAY THAT READS 'MR GRANT' AND SEARCHES THROUGH SOME EXAM PAPERS) Right, Samantha, Samantha, Samantha. Samantha, Samantha Carver, ah, yes. Samantha Grant. Yes. I mean overall it's been a good three months of marriage for Samantha, um, she's a very clever girl. She's got a lot to say for herself, sometimes a little too much. And her work can sometimes be a little slapdash.

ADRIAN: What do you mean?

EDWARD: Well, um, take this for example. I mean she's dusted it, obviously at the last minute, and she's missed around the edges. So I had to give her six out of ten. Er, could you bring in the wine now please, Samantha. (SAMANTHA DASHES IN) Walk, don't run!

SAMANTHA: Sorry, still cooking.

JEANETTE: Smells lovely, dear. Oh, we've missed you pet.

SAMANTHA KISSES HER PARENTS.

SAMANTHA: Hello, Dad.

ADRIAN: Hello, stranger.

Ah, c'est formidable.
Samantha's very good at oral.

EDWARD: How might one order a bottle of wine in France? Samantha?

SAMANTHA: Oh, 'Une bouteille de vin, s'il vous plaît'.

EDWARD: Ah, c'est formidable. Samantha's very good at oral.

BERNARD CHUMLEY — UNDERTAKER

TOM V/O: Meanwhile, it is a sad day at Sandi Toksvig House.

INT. FLATS. AN UNDERTAKER ARRIVES AT A FLAT WITH BEARERS AND COFFIN. HE KNOCKS ON THE DOOR, SIR BERNARD OPENS IT WEARING A BLACK WIG.

UNDERTAKER: We're very sorry for your loss.

SIR BERNARD: Thank you. Do come in.

THEY GO IN.

SIR BERNARD: She's just through there. It sounds awful to say, but in a way it's a relief.

UNDERTAKER: Yes.

SIR BERNARD: She'd been very ill for many years and we'd had so many scares. So in the end it was just very peaceful.

MAN: Mr Garfield.

UNDERTAKER: Yes?

MAN: Can you come in here please a moment?

UNDERTAKER: Excuse me.

SIR BERNARD: Of course.

THEY GO INTO ANOTHER ROOM, LEAVING SIR BERNARD ALONE.

SIR BERNARD: Come on, Bernard. Kitty wouldn't want you to cry.

THE MEN RETURN.

UNDERTAKER: Mr Chumley?

SIR BERNARD: Yes?

UNDERTAKER: She's not dead.

SIR BERNARD: No, I know. Any chance you could take her anyway?

THE UNDERTAKER GLARES AT SIR BERNARD. THEY TAKE THE COFFIN BACK OUT. HE HEARS BANGING FROM NEXT DOOR.

SIR BERNARD: Yes. All right, Kitty!

She's not dead.

MATTHEW WATERHOUSE — BOARD GAMES

EXT. OUTSIDE A FACTORY A MAN IS CHATTING AWAY TO ANOTHER 'MAN' WHO TURNS OUT TO BE A DUMMY
WHICH KEELS OVER.

TOM V/O: Over ten board games are sold every day in Britain. The most popular
are 'Ask Alan', 'Frobisher's Fingers', and 'Pigdog'.

INT. OFFICE. A MAN SITS AT HIS DESK. WATERHOUSE BURSTS IN.

MATTHEW: This is the big one. It's called 'Snakes and Snakes'.

MANAGER: Right.

MATTHEW: You know 'Snakes and Ladders'?

MANAGER: Yeah.

MATTHEW: Well, it's like 'Snakes and Ladders', but with snakes.

MANAGER: Right.

WATERHOUSE PULLS OUT A HOME-MADE GAMES BOARD.

MATTHEW: There is a snake on every square, devilishly difficult – no one's ever finished it.
How's that for starters? Got another one. 'Milk Round'.

WATERHOUSE PRODUCES ANOTHER BOARD, DICE, GAME PIECES, ETC.

MANAGER: Right. How does 'Milk Round' work?

MATTHEW: You are a milkman delivering milk, or a woman, to a house from your van,
or a flat. Right. You be the milk bottle, I will be the loaf of bread. Right, pick a card.

THE MANAGER DOES SO.

MANAGER: Er . . .

MATTHEW: What's it say?

MANAGER: Two pints of milk please.

MATTHEW: Right, what that means is: please, two pints of milk, please, for house number one,
right. Roll the dice. (WATERHOUSE SHAKES SOME DICE, AS IF ABOUT TO ROLL. PAUSE) I said roll the dice.

MANAGER: Oh, sorry.

THE MANAGER ROLLS.

Well, it's like 'Snakes and Ladders', but with snakes.

MATTHEW: Six, ignore it. Right, what are you again?

MANAGER: Er, I think I'm the milk bottle.

MATTHEW: I wanted to be the milk bottle.

MANAGER: Right, well this is all very interesting.

MATTHEW: Right, got another one.

GETS A PIECE OF WOOD OUT.

MATTHEW: 'Scratch Wood Scratch'. (WATERHOUSE SCRATCHES IT) Your go.

MANAGER: No. I don't even know what the . . . I don't know.

THE MANAGER SHRUGS AND SCRATCHES THE PIECE OF WOOD.

MATTHEW: Well I've never seen that move before! Let me just check the rule book. (WATERHOUSE FLICKS THROUGH A THICK BOOK. PAUSE) Yeah, you've won. You're a clever one, I'll give you that. Right, got another one. 'Throw Baby, Catch Baby'.

MANAGER: Right.

MATTHEW: But you need a real baby.

MANAGER: No.

MATTHEW: Cards?

MANAGER: No.

MATTHEW: Fighting?

MANAGER: How can I put this? I'm very sorry, there seems to have been some sort of misunderstanding here. Um, we are not a games manufacturer. You do know that?

MATTHEW: Yeah.

MANAGER: And we've never made games here. We import tyres – you do know that?

MATTHEW: Yeah. Your point being?

KELSEY GRAMMAR SCHOOL

TOM V/O: At Kelsey Grammar School, a new term is beginning.

INT. CLASSROOM. THE TEACHER ENTERS. THE CLASS STANDS.

TEACHER: You may sit. Right, let me introduce myself. My name is Mr Cleaves, and I will be teaching you biology.

THE TEACHER WRITES 'MR WELLS, FRENCH' ON THE BLACKBOARD.

EDWARD AND SAMANTHA - PARENTS' EVENING 2

INT. LIVING ROOM. EDWARD AND SAMANTHA AND SAMANTHA'S PARENTS, ADRIAN AND JEANETTE, ARE EATING DINNER.

EDWARD: . . . and he never took an assembly again.

HE LAUGHS AT HIS OWN JOKE.

JEANETTE: This sorbet is delicious. Did you make it yourself?

SAMANTHA: Yes, with a little help from Nigella.

EDWARD: What?

SAMANTHA: I got it out of Nigella Lawson's book.

EDWARD: You copied it from Nigella?

SAMANTHA: Well . . .

EDWARD: You took the work of another girl and passed it off as your own?
Right, in the bin!

HE THROWS AWAY THE DESSERT.

There we are. I think it's wonderful they still do this free milk.

ADRIAN: I was enjoying that.

EDWARD: Yes, well, no one likes a cheat.

EDWARD LEAVES.

SAMANTHA: Sorry about that. He doesn't always treat me like I'm still at school.

EDWARD (OFF-CAMERA)**:** Coffee anyone?

SAMANTHA: Oh, yes please, darling, that would be lovely.

ADRIAN: Yes, please. Thank you.

EDWARD RETURNS WITH COFFEE FOR THREE. HE PUTS A SMALL BOTTLE OF MILK IN FRONT OF SAMANTHA.

EDWARD: There we are. I think it's wonderful they still do this free milk.

SANDRA AND RALPH — WAITING ROOM

TOM V/O: Child labour is thankfully alive and well in Britain. Today some child actors are auditioning for a production of *Bugsy Malone*.

INT. WAITING ROOM. PARENTS AND CHILDREN ARE WAITING FOR THEIR AUDITION. SANDRA BRINGS UP SOME PHLEGM INTO A TISSUE AND WIPES RALPH'S FACE.

MELANIE: James Wilton and Ralph Patterson.

SANDRA: It's 'Raif'. (TO RALPH) No pressure, but if you don't get it, we'll have to sell the rabbit.

RALPH: OK, Mum, I'll do my best.

SANDRA: OK, good luck, love. Oh, don't forget your tap shoes and tell them your cousin was on 'Double Dare'.

RALPH GOES INTO THE AUDITION ROOM. SANDRA EDGES OVER TO MITCH.

SANDRA: (TO ANOTHER PARENT, MITCH) Does your boy go up for much?

MITCH: Oh, no no, this is his first, you know, apart from the school play like.

SANDRA: Oh, so he's not at stage school?

MITCH: Oh no no, just normal school.

SANDRA: He don't stand a chance then. (SANDRA SITS NEXT TO MITCH) What you gotta do is you got to get him into a stage school.

MITCH: Are they not quite dear?

SANDRA: Yeah, but you gotta make sacrifices. Look, I sold me shoes. And I'm on the game. Just so Raif can go to Italia Conti.

MITCH: So it's good then?

SANDRA: Oh it's worth every penny. He got down to the last twelve for Dairylea, and he had a callback for 'Bodger and Badger'.

MITCH: Really?

SANDRA: Yes, I'm not a liar!

MITCH: Well, er, thanks for all your advice like.

SANDRA: Of course, we always knew he was going to be an actor, ever since before he was born, yeah. He's so talented. They say he gets it from me.

MITCH: Right.

SANDRA: Of course I would have loved to have gone to a stage school, but my mother wasn't prepared to make the sacrifices I've made. Still, she's blind now – that gives me some comfort. So are you single, or . . .?

MELANIE ENTERS, WITH THE TWO BOYS.

MELANIE: Mr Wilton, we'd like to recall James for this afternoon. Mrs Patterson, thank you, you are free to go.

MITCH: Well done, lad.

SANDRA: Yeah, well done. Really really well done!

SANDRA SCRATCHES JAMES'S FACE.

JAMES: Argh!

JAMES STARTS TO CRY.

SANDRA: Oh, is he all right?

MITCH: He's bleeding!

SANDRA: Oh, he won't be Bugsy Malone now will he? Come on, better luck next time, eh.

MITCH: Oh. Crazy! You'll be all right. Are you OK? Let's have a look, let's have a look. Oh dear. Oh dear, we'll go and get it cleaned up, right, we'll get it cleaned up.

IN THE BACKGROUND WE SEE SANDRA SEVERELY REPRIMANDING HER SON.

SEBASTIAN AND MICHAEL – HOTEL

TOM V/O: It's party conference time and late at night, in his hotel room, the Prime Minister is making some final changes to his big speech. I love party conferences, they're brilliant! I've got them all on video.

INT. HOTEL SUITE. MICHAEL, SEBASTIAN AND TWO AIDES ARE HAVING A MEETING.

MICHAEL: That all seems fine. Just punch out the stuff about education reform. Let's, let's call it a night.

ADVISER 1: OK. Well, we'll get to work on that and we'll see you in the conference hall in the morning. Good night, Prime Minister.

MICHAEL: Good night.

THEY GO.

SEBASTIAN: Oh, I thought they'd never leave!

THE PRIME MINISTER IS SURPRISED THAT SEBASTIAN HASN'T LEFT WITH THEM.

MICHAEL: Is there something else you wanted to talk about?

SEBASTIAN: Not really, no. Oh, I'm shattered.

HE SLUMPS ON THE SOFA. THE PHONE RINGS.

MICHAEL: It's probably the Japanese Prime Minister, would you mind?

SEBASTIAN: Can I just use your loo?

MICHAEL: Yes.

SEBASTIAN: Thank you.

SEBASTIAN DISAPPEARS INTO THE EN-SUITE.

MICHAEL: Kazuko, 'Koninichiwa'. Yes, yes, it's coming along. Look, I've got the treaty right here. What exactly are your objections to it?

SEBASTIAN COMES OUT OF THE BATHROOM IN A BATHROBE CLEANING HIS TEETH.

MICHAEL: Yeah, no, I do realize it's a very sensitive issue for your people. Yeah. No, no, I appreciate your concerns about the second clause. Well perhaps we could look at making an amendment that everybody would agree with.

SEBASTIAN STRIPS OFF AND GETS INTO BED.

MICHAEL: Yes. No, I shall be meeting with the Cabinet tomorrow and I think we'll get a much clearer picture of where we are. No, I think it's, it's very nearly there, it's just a couple of details isn't it? Hmm? No, I, I take it you'll be at the summit on the fifteenth? Well I think it's very important that we have it resolved before –

SEBASTIAN PICKS UP THE EXTENSION PHONE.

SEBASTIAN: Are you guys going to be long?

MICHAEL TURNS ROUND. SEBASTIAN PATS THE BED.

SEBASTIAN: He'll call you back.

SEBASTIAN PUTS THE PHONE DOWN AND LIFTS THE BED COVER.

SEBASTIAN: Be gentle with me, Prime Minister.

LOU AND ANDY — NEW WHEELCHAIR

TOM V/O: At his home in Herby, Andy is busy eating his own body weight in nuts.

INT. ANDY'S LIVING ROOM. ANDY IS WATCHING TELLY AND EATING NUTS. LOU ENTERS, PUSHING IN A NEW WHEELCHAIR.

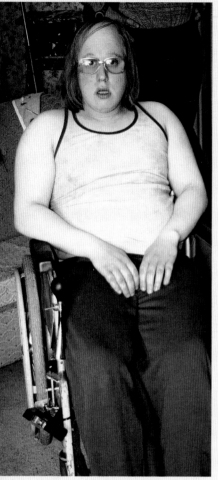

LOU: What are you watching, *Monster Trucks*?

ANDY: *Monster Trucks*, yeah.

LOU: Well, I have got something rather special for you.

ANDY: What is it?

LOU: It's the new chair you wanted.

ANDY: Yeah, I know.

LOU: I had to go all the way down to Cranmouth for it – it was a right kerfuffle. Right, let's, let's pop you in it. (PAUSE) (LOU STRUGGLES TO LIFT ANDY) One, two, aaah! That's got you, that's got you, that's got you. That's got you, that's got you.

ANDY: I don't like it.

LOU: Give it a chance.

ANDY: I wanna get out.

LOU: Well maybe you just need a cushion or something. Look, I'll go and pop your tea on and then I'll come back and sort it out.

WHILE LOU IS OUT OF THE ROOM ANDY GETS OUT OF THE WHEELCHAIR. HE TIPS THE NEW ONE OVER AND GETS BACK INTO HIS OLD ONE.

LOU (OFF-SCREEN)**:** Everything all right?

ANDY: Yeah, fine.

TOY SHOP 2

INT. TOY SHOP. MR MANN IS STILL WAITING FOR HIS PIRATE MEMORY GAME.

MARGARET (OFF-CAMERA)**:** Roy?

ROY: Yes, Margaret?

MARGARET (OFF-CAMERA)**:** Is the pirate memory game man still there?

ROY: Yes, Margaret.

MARGARET (OFF-CAMERA)**:** Because I think I've found something.

ROY: Oh.

HE GOES TO THE BACK AND RETURNS WITH A DUSTY OLD BOX.

ROY: Oh my word, how funny. 'Cap'n Jack's Pirate Memory Game', ages – oh, how funny – ages four to eight. And it does look a little less piratey than the other one.

MARGARET (OFF-CAMERA)**:** Well, what does he reckon?

ROY: Well, what do you reckon?

PAUSE.

MR MANN: Can I have a look at the other one again?

ROY: Yes, of course – there you go.

PAUSE.

MR MANN: And how much is this one again?

ROY: They both retail at £4.95.

MR MANN: Oh.

ROY: Oh, is there a problem?

MR MANN: I was hoping to spend around £4.80. I'll be getting some money for me birthday next week. I'll buy it then.

ROY: Yes.

MR MANN SIGHS AND CONTINUES TO STAND THERE WAITING.

JASON AND NAN – SHOPPING

EXT. JIM SWEENEY HOUSE. JASON AND GARY APPROACH NAN'S FLAT, WITH SHOPPING BAGS.

TOM V/O: Sheltered accommodation is where people who are too old and lazy to do things for themselves are kept.

JASON: Do I look all right?

GARY: Yeah, you look fine.

GARY RINGS THE DOORBELL.

JASON: So, no Granddad in the frame?

GARY: No, no he died ten years ago.

JASON: Oh great . . . great shock that must have been.

THE DOOR OPENS. NAN IN HER NIGHTIE IS STANDING IN THE CORRIDOR.

NAN: Oh hello, love.

GARY: Hello. Nan.

NAN: Sorry to keep you. Me hip's playing up again.

GARY: You remember Jason?

NAN: Yes.

NAN IS SEEN IN SOFT FOCUS, WITH MAKE-UP, ETC. MUSIC.

JASON: Hello.

JASON SNOGS NAN.

NAN: Oh! Mind my bag, it's nearly full.

GARY: We've got your shopping.

NAN: Oh you are good. Come in. Come in.

NAN: I'm sorry I'm in my nightie.

JASON: That's all right. You've got the figure for it.

NAN: Oh thanks.

GARY: We'll, we'll just put these away for you.

GARY GOES TO PUT THE SHOPPING AWAY.

JASON: Oh thanks.

GARY (SARCASTIC)**:** Cheers.

JASON SHUTS THE DOOR.

NAN: Thanks for helping with the shopping. You are a good boy.

JASON: I can be a bad boy sometimes. It's hot in here.

NAN: I like it nice and warm.

JASON: Workin' up quite a sweat.

JASON TAKES OFF HIS TRACKSUIT TOP.

NAN: You couldn't pass me that pouffe could you dear? Me feet are killing me.

JASON PROPS UP NAN'S FEET AND PULLS OFF HER SLIPPERS. HE STARTS TO MASSAGE HER FEET.

JASON: Oh baby. Is that nice?

NAN: Oh yeah.

JASON: What about here?

NAN: Hmm.

HE STARTS TO SUCK HER TOES. THE DOOR OPENS AND GARY COMES IN.

GARY: Don't know if you wanted sugar, Jase – (GARY SURVEYS THE SCENE) What's going on?

JASON LOOKS UP IN PANIC.

JASON: It's not what it looks like.

GARY: Get out, Get out!

AS JASON LEAVES HE MOUTHS 'CALL ME' TO NAN.

NAN: Is he a trained chiropodist?

EDWARD AND SAMANTHA — FILLING IN

EDWARD AND SAMANTHA ARE LYING IN BED.

EDWARD: Oh, I forgot to say, I won't be here tomorrow night. Mr Jackson will be filling in for me.

WORLD RECORD ATTEMPT — WORLD'S LARGEST MINCE PIE

INT. CONFERENCE HALL. THE TWO IANS HAVE MADE A HUGE MINCE PIE THAT IS FAR TOO BIG FOR THE OVEN.

IAN 1: Right, I think that's ready to go in the oven now.

IAN 2: Got it, got it. Oh, I've got it, I've got it. Got it, got it. Yeah, yeah. Bit lower. Try it round this way.

CREDITS ROLL...

TOM V/O: And so we have reached the end of this evening's television programme. And what a remarkable array of Britons we've met. My favourites were the little kicking boy, Beefy Bill and Dicky Snapples – the dwarf who hides apples. Until next time, goodbive.

Thursday 5th July

Dear Diary,

As I write these words one's head is spinning from all the events of the day. Oh, what a glorious day it was. How I love this season, when all the pretty debutantes come out to play.

Today was the Henley Regatta. Being a lady, which I very much am, I awoke early with a wonderful morning glory and partook of my dainty ladies' breakfast - sausages, eggs, beans, hash browns, mushrooms and three Weetabix. After my ladies' morning bath in rosewater I had a shave and got dressed in all my ladies' finery - knickerbockers, petticoat, petite lace booties, a shawl, a bonnet, all the gear. Then I took the omnibus to the station. The driver was very rude and for some strange reason kept on calling me 'mate'. Upon arrival at the station I purchased a ladies' ticket to Henley and proceeded to find a ladies' seat. The ticket collector was a very queer fellow and insisted on addressing me as 'sir'. I suppose it takes all sorts!

I had a can of lager and a chunky KitKat on the train and arrived in Henley at eleven sharp. The weather was quite quite glorious. The sun was shining, the birds were singing and the water was glistening but I was dying for a shit so I had to find one of those Portaloo thingummyjigs. Then I went to observe the rowing. My, what strength these men have! I could never hope to row. I am a lady, you see, and I do ladies' things, like collect thimbles, wave at soldiers and arrange paper doilies on dressing tables.

After the races I placed my picnic blanket upon the ground and opened my Fortnum & Mason's ladies' hamper. Oh what delicacies laid within! A Peppuami and a pack of Cleavers. I could see lots of gentlemen staring at me. It was enough to make a lady blush, which I am – a lady, that is, not a blush. Some people were finding me so beautiful they actually moved away. After Luncheon I took a stroll over to the Stewards' tent and helped myself to a Pimms. There were lots of VIPs in there, including that actress I so admire and in many ways aspire to be, Helen Bonham Carter. Oh, the number of occasions I've marvelled at those Merchant Ivory costume dramas she's appeared in, like 'Fight Club' and 'Planet of the Apes.' In fact when I saw her in 'Planet of the Apes' I thought, 'She's never looked lovelier.' In real life, it occurred to me, She's quite hairy and for a moment I thought she might actually be a man dressed up as a lady – you do hear of such things. However when I put this to her she seemed most displeased.

Following my ejection from the tent, and by now, I confess, being not a little merry, I abandoned all my clothes and jumped into the river, which I think, on reflection, may have been a mistake. Like many ladies I suffer rather from an excess of back hair, which might explain the alarm my in flagrante appearance evidently caused. However, the police were very kind and I was released without charge within a few hours.

As I write to you now, I am tucked up at home, in bed, in my ladies' nightgown, with just a drop of my favourite tipple – a sweet sherry – and my pipe for company. Tomorrow is Ascot, and I will be sure to wake early in the morning for I must go into town and collect my hat from the milliner. I have requested an intricate design depicting scenes from the film '2 Fast 2 Furious.' Oh what a belle I shall be!

Emily Howard (a lady)

EPISODE *eight*

TOM V/O: Brighton, Brighton, Brigh– oh. Britain, Britain, Britain, birthplace of William Shakespeare, Mahatma Gandhi, and Big Bird. But what of the ordinary people of Britain? What about them and all their stuff? We aim to find out in what I promise is the final episode of this series. Oh my sweet potatoes!

EMILY HOWARD — ICE-CREAM VAN

EXT. SEA FRONT – AN ICE-CREAM VAN HAS STALLED. EMILY PASSES BY.

TOM V/O: Transvestism in Britain is as popular today as it has always been. I myself am currently wearing a lovely dress that used to belong to my father.

DRIVER: Oi, mate? (EMILY PRETENDS NOT TO HEAR) You in the skirt.

EMILY: Yes?

DRIVER: You couldn't give me a push could you?

EMILY: But I'm a lady.

DRIVER: Please?

EMILY: Ladies don't push.

DRIVER: Oh go on, pal.

EMILY: All right then. A little lady's push.

EMILY WEAKLY PUSHES THE VAN.

DRIVER: You couldn't push a bit harder could you?

EMILY: It sounds like you've flooded the engine.

DRIVER: Oh no, have I?

EMILY: Being a lady, I wouldn't really know, but it sounds like you've had the choke out too long.

DRIVER: Really?

EMILY: Oui oui. Ouvrez le bonnet.

All right then.

A little lady's push.

EMILY LOOKS UNDER THE BONNET, WHICH OBSCURES HER FACE. WE HEAR A MAN'S VOICE.

EMILY: Oh yeah, you've got a faulty connection with your starter motor.
(EMILY GOES UP TO THE DRIVER) Try it now.

THE VAN STARTS.

DRIVER: Oh, thanks.

EMILY: Pleasure's all mine.

DRIVER: You certainly know your stuff.

EMILY: I grew up with three brothers, so I suppose I am a bit of a tomboy!

DRIVER: Yeah, I bet you are.

HE DRIVES AWAY – EMILY WALKS OFF COQUETTISHLY.

DAFFYD – MYFANWY COMES OUT

EXT. PUB. NIGHT. ON ONE TABLE ARE THREE SCIENTISTS, IN WHITE COATS, WITH TEST TUBES, ETC.
A MINER EXITS THE PUB CARRYING A TRAY WITH THREE PINTS ON IT. HE JOINS THE OTHER MINERS.

TOM V/O: It's twenty to Toby and we're in Wales, which is apparently a part of Britain.

INT. PUB. DAFFYD SITS AT THE BAR READING A COPY OF BOY GEORGE'S AUTOBIOGRAPHY.

DAFFYD: Absolutely fascinating! It says in here Boy George is a gay. Can I have another Bacardi and Coke please, Myfanwy?

MYFANWY: Is it all right if Miss Fitzwilliams serves you, only I'm leaving now?

DAFFYD: Oh yes, where are you going?

MYFANWY: Well, I got a date see.

DAFFYD: Ooooh! Oh, a date. I'd love to go on a date, but I can't as I'm the only gay in the village.

MYFANWY: Yes, of course you are. Right, see you tomorrow.

DAFFYD: So, who's the lucky fellah?

MYFANWY: I don't want to miss my bus.

DAFFYD: No, come on, who is he?

MYFANWY: Well, I wasn't planning on telling you tonight, but I suppose you may as well know.
I'm actually going on a date with another woman.

DAFFYD: Oh I see – girls' night out is it?

MYFANWY: Look, Daffyd, I'll make no bones about it. I've actually been seeing this girl for a while now.

DAFFYD: What?

MYFANWY: I suppose I'm finally coming to terms with the fact that I am a lesbian. Ta-ra.

Just a bit of **fanny fun**.

MYFANWY HEADS FOR THE DOOR.

DAFFYD: Hang on just a minute.

MYFANWY: What?

DAFFYD: You are not a gay.

MYFANWY: I am.

DAFFYD: No, I'm the gay in this village.

MYFANWY: Well I'm gay too. Bye.

DAFFYD: Well let's just talk about this!

MYFANWY: Well, can we do it later, only Rhiannon's waiting for me?

DAFFYD: Rhiannon? Rhiannon? And how far have you gone with this Rhiannon?

MYFANWY: Just a bit of fanny fun.

DAFFYD: Can I have a large brandy please, Miss Fitzwilliams?

MYFANWY: Look, Daffyd, I got to go. Only Rhiannon's minge is going to get cold.

MYFANWY EXITS. MISS FITZWILLIAMS GIVES DAFFYD HIS DRINK.

MISS FITZWILLIAMS: There you go, Daffyd.

DAFFYD: Oh, thank you. So did you have any idea Myfanwy is a gay?

MISS FITZWILLIAMS: Not until she joined my lesbian pottery class, no.

DAFFYD SPITS OUT HIS DRINK.

BORIS THE BABYSITTER 1

TOM V/O: When it comes to getting ready to go out, women in Britain take on average six months longer than men. At this house in Quimby, woman Helen is finally ready.

INT. MIDDLE-CLASS LIVING ROOM. HELEN PUTS ON HER LIPSTICK IN THE MIRROR, NEXT TO A COT WHERE A BABY IS SLEEPING. HER HUSBAND PETER ENTERS.

HELEN: Ssh, he's just going off.

PETER: Come on, Helen, we're going to be late.

HELEN: All right. Well the babysitter isn't even here yet.

PETER: Is it Saskia again?

I will make sure nothing happens to your baby. I SWEAR ON YOUR LIFE

HELEN: No no, she wasn't available. The agency's sending somebody else. Are these shoes all right with this dress?

PETER: Yes, I told you, they're fine.

THE DOORBELL RINGS.

HELEN: Oh, at last.

SHE OPENS THE DOOR. BORIS, A GIANT BRUTE OF A MAN IS STANDING THERE. HE HAS A HEAVY EASTERN-EUROPEAN ACCENT.

HELEN: Are you the babysitter?

BORIS: Babysitter, yes.

HELEN: Have you done this before?

BORIS: Yes, I sit baby real good.

PETER CALLS OUT.

PETER: Bring her in.

BORIS ENTERS.

PETER: Oh. Hello. I'm Peter.

BORIS: Ah, Pietka. That was my mother's name.

BORIS KISSES PETER.

PETER: And you've, you've met my wife Helen.

BORIS: Ah, Helen, that was not my mother's name.

BORIS HUGS HELEN TIGHTLY.

HELEN: Actually darling, I'm not really feeling very well.

PETER: Oh come on, this is important. Everyone from the office is going to be there.

BORIS: Important, office, huh.

HELEN: All right.

PETER: Harvey's over here. He's fine at the moment, but any problems and our mobile numbers are on the table. So.

BORIS: I will make sure nothing happens to your baby. I swear on your life.

PETER: Oh, thank you.

EPISODE

BORIS: If anybody tries to hurt him.

HE MIMES THROAT SLITTING.

PETER AND HELEN: Well we, er, we shouldn't be too long. We won't be long, no.

BORIS: Sssh. Is nothing. You go, you go. Enjoy.

EXT. DRIVE. PETER AND HELEN GO TO THEIR CAR. HELEN'S MOBILE RINGS AND BORIS AND BABY APPEAR AT THE WINDOW.

HELEN: Hello?

BORIS (AT WINDOW)**:** Your baby is fine.

HELEN: Thank you.

BORIS (AT WINDOW)**:** If anything happens to your baby, I will phone you immediately.

HELEN: Thank you, Boris.

THE PHONE RINGS AGAIN.

HELEN: Hello?

BORIS (AT WINDOW)**:** Your baby is fine.

VICKY POLLARD — REFORMED CHARACTER

EXT. SCHOOL. IN THE PLAYGROUND, A FEW SMALL KIDS PLAY WITH A FOOTBALL. TWO TEACHERS RUN TOWARDS THEM, NICK THE BALL, AND START PLAYING THEIR OWN GAME.

SCHOOLMASTER: Right, give me the ball. Go and stand over there!

TOM V/O: Back at one of her old schools, reformed character Vicky Pollard has been asked to give a speech to her old classmates.

INT. CLASSROOM. VICKY STANDS NEXT TO MR COLLIER AT THE FRONT OF THE CLASSROOM, WITH HER PRAM.

MR COLLIER: OK gang. Now for today's General Studies, I've invited someone along who used to be a pupil at this school. Her name is Vicky Pollard. Some of you may remember her.

LAURA IS WEARING AN EYE PATCH. SHE LOOKS AT VICKY ACCUSINGLY.

VICKY: (MOUTHS) I said sorry!

MR COLLIER: Now I'm sure Vicky won't mind me saying that she used to be a bit of a tearaway. She got caught shoplifting, was sent to a young offenders' institution, became pregnant at fourteen, and had the baby taken into care. But, she's turned her life around, um, she's now got a job at Boots, a small flat, and is taking a part-time course in, what is it?

VICKY: Reading.

MR COLLIER: Reading. And she's here today to tell us all a little bit about her experiences. So, all right. Over to you, Vicky.

VICKY: (READS) Shut up I ain't done nuffin' and if anyone says I did they get beatings.

MR COLLIER: Right, thanks. Um. Has anybody got any questions they want to ask? Yeah, Jordan?

JORDAN: Yeah. What d'you nick?

VICKY: Shut up! I never nicked nuffin' apart from like one fing and like one ever fing and like a few other fings but apart from that I never nicked nuffin'. Have you been speaking to Wayne Duggan 'cause let me tell you about Wayne Duggan right. Wayne Duggan bunked off PE and went in the locker and took a slash all over Elliot Nathan's *brand new Adidas bag* and now Elliot Nathan said he's gonna tell the whole of year nine that Wayne Duggan sniffs highlighter pens.

MR COLLIER: OK. Let's have another one. Harmony?

HARMONY: Have you got a criminal record?

VICKY: Yeah but you just lie about it because you know Misha? Well she reckons her dad killed this man but he just lied and said he never and now he's got this really good job putting the jam in Jammy Dodgers.

MR COLLIER: OK. One more, yes, Dean?

Bonfires in Britain are a great way of getting rid of those old things lying around that you don't need any more. Only last week I found an old bonfire I never use and put that on the bonfire.

DEAN: What's borstal like?

VICKY: Oh my God it's like sooo brilliant. It's so much better than school 'cause there's no lessons or homework or nuffin' and like there's people getting beaten up and once this really funny fing happened because this girl got locked in the fridge and nearly died.

MR COLLIER: OK. Thanks a lot, Vicky. There's a lot for us to think about there and how we can apply it all to our own lives. Oh sorry, Kelly, did you have a question?

KELLY: Did you get that Tommy I asked you for?

VICKY CHUCKS KELLY A BOTTLE OF PERFUME.

VICKY: Anyone else wants anything, they can just let me know.

MR COLLIER: Thanks a lot, Vicky. Right, you can go.

VICKY: Go? Alright . . .

VICKY HEADS FOR THE DOOR.

MR COLLIER: Your baby?

VICKY: Huh? Oh, it's all right, you can keep it. I've got loads more at home anyway.

VICKY EXITS.

LOU AND ANDY – BONFIRE

TOM V/O: Bonfires in Britain are a great way of getting rid of those old things lying around that you don't need any more. Only last week I found an old bonfire I never use and put that on the bonfire.

EXT. ANDY'S BACK YARD. LOU IS GATHERING THINGS FOR THE BONFIRE. ANDY IS LOOKING ON FROM HIS WHEELCHAIR.

LOU: Right. This is the last of the boxes. Now are you sure you want all this stuff burnt?

ANDY: Yeah.

LOU: Got all your old books and your games in here – are you sure you don't want them?

ANDY: Yeah.

LOU: You want it all put on the fire?

ANDY: Yeah, burn it up.

LOU: Yeah. 'Cause once I burn it, you can't have it back, you do know that?

ANDY: Yeah, I know.

LOU: You want it all burnt?

ANDY: Yeah.

CUT TO: EXT. ANDY'S BACK YARD. THE PAIR WATCH AS ANDY'S BELONGINGS ARE BURNING.

ANDY: I want me stuff back.

BORIS THE BABYSITTER 2

INT. LIVING ROOM. BORIS HAS A BALALAIKA.

BORIS: So, my little friend, what shall we do?

BORIS DANCES AROUND WITH THE BABY. WE SEE A MONTAGE OF HIS CHILD CARE – WATCHING 'BATTLESHIP POTEMKIN', DOING A PUPPET SHOW WITH STALIN AND LENIN, SINGING, ETC.

BORIS: (SINGING) 'Babushka, Babushka.'

PETER AND HELEN RETURN.

HELEN (OFF-CAMERA)**:** Hello?

PETER (OFF-CAMERA)**:** We're here.

BORIS: Oh sssh. Baby sleeping.

HELEN: Oh. How has he been?

BORIS: He very hungry.

PETER: Right. What did you give him?

BORIS: Meat.

PETER: What kind of meat?

BORIS: Good meat.

HELEN: Did you give him any milk?

BORIS: Yes, he very thirsty baby.

HELEN: Oh. There was some milk in the fridge. Did you find that all right?

BORIS: No, I use my own.

HE CLUTCHES HIS BREAST.

PETER: Right. Did you, did you, did you have to change him?

BORIS: No, is same baby.

PETER: Right. Well, we were gone, what, about three hours, so is fifteen pounds OK?

Sssh.
Baby sleeping.

BORIS (EMOTIONAL)**:** Oh, thank you, thank you! Fifteen pounds! Where I come from, you have to babysit three hours to earn fifteen pounds. I will send it home to my mother.

HELEN: Oh, that's good.

BORIS: It is not good, she is dead.

HE CLOSES HELEN'S EYES.

HELEN: Oh. Well, it's getting rather late. I imagine you'll want to be getting back.

BORIS: Yes. If ever you need babysitter and Boris is not available, please remember, I have brother; Josef.

PETER: Oh yes?

BORIS: He is a very bad man, but he wants to be good in his heart.

PETER: Well we'll, er, we'll bear that in mind.

BORIS: Remember him!

PETER: We will, we will.

BORIS GOES TO LEAVE.

BORIS: Sssh.

BORIS EXITS. PETER AND HELEN RETURN TO THE COT.

PETER: Hello, Harvey.

HELEN: Oh, I think he's going to say something.

HARVEY: Comrade Stalin salutes you!

KELSEY GRAMMAR SCHOOL

TOM V/O: At Kelsey Grammar School in Flange, it is break time.

EXT. AS BEFORE, BREAK LASTS ABOUT TEN SECONDS.

INT. CLASSROOM. THE CLASS STAND.

TEACHER: Sit. (PAUSE) (THEY DO SO) Yesterday's test did not make for happy reading. Meacher. The answer to question two was Golden Wonder, not KP.

HE THROWS MEACHER THE BOOK.

TEACHER: Philips, how many times do you need to be told? Red for ready salted, blue for salt 'n' vinegar.

HE THROWS THE BOOK AT HIM.

TEACHER: Patel, the two variables on the graph were pickled onion and prawn cocktail.

HE THROWS THE BOOK BEHIND HIM.

TEACHER: Wilson, you could have had Cheese 'n' Owen or Smoky Beckham. There is no such flavour as Prawn Collymore.

THE CLASS LAUGH. HE THROWS THE BOOK DOWN.

TEACHER: Papathasaniou, please note Monster Munch is maize-based. This was all covered in the first term.

PAPATHASANIOU: I put maize.

THE TEACHER THROWS THE BOOK AT HIM FROM BETWEEN HIS LEGS.

TEACHER: Frazzles, Denton, not Quavers. They look like rashers, for Pete's sake. The clue is in the bag.

MORE BOOK THROWING.

TEACHER: Nash, you got ninety-five per cent – well done. I particularly enjoyed your diagram of a Wotsit.

THE BOOK GETS THROWN AND FALLS APART.

TEACHER: Irving, number five was Oxbow lakes, otherwise good.

THE TEACHER LOOKS UP.

TEACHER: Where is Irving?

NASH: He's having his tonsils out, sir.

HE THROWS THE BOOK OUT OF THE WINDOW. IT LANDS IN A HOSPITAL WARD, ON IRVING'S BED.

EPISODE

Nash, you got ninety-five per cent – well done. I particularly enjoyed your diagram of a Wotsit.

TEACHER: And finally, Palfrey, best before . . .?

CLASS: See base of pack.

TEACHER: Hmm.

THE TEACHER HOLDS THE BOOK OUT. PALFREY COMES TO COLLECT IT, BUT THE TEACHER THROWS IT INSTEAD.

RAY McCOONEY — TAX INSPECTOR

EXT. HOTEL. COUPLE LIE OUTSIDE ON SUNBEDS WEARING SWIMMING COSTUMES DESPITE BAD WEATHER.

TOM V/O: Weather-wise, the best time to visit Scotland is Tuesday 12th June, around 2.30.

A THUNDERSTORM IS RAGING OUTSIDE.

INT. HOTEL. RAY IS BEHIND HIS COUNTER. A DOUR-LOOKING INSPECTOR AND HIS FEMALE ASSISTANT ADDRESS RAY.

INSPECTOR: Mr McCooney, you have tax payments overdue of nearly twenty-four thousand pounds. Can you give us a cheque today?

RAY: Maybe I can and maybe I can't.

HE PLAYS THE FLUTE.

WOMAN: Please, we've had all of this last year, Mr McCooney. You've got to take this seriously.

RAY: Yeeeees.

WOMAN: Can you give us the cheque today?

RAY PLAYS 'WHO DO YOU THINK YOU ARE KIDDING MR HITLER?' ON THE PAN PIPES.

WOMAN: That's not the answer I'm looking for.

HE PLAYS 'LAST OF THE SUMMER WINE' ON THE MANDOLIN.

INSPECTOR: You'd help yourself a lot more, Mr McCooney, if you started giving us some straight answers. Your form here is incomplete. Gross income: yes. Net income: yes.

RAY: No, it's not 'yes', it's 'yeeeees'.

INSPECTOR: You can't just put down 'yeeeees'. You do know that, don't you?

RAY: Yes.

WOMAN: So, can you give us some payment today?

RAY: What if I were to offer you six magic beans?

HE DOES SO.

WOMAN: Probably wouldn't be interested.

RAY: Seven magic beans?

HE DOES SO.

WOMAN: Nope.

RAY: (INDICATES A RADIO) How about a talking noisy-box? Inside there are tiny sprites a-talkin' to you. But they cannae hear ye, mind, unless they're doing a phone-in.

WOMAN: No.

RAY: You want the piccalillo, don't you?

HE PLAYS THE FLUTE AGAIN.

RAY: You'll never take it! Never! Oh, have it, have it, and be gone!

INSPECTOR: I tell you what, Mr McCooney. Why don't you pick up your quill . . .

RAY: Yeeees.

HE PICKS UP A PEN.

INSPECTOR: And your magic money-paper.

RAY: Oh yes.

HE PICKS UP A CHEQUE BOOK.

INSPECTOR: Put your mark upon it.

RAY: Yeeeees.

HE SIGNS IT.

INSPECTOR: And we'll do the rest.

RAY: Yes, yes, yes, yes, yes.

HE HANDS THEM THE CHEQUE.

INSPECTOR: Good day.

RAY: Fare thee well, keepers of the purse.

THEY EXIT. HE PLAYS THE FLUTE. HE SUDDENLY REALISES WHAT HAS JUST HAPPENED.

RAY: Shit!

No, it's not 'yes', it's 'YEEEES'.

Make sure you get down every part of this, Miss Grace.

DAME SALLY MARKHAM

EXT. DAY. STATELY HOME SET IN ACRES OF LAND. A GARDENER IS TRIMMING A HEDGE IN THE SHAPE
OF A PAIR OF BREASTS.

TOM V/O: Country house, blah blah blah, novelist, blah blah blah, cue the
rude topiary.

INT. STATELY HOME. MISS GRACE IS TAKING DICTATION.

DAME SALLY: Make sure you get down every part of this, Miss Grace.

DAME SALLY MIMES TO THE RADIO.

RADIO VOICE 1: There's a tailback stretching a mile and a half, so avoid like
the plague. The Dartford Tunnel jam-packed as usual.

DAME SALLY: 'Said James.'

RADIO VOICE: . . . at twenty past. In the meantime, remember this?

DAME SALLY: (MIMES TO WHAM'S 'WAKE ME UP BEFORE YOU GO-GO') (SHE TURNS THE RADIO
DOWN) 'Said Lady Asquith.'

MARJORIE DAWES/FATFIGHTERS —
MRS HARRISON

EXT. COMMUNITY CENTRE. GUY FAWKES AND SOME ACCOMPLICES, IN FULL PERIOD COSTUME,
CARRYING BARRELS MARKED 'GUNPOWDER', EXIT THE BUILDING.

TOM V/O: It's all change at the community centre. One group has
finished their weekly meeting, whilst another is just beginning.
FatFighters meets once a week. Those in attendance have managed to
steal themselves away from eating for just an hour to talk about food.
The greedy fuckers!

INT. FATFIGHTERS. MARJORIE ADDRESSES THE GROUP.

MARJORIE: Or just some low-fat cottage cheese if you're a vegelesbian.
Now, before we go any further, I want to introduce you to a noo face.
She is a noo face. She is in fact from FatFighters head office. Now her
name is Mrs Harrison. Mrs Harrison has come here today to check that
I'm running the meetings OK. So you can all tell her how brilliant I am.
What happened? Did someone make a complaint or . . .?

MRS HARRISON: It could be one complaint, it could be a series of
complaints.

MARJORIE: Oh, right. Who was it? Was it him? (SHE POINTS AT PAUL) You can't say, you can't say. Was it her? (SHE POINTS AT MEERA) Was it written in Indian? You can't say. Bastards. Okay, let's start with the weigh-in. Paul, would you like to . . .

MRS HARRISON: Excuse me, Marjorie.

MARJORIE: Yes, Mrs Harrison?

MRS HARRISON: Haven't you forgotten something? The course leader weighs themselves first.

MARJORIE: Oh no, that's OK Mrs Harrison. I weighed myself at home to save time. (MRS HARRISON GLARES AT MARJORIE) Eight stone five. What? Right. Oh this? (MARJORIE POINTS TO THE SCALES) Oh sorry. Right. I'm sorry, wasn't sure. What, do I get up do I?

MARJORIE STANDS ON THE SCALES.

MRS HARRISON: You *were* fourteen stone and four pounds.

MARJORIE: Oh ho, I was big, wasn't I?

MRS HARRISON: You *are* fifteen stone and eleven pounds.

MARJORIE: Oh. Well, er . . .

MARJORIE TAKES HER SHOES OFF.

MEERA: You don't allow us to take shoes off.

MARJORIE: Yes, thank you, Miri. I don't know how you do things in India, but over here . . .

SHE STEPS BACK ON THE SCALES.

MRS HARRISON: Fifteen stone ten.

MARJORIE: See, it's dropping, dropping. This jacket's very very heavy. I don't need these.

SHE TAKES HER JACKET AND CULOTTES OFF.

MARJORIE: This can go.

SHE TAKES OFF HER BLOUSE.

MRS HARRISON: Fifteen stone eight and a half.

MARJORIE: Oh well, this has got a lot of underwiring. (SHE GOES TO UNDO HER BRA)

MRS HARRISON: Marjorie, I think we've seen enough.

PAUL: Yeah!

MRS HARRISON TAKES MARJORIE TO ONE SIDE AND SPEAKS QUIETLY.

Now, before we go any further, I want to introduce you to a noo face. She is a noo face. She is in fact from Fatfighters head office. Now her name is Mrs Harrison. Mrs Harrison has come here today to check that I'm running the meetings OK. So you can all tell her how brilliant I am. What happened? Did someone make a complaint?

MRS HARRISON: Marjorie, this isn't easy for me to say, but because you've put on so much weight I'm afraid I have no option but to suspend you for a while.

MARJORIE: You what?!

MRS HARRISON: Just until you've lost some of the weight. It really doesn't set a good example.

MARJORIE: Look who's talking! You're no spring onion yourself!

MRS HARRISON: Marjorie, we'll discuss this later.

MARJORIE: No! Let's have it out now!

MRS HARRISON: Marjorie, you're making an exhibition of yourself.

MARJORIE: Oh am I really?! Well you can take your FatFighters and you can shove it up your fat arse! That's right, SC-REW YOU!

SHE EXITS AND SLAMS THE DOOR TRIUMPHANTLY.

PAUSE.

MARJORIE COMES BACK IN SHEEPISHLY TO GET HER CLOTHES.

PIANIST

A PIANIST IS PLAYING AT THE ROYAL ALBERT HALL. A VERY LOUD TEXT BEEPING COMES THROUGH ON HIS MOBILE PHONE. HE LAUGHS AT THE DIRTY TEXT HE'S BEEN SENT AND REPLIES. HE THEN STARTS PLAYING AGAIN.

JASON AND NAN – PRESENTS

TOM V/O: When I'm old, I hope I have the good manners to throw myself out of the window. But some people are selfish and go on living, like this old bitch.

INT. NAN'S LIVING ROOM. NAN IS WATCHING 'THE GOOD LIFE' ON TV. WE HEAR THE NINETIES CLUB ANTHEM 'GOOD LIFE' PLAYING, AS IF IT WAS THE THEME. THE DOOR BELL RINGS. NAN TURNS OFF THE TV. NAN OPENS THE DOOR TO JASON. JASON SEES NAN IN HIS ROMANTIC IMAGE, AS USUAL.

NAN: Oh hello, Jason. Er, Gary not with you?

JASON: No, I don't see so much of Gary these days.

NAN: Oh that's a shame. Well, come in.

THEY GO INTO THE LIVING ROOM.

JASON: I, er, brought you some things.

JASON GIVES NAN A PLASTIC BAG.

NAN: Oh thank you. Oh, oh, I like this. Nice.

HE HAS BROUGHT HER A TUB OF HÄAGEN- DAZS AND A VIDEO OF *NINE AND A HALF WEEKS*.

NAN: What's this? Nine and a Half Weeks. Oh. Right, now.

SHE PULLS OUT A TUBE OF LUBRICATING JELLY.

NAN: Oh, I can't have jelly. I'm diabetic. Never mind, this bag will come in useful.

JASON: Why don't you, er, open the ice cream now? It's fun to share.

NAN: Not for me thanks love, I've just had a nectarine. But you have some.

You never told me you had an older sister.

THE DOORBELL RINGS.

NAN: Oh, that'll be Winnie. I won't be a mo.

NAN GOES TO ANSWER THE DOOR.

JASON: Okay. (MUTTERS) Oh great!

NAN OPENS THE DOOR.

NAN (OFF-CAMERA)**:** I've got somebody with me.

WINNIE (OFF-CAMERA)**:** Oh.

NAN: And he's a lovely boy. He's a friend of Gary's. Winnie, this is Jason.

WINNIE: Hello, love.

WE SEE WINNIE, ANOTHER OLD LADY.

JASON: Hello!

NAN: Can you see the family resemblance?

JASON: Yeah. You never told me you had an older sister.

NAN: Lovely to see you, dear.

NAN AND WINNIE KISS. JASON IMAGINES THE TWO OLD LADIES HAVING A PASSIONATE SNOG.

NAN: Fancy a sandwich, Jason?

JASON LOOKS UP TO HEAVEN AND MOUTHS 'THANK YOU'.

EPISODE

LIZ AND CLIVE — MOLLIE SUGDEN

A MAN IS HAVING A WEE IN A TOILET IN THE STREET WITH A SIGN 'PUBLIC TOILET'. HE SWOPS HANDS TO SHAKE HANDS WITH A FRIEND.

TOM V/O: Chinese food has been so popular in Britain, it has been exported as far afield as China.

INT. CHINESE RESTAURANT. LIZ AND CLIVE ARE HAVING A MEAL.

LIZ: They repeated it last night, it was very funny. Mollie came in, she shook her brolly and said her pussy had got all wet in the rain.

CLIVE: (BORED) Really?

LIZ: It's funny, 'cause it rained at her wedding and my bridesmaid's outfit got soaked. Everybody.

CLIVE: This duck's very fatty. Do you think I should send it back?

LIZ: Yes.

CLIVE SUDDENLY SPOTS SOMETHING.

CLIVE: Oh my word, you'll never guess who's just walked in.

LIZ: Who?

CLIVE: Mollie Sugden.

LIZ: Don't be silly, Clive.

CLIVE: Yeah, that's definitely her.

LIZ TURNS ROUND TO SEE MOLLIE SUGDEN AND FRIENDS JUST SITTING DOWN.

CLIVE: Go and say hello.

LIZ: No, Clive. She doesn't want to be bothered.

CLIVE: What are you talking about? You were bridesmaid at her wedding. Of course she'll want to be bothered!

LIZ: No, Clive, no.

CLIVE: All right.

LIZ: Let's go somewhere else. I don't like it here.

THE WAITER RUSHES OVER.

WAITER: Have you seen who's just come in? Your friend, Mollie Sugden.

CLIVE: Oh come on, you haven't seen her for years. I'll bring her over.

LIZ: Clive!

IT'S TOO LATE.

CLIVE: Excuse me, er, Mrs Sugden?

MOLLIE: Yes?

CLIVE: I'm so sorry to bother you. I just thought you might like to know that I'm here today with my wife Liz, who used to be Liz Bendall.

MOLLIE: Sorry?

CLIVE: Liz Bendall. She was the bridesmaid at your wedding.

MOLLIE: Well I don't know anyone called Liz. My friend Helen was the only bridesmaid at my wedd– . . .

MOLLIE SLUMPS FORWARD; A KNIFE LODGES IN HER BACK – THROWN BY LIZ.

SEBASTIAN AND MICHAEL – ITALIAN PM

EXT. 10 DOWNING ST. THE POLICEMAN USHERS ANOTHER POLICEMAN OVER. AS SOON AS HE ARRIVES, THE FIRST POLICEMAN DASHES OFF, LEAVING THE SECOND STRANDED.

TOM V/O: Inside 10 Downing Street, the Prime Minister is having an urgent meeting with his Italian counterpart. I actually lived in Italy for a few years, while I was Pope.

INT. PM'S OFFICE. MICHAEL SITS AT HIS DESK OPPOSITE HIS ITALIAN COUNTERPART AND AN INTERPRETER.

MICHAEL: And Prime Minister, I believe that . . .

INTERPRETER: *Il nominstro* . . .

MICHAEL: . . . a very special bond between our two nations . . .

INTERPRETER: *Credo che il vincolo speciale tra le nostre due nazioni* . . .

MICHAEL: . . . can only grow stronger in this difficult time.

INTERPRETER: *Possa crescere soltanto piu forte a questo tempo difficile.*

MICHAEL: As you know, this evening I will be having talks with the President of France. I believe . . .

INTERPRETER: *Come sepete, questa sera avro dei discorsi col presidente di Francia* . . .

SEBASTIAN ENTERS.

SEBASTIAN: Hiya!

MICHAEL: Sebastian . . . erm . . .

INTERPRETER: Sebastian.

MICHAEL: I'm in a very important meeting. Can't it wait?

INTERPRETER: *Una meeting molto importante. Non puo attendere?*

SEBASTIAN: No, Prime Minister, it can't. What's all this about you flying off to China tomorrow? We're supposed to be having a meeting.

THE INTERPRETER CONTINUES INTERPRETING.

MICHAEL: Well it's a matter of grave international importance. And I'm afraid the meeting about your agricultural report will have to wait.

SEBASTIAN: I had my hair done and everything!

SEBASTIAN POINTS TO HIS HAIR. THE INTERPRETER MIMICS HIM.

Lei me usa appena quando lei vuole, Michael, e poi lei butta via . . .

INTERPRETER: *Ho avuto i miei capelli fatti e tutto!*

MICHAEL: Sebastian, Sebastian, please.

INTERPRETER: *Sebastian per favore.*

SEBASTIAN: You just use me when you want, Michael, then you just throw me away!

SEBASTIAN WAVES HIS ARMS DEMONSTRATIVELY. THE INTERPRETER MIMICS HIM.

INTERPRETER: *Lei me usa appena quando lei vuole, Michael, e poi lei butta via . . .*

MICHAEL: Can you please stop translating this?

INTERPRETER: *'Is metiamo'.*

MICHAEL: Thank you. Come here.

SEBASTIAN: Don't touch me!

MICHAEL PULLS SEBASTIAN TO ONE SIDE.

MICHAEL: I could do without the hysterics.

SEBASTIAN: Oh, I'm being hysterical, am I?

MICHAEL: Sssh.

SEBASTIAN: No, I'm not going to sssh. I think Prime Minister Carluccio should know what you're really like.

MICHAEL: The meeting tomorrow is off.

SEBASTIAN: Oh, well I've got other plans now anyway.

MICHAEL: Oh, have you?

SEBASTIAN: Yeah, um, the leader of the Opposition has invited me round for tea. So just think about that when you're on your little plane tomorrow!

MICHAEL: Goodbye, Sebastian.

SEBASTIAN: Whatever. Goodbye Mr Italian Prime Minister.

ITALIAN PM: *Ciao.*

SEBASTIAN: Oh, *ciao. Ciao.*

SEBASTIAN MAKES A BIG DISPLAY OF SAYING GOODBYE.

MICHAEL: Get out!

HE GOES.

MICHAEL: Sorry about that.

INTERPRETER: *Dolente.*

ITALIAN PRESIDENT: *Se lei l'ama, va dopo lui.*

MICHAEL: What did he say?

INTERPRETER: The Prime Minister say; 'If you love him, go after him'.

'If you love him, go after him'

EPISODE

LOU AND ANDY — SUPERMARKET

TOM V/O: At this really supermarket in Herby, Lou is taking Andy on his weekly shop.

INT. SUPERMARKET. LOU WHEELS ANDY DOWN THE AISLE.

LOU: Now, which soup do you want for your tea?

ANDY: That one.

ANDY POINTS INDISCRIMINATELY.

LOU: That one?

ANDY: Yeah.

LOU: But that's whole sweet red peppers.

ANDY: Yeah, I know.

LOU: Well I'll get you some cream of tomato. You like cream of tomato, don't you? (ANDY SLIPS SOMETHING INTO HIS TROUSERS. LOU SPOTS HIM) Here, what are you doing?

ANDY: Robbing.

LOU: It's very wrong to steal. You do know that, don't you?

ANDY: Yeah, I know.

LOU: Well put that back then.

ANDY DOES.

LOU: I am very disappointed in you, Andy Pipkin. I don't ever want to see you do anything like that ever again. Do you hear?

ANDY: Sorry.

LOU: Right, now, we're all out of beans. Now I could get you the normal ones or the ones with the little chipolatas in.

ANDY STEALS SOMETHING ELSE, BUT IS SPOTTED BY A SECURITY GUARD. HE LEAPS OUT OF HIS WHEELCHAIR AND RUNS OFF. LOU REMAINS ENGROSSED IN HIS SHOPPING.

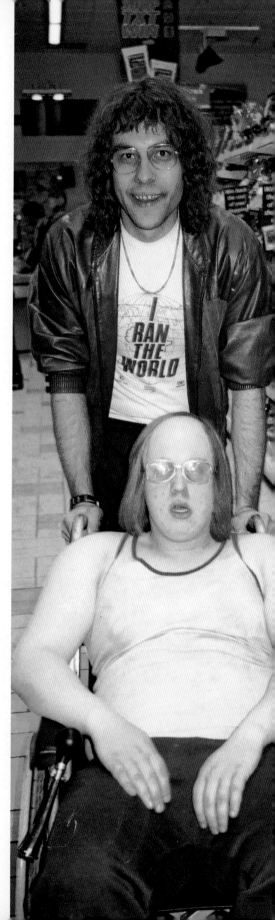

LOU: Oh. They're doing a special offer on Alphabetti Spaghetti. I'll get that instead.

LOU TURNS AND SEES THE WHEELCHAIR IS EMPTY. HE IS BAFFLED.

LOU: Andy? Andy? Andy?

WORLD RECORD ATTEMPT – MOST PEOPLE IN A MINI

INT. CONFERENCE CENTRE. THE TWO IANS AND TWO OF THEIR FRIENDS SIT IN A MINI.

IAN 1: What's the record?

IAN 2: Sixteen.

IAN 1: We haven't got any more seats.

IAN 2: Probably room for one more small one.

WE PULL BACK TO REVEAL A QUEUE OF IANS BENEATH A BANNER THAT READS 'MOST PEOPLE IN A MINI – WORLD RECORD ATTEMPT'. A CHILD IAN (COMPLETE WITH BEARD AND GLASSES) JOINS THE GROUP IN THE MINI. PAUSE. SUDDENLY IAN 3, SQUEEZED IN THE BACK, STARTS TO PANIC.

IAN 1: Ian?

IAN 3: No, it's no use, I've got to get out. Come on, I can't breathe. Let me out.

THE CREDITS ROLL, AS THE GROUP QUICKLY CLIMB OUT OF THE CAR.

TOM V/O: And so this remarkable series draws to a close. I think it's fair to say that this has been arguably the finest programme ever broadcast. And that I am some kind of god, who should be worshipped as such. Next week, *Coupling* or something. Goodbibe.

AS THE THEME DRAWS TO A CLOSE, WE HEAR IT SLOW DOWN, TUNELESSLY.

EPISODE

pilot episode

TOM V/O: Britain. Britain. Britain. Population: one millions. Number of towns: nine. Average height: thirty. Shoe size . . . But just who are Britain? Over the next eleventen weeks, we aim to find out – by following the lives of ordinary British folk. What do they? Who is them? And why?

OPENING CREDITS: WE SEE A MONTAGE OF FOOTAGE DEPICTING BRITISH LIFE. WE PULL BACK TO REVEAL THAT THESE MOVING IMAGES ACTUALLY APPEAR ON POSTCARDS, IN A DISPLAY CAROUSEL INSIDE A SMALL SHOP.

LATYMER 1

INT. THERAPY ROOM. LATYMER, A SOUTH AFRICAN MASSEUR WITH DARK BROWN SKIN AND BLOND HAIR IS GIVING A MASSAGE. HE SPEAKS CALMLY AND QUIETLY.

LATYMER: Oh yes, you're very tense here, aren't you, Jonathan? (PAUSE) I think the thing to do is to try and think of something relaxing. When I want to relax I like to think of a herd of marauding buffalo, trampling through a village. The villagers are fleeing. Perhaps one or two people are caught in the mêlée. (PAUSE) Ooh, you still seem very tense.

EMILY HOWARD – SWIMMING POOL

EXT. SWIMMING POOL. WE SEE A WOMAN IN SOME STOCKS.

TOM V/O: We begin our journey in Merkin, a happy town just north of Troot.

INT. LOBBY OF SWIMMING POOL – TICKET OFFICE. EMILY IS OBVIOUSLY A MAN, BUT WEARS ASSORTED, ILL-FITTING LADIES' CLOTHING IN A VICTORIAN STYLE AND CARRIES A PARASOL. HE GOES TO THE FRONT OF THE QUEUE, PUSHING A MAN OUT OF THE WAY.

TOM V/O: It's midday and rubbish transvestite Emily Howard is paying a visit to his local swimming pool.

When I want to relax I like to think of a herd of marauding buffalo, trampling through a village.

EMILY: First thing first! I am a lady and I would like a ladies' swim, please.

TICKET SELLER: Er, yeah, men, women, whatever, it's two pounds sixty.

EMILY: Yes, a ladies' swim. Oh, where's my purse? Oh, it's in my ladies' handbag. That I bought from a ladies' shop. From a lady.

EMILY ROOTS THROUGH HIS HANDBAG.

EMILY: Oh, these coins are so heavy. Of course, you wouldn't notice, being a man, ha ha. Heaven knows what that is like. I do not. How could I? I am a lady. Tell me, is there a poo-el reserved for womenfolk?

TICKET SELLER: No, there's just one pool. It's mixed.

EMILY: No, really?

EMILY GIGGLES AT THE VERY IDEA.

TICKET SELLER: Yeah. There is a 'ladies only' swim on Tuesday nights.

EMILY: Tuesday nights you say?

EMILY GETS OUT A TINY, SUITABLY OLD-FASHIONED DIARY AND PENCIL AND LEAFS THROUGH.

TICKET SELLER: Yeah so you can't come . . . then.

EMILY: (QUIETLY IN AGREEMENT) No, you're right. I can't come then. I'm doing ladies' things that night, that ladies do. Because that's what I am – a lady.

EMILY DELIBERATELY DROPS HIS HANDKERCHIEF ON THE FLOOR.

EMILY: Ooh, I've dropped my lace handkerchief on the floor.

EMILY TURNS TO THE MAN BEHIND HIM. THE MAN SIGHS AND RELUCTANTLY PICKS UP THE HANDKERCHIEF AND HANDS IT TO EMILY.

MAN: There you are, mate.

EMILY POINTS TO THE HANDKERCHIEF.

EMILY: I bet you're wondering what those initials stand for? 'E.H.' It's Emily, Emily Howard. I have a lady's name because that's what I am – a lady.

TICKET SELLER: Yeah . . . the pool's that way.

EMILY: Thank you. Where are the changing rooms?

TICKET SELLER: The men's changing rooms are just over there.

EMILY: Oh, so you have changing rooms for men. Very good. And the ladies'?

TICKET SELLER: Well the ladies' – which is for ladies only – is right next door.

EMILY: Merci, monsieur!

EMILY WALKS SELF-CONSCIOUSLY TOWARDS THE CHANGING ROOMS.

TICKET SELLER: (CALLING AFTER EMILY) . . . SO men can't go in there. They get thrown out.

EMILY: I should hope so!

EMILY GOES TOWARDS THE LADIES' CHANGING ROOM.

EMILY: Thank you! I've found it.

EMILY LINGERS NERVOUSLY BY THE LADIES' CHANGING ROOMS, BIDING TIME, EVENTUALLY GIVING UP AND STOMPING OFF INTO THE MEN'S.

SCENES FROM

LATYMER 2

INT. THERAPY ROOM. AS BEFORE.

LATYMER: Ooh, there are a lot of stress knots in your ear . . . Imagine a gang of children throwing stones at a pensioner. He is weeping softly as they lift him and put him into a wheelie bin. (PAUSE) The wheelie bin is being pushed down a hill now, and the children have let go. It's careering towards a busy road. (PAUSE) Relax.

MARJORIE DAWES/FATFIGHTERS

INT. MARJORIE DAWES' LIVING ROOM – A FAIRLY STANDARD SUBURBAN LOUNGE.

TOM V/O: If there is one thing that brings this country down it's fat people. They're heavy, they're rude, and in summer they smell.

A GROUP OF PEOPLE ARE WAITING IN EMBARRASSED SILENCE, WHILE MARJORIE IS ON THE PHONE.

MARJORIE: I know. Well, they're all the same. (PAUSE) Well, anyway, I'd better go, I've got my fat people round. All right. Bye bye.

MARJORIE: OK. Sorry about that. So welcome to FatFighters. I've been really looking forward to finding out how we've all been doing this week in our fight against the flab.

MARJORIE SITS DOWN, IN FRONT OF THE GROUP, IN A SLIGHTLY HIGHER CHAIR THAN THE OTHERS.

MARJORIE: So let's start by going round the circle. Paul?

PAUL: Hello, I'm Paul. And I'm three stone off my target weight.

PAT: Hi, I'm Pat. I am five stones and one pound off my target weight.

MEERA: My name is Meera and I am one stone off my target weight.

MARJORIE: And I am Marjorie and I am my target weight. OK, so it's a special day today at FatFighters because we have a noo member. He is a noo member. His name is Christopher Halliday and he's just turned thirteen and he's got a little bit of a problem with food. Now we're all friends here at FatFighters and we're all here to help each other, all right?

WE FOCUS ON AN UNCOMFORTABLE-LOOKING CHRISTOPHER.

MARJORIE: . . . and I've promised his mum we're all gonna be extra special nice to him, aren't we, FatFighters?

GROUP: (SMILING, FRIENDLY) Yeah, hello, hi, (ETC.)

MARJORIE: So, Chris, I hear they bully you at school. What do they say, Chris? What do they call you?

CHRISTOPHER: Fatty.

MARJORIE: Fatty. (MARJORIE LOOKS AT THE GROUP WITH SADNESS) Not Fatty bum-bum?

CHRIS: No.

MARJORIE: They don't go 'Ooh fatty bum-bum. Fatty fatty bum-bum'?

CHRIS: No.

MARJORIE: No. Just Fatty. (PAUSE) Incredible Bulk? Piggy? Pigs In Space?

CHRIS AND MARJORIE: No.

MARJORIE: Ooh, Chubby Checker? Fat Greedy Boy? Cracker?

BOTH: No.

CHRISTOPHER: They don't ALL make fun of me being fat.

MARJORIE: No, but the others will be thinking it. So what advice can we give to Fatty Halliday about losing some of this excess weight? Paul?

PAUL: Eat sensibly.

MARJORIE: Oh that's rich coming from you. Anyone else?

PAT: Don't eat too much chocolate.

MARJORIE: What do you mean – 'Don't eat too much chocolate'? All the other kids hate him. Chocolate's the only friend he's got. Meera?

MEERA: Exercise.

MARJORIE: No I can't . . . what?

MEERA: Exercise.

MARJORIE: What? Do it again . . .

MEERA: Exercise.

MARJORIE: No I can't understand . . . do it again.

MEERA: Exercise.

MARJORIE: One more?

MEERA: Exercise.

MARJORIE TRIES TO SHARE A MOCKING LOOK WITH THE OTHERS, WHO DO NOT RESPOND.

MARJORIE: No, I'll tell you what you *should* be doing, Chris, and that's getting some

kind of exercise! (TO MEERA) Ooh, that reminds me. Lot of hidden calories in curry. (TO CHRISTOPHER) Yeah? Exercise. Anything really – football, jogging, football. I do ten minutes of step-aerobics every month and that's why I'm so thin.

CHRISTOPHER: You're not thin, you're fat.

MARJORIE: I'm sorry?!

PAUL: He said you're not thin, you're fat . . .

MARJORIE: Yeah, I heard what he said. (TO CHRISTOPHER) There will be no name-calling in this class. (VOICE STARTS TO CRACK) Do you hear me?

MARJORIE GETS UP AND MOVES TO THE WINDOW, HER BACK TO THE GROUP.

MARJORIE: Ooh. That hurt. That really did hurt. (MARJORIE REALISES ONE OF HER ORNAMENTS IS OUT OF PLACE AND MOVES IT. SHE TURNS BACK TO THE GROUP) I know you're noo, Christopher, but that's not really how we do things at FatFighters. All right?

THEN SHE SNAPS HERSELF OUT OF IT, VERY DEMONSTRATIVELY.

MARJORIE: We'll move on. Let's put it behind us.

MARJORIE SPOTS THE BOARD.

MARJORIE: Our presentation topic is 'Legal and Illegal Foods'. (TO CHRISTOPHER) Chrissy, can you give me a hand with the board?

MARJORIE AND CHRISTOPHER GET UP AND GO TO THE CORNER OF THE ROOM WHERE THERE IS AN EASEL. MARJORIE WHISPERS TO CHRISTOPHER.

MARJORIE: If you ever do anything like that again, I'm gonna kill your mum.

WITHDRAWN

DENNIS WATERMAN

EXT. THEATRICAL OFFICE IN THE WEST END OF LONDON. SOME VICTORIAN PROSTITUTES PLY THEIR TRADE.

TOM V/O: It's late noon in Britain's capital city . . .

INT. JEREMY RENT'S OFFICE. WE SEE PLAYBILLS AND OTHER SUITABLE THEATRICAL EPHEMERA. JEREMY IS SEATED AT HIS DESK LEAFING THROUGH A COPY OF *SPOTLIGHT*. THE INTERCOM ON HIS DESK BUZZES.

TOM V/O: . . . and theatrical agent Jeremy Rent receives a visit from one of his clients.

SECRETARY: (OVER INTERCOM) Dennis Waterman's arrived.

JEREMY: Excellent news. Send him in.

THE DOOR OPENS. DENNIS POPS HIS HEAD ROUND.

DENNIS: Hello.

JEREMY: Dennis, lovely to see you, dear heart. Come in. Do take a seat.

DENNIS ENTERS AND SITS DOWN. WE SEE FOR THE FIRST TIME THAT HE IS VERY SMALL.

JEREMY: How does this grab you? Comedy drama, Granada, June, July – maybe August – depends. It's a lead. You play John. Escaped convict. He's on the run, he wins the Lottery. It's called *Lucky Runnings*. Miriam Margolyes . . .

DENNIS: The fat one?

JEREMY: Yes.

DENNIS: I like her.

JEREMY: Pete Davidson . . .

DENNIS: Off the telly?

JEREMY: That's right. Les Grantham, Ru Madoc, Dave Yip. It's a nice one, Den. The scripts are good . . .

DENNIS TAKES THE SCRIPTS FROM JEREMY WITH HIS LITTLE CHILD'S HANDS. THEY GROW IN SIZE.

DENNIS: Ooh, they're heavy.

JEREMY: . . . and the money's great.

DENNIS: Oh, that's nice. So they want me to star in it, write the theme toon, sing the theme toon . . .

JEREMY: No, I think they just want you to be in it this time.

(PAUSE)

DENNIS: Oh, so someone else is writing it but I'll sing it?

JEREMY: No, they, er, they seem to have got that one all sorted out.

PAUSE. DENNIS LOOKS UPSET.

JEREMY: Now why don't I give them a ring then we can let them know you've had the . . . you alright, Dennis?

DENNIS: Not doing it.

JEREMY: Why not?

DENNIS: Don't want to. It's rubbish. Scripts are stu-pid.

DENNIS DISCARDS THE SCRIPTS.

JEREMY: You haven't even read them yet.

(PAUSE)

JEREMY: Dennis?

DENNIS: (SINGING TO THE THEME TUNE FROM *MINDER*)

'I'm an escaped convict on the ru-un – da da da da da
I've won the Lottery and I'm having fun – da da da da da
I'm running much too fast
Can't escape from the past
I'd be so good for . . . Lucky Runnings.'

PAUSE. JEREMY ROLLS HIS EYES.

JEREMY: Dennis, this insistence of yours on always writing and singing the theme tune really isn't doing us any favours . . .

DENNIS: Oh, so you're saying I should give up the acting and concentrate on the singing?

JEREMY: No, Dennis! You could have been in the new Indiana Jones film! They wanted you to play his brother! You know who that part went to? Ralph Fiennes!

DENNIS: Well *he's* no singer . . .

TELEPHONE RINGS.

JEREMY: Hello? (TO DENNIS, WITH HAND OVER RECEIVER) It's the Indiana Jones people. Ralph Fiennes has been decapitated in a stunt . . . Yes, Dennis is still available, in fact he's right here, I'll pass him over.

JEREMY PASSES OVER THE 'PHONE WHICH IS MUCH BIGGER IN DENNIS'S WORLD.

DENNIS: Ooh, let me speak to them . . .

Hello? Yes I'm fine! (SINGS) 'I am Indiana Jones's brother . . . ' Hello?

LATYMER 3

INT. THERAPY ROOM.

LATYMER: Yes, I've just found some stress knots in the perineum which I'm going to work on and . . . tell you what, why don't you have a little nap? I'll sing you a lullaby as you drift off. (SINGS SOFTLY AT FIRST BUT IT RISES TO A DEAFENING DISCORDANT CRESCENDO) 'Go to sleep, go to sleep, go to sleep, go to sleep, go to sleep. (PAUSE) Jonathan, are you asleep?'

DOMINOES

INT. LARGE EXHIBITION HALL. WE SEE A BANNER ON THE WALL THAT READS 'DOMINO TOPPLING WORLD RECORD ATTEMPT'. WE SEE A CLOSE-UP SHOT OF IAN 1 CAREFULLY PLACING DOMINOES IN A CHAIN. HE RUNS OUT OF DOMINOES.

IAN 1: Ian, we're gonna need another box.

WE SEE HIS FRIEND, IAN 2, HEAD FOR THE DOOR AND THEN SEE THAT THE CHAIN IS ONLY TWENTY DOMINOES LONG. HE HAS ONE SMALL EMPTY BOX BESIDE HIM.

TOM V/O: If you have enjoyed this programme you may like to know that there is a fact sheet available which accompanies the series, containing recipes from the show, quizzes, knitting patterns, and pornographic pictures I have drawn of myself. Goodbine.

Little Britain series one

Written and performed by: Matt Lucas and David Walliams

Director: Steve Bendelack

Producer: Myfanwy Moore

Script Editor: Mark Gatiss

Music: David Arnold

Location Manager: Jodi Moore

Sound: Bob Newton and Lawrie Taylor

Makeup Designer: Lisa Cavalli-Green

Costume Designer: Annie Hardinge

Camerman: Dave Bowden and Martin Hawkins

Vision Mixer: Naomi Neufeld

1st Assistant Director: Mel Nortcliffe

Casting Director: Tracey Gillham

Production Secretary: Nerys Evans

Scripts Supervisor: Chrissie Bibby

Assistant Producer: Andrew Wilshire

Production Executive: Jez Nightingale

Dubbing Mixer: Nigel Heath

Executive Producer: Jon Plowman

Production Manager: Julia Weedon

Editor: Mykola Pawluk

Production Designer: Denis de Groot

Director of Photography: Rob Kitzman

With the voice of: Tom Baker

Special Guests: Antony Head, Les McKeown,
 David Soul, Mollie Sugden

Featuring

Abi Eniola, Adam Dankin, Amanda Root, Anjal Mya Chadha,
Charaubala Chokshi, Christian Coulson, Dann Condon, David Arnold, David Foxxe,
Di Botcher, Evie Garratt, Ewen MacIntosh, Georgie Glen, Giovanni Del Vecchio,
Graham Beasley, Gwenllian Gavies, Helen Coker, Hilda Schroder, Jack Stanley,
Jeanne Mockford, Jeillo Edwards, Jennie Bond, Joanne Condon, Joseph Lang,
Karen Seacombe, Mark Morriss, Menna Trussler, Olivia Jardith, Paul Putner,
Philip Jackson, Ruth Jones, Sally Bankes, Sally Hawkins, Sally Rogers,
Siobhan Haye, Stephen Aintree, Steve Furst, Stirling Gallacher, Ted Robbins,
Timothy Mark Chipping, Tom Fallows, Tony Tang, Veronica Roberts, Wendy Baxter.

omplete first BBC series is also available on DVD and VHS, and the
al Radio 4 radio series is available on BBC audio CD and cassette

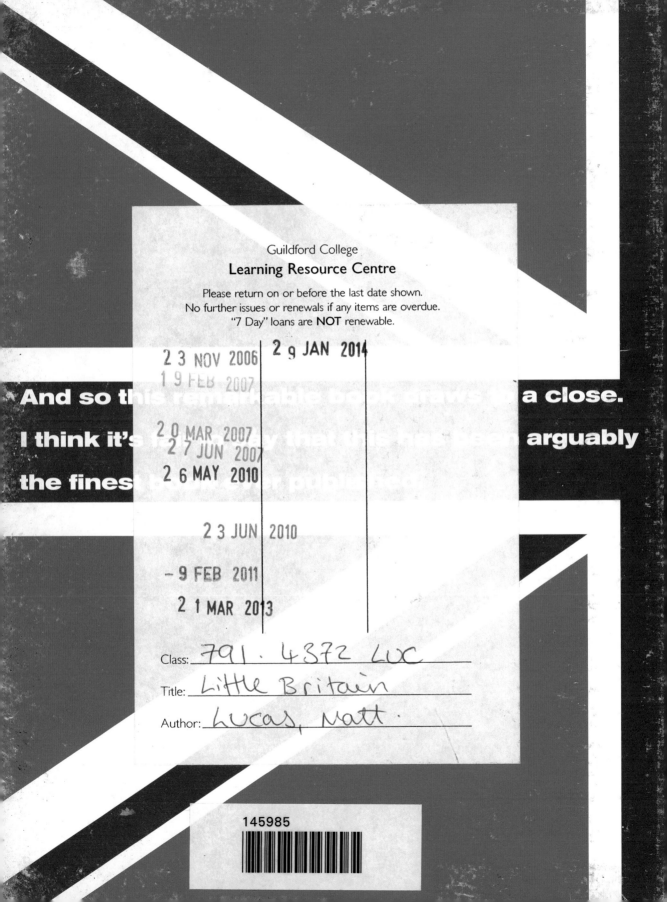

Guildford College
Learning Resource Centre

Please return on or before the last date shown.
No further issues or renewals if any items are overdue.
"7 Day" loans are **NOT** renewable.

2 3 NOV 2006   2 9 JAN 2014
1 9 FEB 2007

2 0 MAR 2007
2 7 JUN 2007
2 6 MAY 2010

2 3 JUN 2010

- 9 FEB 2011

2 1 MAR 2013

Class: 791.4372 LUC
Title: Little Britain
Author: Lucas, Matt.

145985

And so this remarkable book draws to a close.

I think it's fair to say that this has been arguably

the fines British television public ser